DATE DUE

Demco, Inc. 38-293

APR 1 8 2012

Success in Six Cups of Coffee

SUCCESS IN SIX CUPS OF COFFEE

How Smart Networking Conquers Hidden Obstacles

DISCARD

Pino Bethencourt

Professor of Leadership and Executive Education,
IE Business School, Spain

palgrave
macmillan

First published in Spanish as *El éxito en seis cafés* in 2008 by Ediciones Gestión 2000

First published in English 2011 by
PALGRAVE MACMILLAN

Palgrave Macmillan in the UK is an imprint of Macmillan Publishers Limited,
registered in England, company number 785998, of Houndmills, Basingstoke,
Hampshire RG21 6XS.

Palgrave Macmillan in the US is a division of St Martin's Press LLC,
175 Fifth Avenue, New York, NY 10010.

Palgrave Macmillan is the global academic imprint of the above companies and has
companies and representatives throughout the world.

Palgrave® and Macmillan® are registered trademarks in the United States,
the United Kingdom, Europe and other countries.

ISBN 978–0–230–34787–8

This book is printed on paper suitable for recycling and made from fully managed and
sustained forest sources. Logging, pulping and manufacturing processes are expected
to conform to the environmental regulations of the country of origin.

A catalogue record for this book is available from the British Library.

A catalog record for this book is available from the Library of Congress.

10 9 8 7 6 5 4 3 2 1
20 19 18 17 16 15 14 13 12 11

Printed and bound in Great Britain by
MPG Group, Bodmin and King's Lynn

CONTENTS

CHAPTER 1

ONLY SIX?

Is it really possible? Can it be that in order to reach the private equity investor you need for your new venture, or to find the employer who will give you the chance of a lifetime, you only need to have six cups of coffee? Research tells us that this is so. There is an average of six intermediate people that form an invisible chain between you and the person who will help you succeed. Every time you sit down in front of a cup of coffee (or tea if you prefer) with an acquaintance, you are opening the door to meeting a new friend or a business colleague from his or her network.

Suppose you were the owner of a small hotel in San Francisco. You would start by discussing your need to redo your marketing image with your caterer Sally on Monday, who would put you in contact with Bob. Bob, a specialist in web design, might suggest a late evening drink on Tuesday, where he would describe what he would do if he were you. When discussing photographs he would mention his great Venezuelan friend Carolina. Carolina and you could then meet for coffee on a sunny terrace on Friday morning to talk about styles, prices, approaches. Carolina, a big fan of social networks, would receive a Twitter message from her Chinese friend Lee just as she finished her coffee, and would immediately connect you. Lee would be difficult to reach over the phone, but when you finally joined her for another cup of coffee with Carolina, she'd bring along her boyfriend, Hakim.

Hakim's experience in brand building with technology ventures would seem unrelated to your project, but you would get on so well that you would meet for coffee again to borrow a comic book on Japanese Manga you both love. Half way through your fifth cup of coffee, Hakim would remember that his friend from high-school in Berlin was crazy about the kind of niche, city center hotel you'd created. Hans, who travelled constantly between Berlin, New York, and London, would be staying the weekend at Hakim's, who'd promised to take him to the best little sushi restaurant in the whole of San Francisco, just off Fillmore Street. Afterwards they would come by to check out your hotel.

Hans would turn out to be looking for a good investment in the hospitality industry and he would totally endorse the design you'd chosen. That sixth coffee would be the first of many, many cups of tea, coffee, and other alcoholic beverages you would share with Hans over the following year, as you became partners in a very successful new travel offer for young business people visiting the bay area from all over Europe.

This is just a small picture of how six cups of coffee could lead you to a very successful opportunity. By sharing this age-old ritual with each connection in the chain, you would reach that one person who would be looking exactly for you. Six degrees of separation is the average distance between any two people in the world. Somewhere out there a stranger is waiting to build something wonderful with you. Six cups of coffee could bring you together.

Our world is more closely connected than it ever was before. A study conducted by Dodds[1] in 2003, with 60,000 email users in 13 countries, showed that the well-known concept of six degrees of separation holds true in the twenty-first century.

Six conversations separate you from any random person in the world: six interactions, whether they be online or in pragmatic coffee shops, sophisticated oriental tea parlors or dim lit, modern DJ-ambianced lounges. Six human contacts lie between you and the person you need in order to succeed.

Our generation builds more international friendships and business relationships than our parents and grandparents ever imagined possible. We travel frequently to all kinds of remote corners, we chat with foreign strangers on the web, and we share our pictures and ideas with kindergarten friends on worldwide social networks.

Still, the principles of trust remain true to our original *Homo Sapiens* design, no matter how many virtual channels we use to interact with each other. Geographical distance obstacles have dissolved, only to show us how very crucial our cultural differences are becoming.

On the internet, new frontiers are being built by the diverse assortment of languages we speak in the world. We run into unwanted conflicts and confusion when we use an English word to describe our country's vision of life to a colleague who interprets his own cultural understanding of the same term. Networking has become a lot trickier than it used to be a few decades back.

1.1 ARE YOU AS GOOD AS YOU THINK YOU ARE?

We all network, of course. We just don't know what we're doing wrong. It's the subtle trap of leadership skills: executives tend to think they excel at them until recurring errors or a huge disappointment draws them to search for the cause in their own actions.

This book is a new, internet enabled, global approach to an age-old human skill: the science of making friends and building influence. The term networking means producing a movement in your network of personal contacts. Sometimes we illustrate this with expressions like "develop your network" or "manage your relationships".

But networking is a lot more than a methodology or a scientifically proven approach. It's a very personal form of expression: the art of building and cultivating win–win relationships with culturally diverse individuals in a strategic way.

It's an art because there is more than one way to develop human bonds. Your network is a mirror of your own unique approach to business and pleasure. It becomes a meticulously customized extension of your brain's neuronal connections, pushing your ideas and requests out towards society, while it pulls in your preferred resources and choices.

Far from offering an array of tricks or recipes about what to say or how to behave, this book will concentrate on helping you understand your strong points and the weaknesses in your character. It will push you to find and take up the uses, customs, and tools that best adapt to your personality in order to succeed.

Building and cultivating personal bonds can seem cold if one doesn't understand the nature of a human connection. Many authors make it sound like a dollar-churning process manual to exploit others a.s.a.p.

But bonding is a millenary ritual of intimate exchange that requires attention to detail and respectful care. Human interactions move our insides and play with our feelings in such a profound manner that we all learn to protect ourselves from hurt or exploitation.

Again, this book will help you comprehend, begin to perceive, and interpret all the emotional, cultural and delicate essences we exchange as we nurture our link to another person.

You will work on two dimensions:

(1) A more methodic and pragmatic approach to spark new behavior patterns and useful thought processes in your head. You'll improve

the way you manage your own resources in your efforts to extend and strengthen your network.

(2) A more abstract or intellectual dimension to help you understand the emotional essence of personal bonds, whether private or work related. You will reflect on the types of reactions triggered on each side, and realize how large systems of human connections are, in fact, a key principle to the very biological design of our species, reappearing once and again in all things natural to ensure the best performance of the environment we live in today.

By absorbing these fundamental concepts that underlie human dynamics, and building your own methods to distribute your energy in the most efficient manner, you will definitely develop a unique networking style. It will make you more attractive in the eyes of your future friends and international allies, precisely because it will flow naturally and confidently from your very own source.

1.2   DO YOU WANT TO IMPROVE?

Networking is perhaps the most critical skill for success in any executive. Several decades of growing awareness of the presence of what has been called emotional intelligence in the business world have gradually increased organizational attention to the basic skills that make up this area of executive talent.

Networking is, in fact, a more elaborate package or cluster of these leadership capacities; a sophisticated soft skill that combines the more elemental abilities described in most emotional intelligence frameworks.

Networking involves listening, perceiving emotions, reading behaviors, assuming risks, being assertive, communicating in an effective manner, negotiating, and using all of these to manage a systemic perception of the business environment.

Through the networker's lens we give up our interpretation of events and persons as isolated dots. By joining these dots we grasp new meanings and interpretations of how such connections trigger the consequences we experience.

This is exactly why it's utterly useless to rely on a list of recipes or supposedly proven solutions. If you let rigid rules and tricks govern your actions you disconnect yourself from the person in front of you. Think of an executive who applies a pushy westernized elevator-pitch speech to an educated Japanese gentleman; not the best approach.

Book stores are full of management books about how to change your life or lose weight, and yet we are getting fatter every year. Any manager dedicated to building and improving his or her soft skills knows that real change doesn't occur while reading, but in a very different place.

Instructions, ideas and knowledge provide new inputs to our rationale, but only people who translate their thoughts into actions obtain real progress. Trying to make yourself apply a rule that comes into conflict with your nature doesn't work.

This manuscript has been designed to provide you with lots of elements to think about. Frameworks and provocative questions will push you to dig in to your own psyche and come up with simple changes and new habits. Comfortable approaches, well suited to your strengths, will enable a better, more efficient approach to others.

This is a virtual mental gymnasium where you can train, with top-notch machines, music and a great atmosphere. But it's up to you to practice your moves. The smallest effort will yield initial results in your day to day, motivating you to keep training and improving your very own art of meeting new people, building enjoyable connections, full of authenticity, brimming with value for you and for those who walk into your life.

1.3 WHAT FOR?

Good networking is useful for almost any goal in life: finding a wife or husband, planning the perfect vacation, selling your house or learning Chinese, for example.

We're going to focus primarily on business goals that most executives pursue in their daily excursions into the jungle of economy. Executives strive for goals that require a carefully articulated networking strategy and a well-trained instinct in order to mobilize the best acquaintances at each moment.

Some typical objectives you may want to target include:

- Leading the company you work for as its CEO; recruiting powerful allies to increase your influence, getting to the right place and time to demonstrate your talent.
- Improving your sales and margins; increasing your client portfolio and sales volume per client.
- Fundraising among private investors and institutions to develop your not-for-profit ventures.

- Finding the perfect job at all times throughout your professional career.
- Consolidating a successful reputation that will open doors in social and economic circles of influence.
- Accelerating your professional learning curve after a significant career move.
- Accessing the delicate details of corporate strategy that are never written anywhere, but without which you don't get it right.
- Finding and involving the best employees in all corners of large multinational firms, helping you solve internal problems faster and with less stress.
- Preparing and executing a delicate negotiation strategy by managing communication through your network around key meetings.
- Increasing your influence and power in any social environment.
- Accessing top management positions and non-executive seats on boards, exploiting your diversity to add value instead of giving it up to imitate the dominant stereotype.
- Raising money for investment funds of all kinds and getting to the best investment opportunities before your competitors.
- Finding shareholders, business angels and other financial backers for an entrepreneurial adventure.
- Accelerating bureaucratic delays in any organization, public or private.
- Starting up a new professional association or even a political party.
- Gaining support from local authorities and public administration or influencing important decisions.
- Promoting innovation by channeling the best new ideas from your networks and by changing the culture to make them happen.

The list of potential applications is as long and varied as that of a manager's possible goals, but don't forget that executives are still people.

Private needs are also an important part of a manager's networking objectives. You probably don't even think of these because you might have already covered them. Making good friends and taking care of family members, who in turn care for you when you're tired, is fundamental to nurture your personal balance.

Your private network is in charge of bringing you laughter, colorful moments and joy-filled experiences, as well as opportunities to build a family around you.

It may seem a little cold to speak bluntly of goals and objectives in such an intimate and personal aspect of your life, but this way of thinking can help you balance and better integrate your personal and professional lives when working on your network development.

Leaving your private self out would make your network diagnostics and action plans unrealistic and fictitious. They would respond to a theoretical robot version of yourself, void of emotions or an emotional life.

By the time you get past these pages, your perspective on life will have changed radically, along with your views of friendship and your career aspirations.

After today your networks will no longer respond to casualty, luck or over-rated spontaneity. They'll also be derived from your strategic thinking and the conscious development of healthy relationships to make you feel well and naturally you, while at the same time leveraging your personal projects to achieve great results.

1.4 EXECUTIVE LEARNING REQUIRES PRACTICE

Because this book means to achieve visible changes in your personal and professional performance, instead of being just a good read, it's going to make you work with exercises and provocative coach-type questions.

Improving executive skills, like sports, is not something you can do by reading. It requires a lot of practice and self-observation to analyze your own mistakes and learn from them.

So this book will commit to you and your goals, only if you commit to yourself as well. To walk the talk right away, please find a white sheet of paper and write the names of five people you met recently on the left margin of the page.

Now reply to the following questions about each person on the list. You can draw a column for each item to fill in your responses as shown on the graph.

In the column named "data," fill in everything you learned about the person: age, profession, address, where he was born, what he likes to eat, etc. If you can't think of anything relevant, just write a question mark.

In the column about the level of trust you were able to generate, named "TrustL" on the graph, write down the impression you think you made. Don't get it wrong, it's not about whether you liked him or her, but rather, the impression you made on the other person.

My recent 5 contacts	Data	TrustL	MainPr.	MyHelp
1) Pepe X	sdlQ	1	?	?
2) Ana M	?	?	?	?
3) Rose G	....	....	....	...
4) Monica C				
5) Albert A				

GRAPH 1.1

Use a score between 1 and 3, with 3 points going to those contacts that were very pleased and showed great interest in you, and one point signifying discomfort or low receptivity during your conversation. Once more, if you can't decide what score to assign, use a question mark.

In the next column, marked as "MainPr," write down the person's most important problem or challenge today. What is he or she trying to achieve over everything else, or what keeps them up at night. Use the question mark if you can't answer.

Finally, the column "Myhelp" is there to reflect what you can do to help out your new friend. Who can you introduce him or her to? Who do you know who could help out? What books can you recommend? Are there any web pages or newspaper articles you can provide to help this person solve the riddle? Write down anything you can think of.

Of course, if you were not able to respond to the previous columns, you will have to write another question mark in this last column.

What did you think of this exercise? Is there anything interesting about your answers? Have your learned anything about your networking prowess?

This exercise has been completed by thousands of executives in courses and seminars about networking, and the great majority of them finish the exercise with lots of question marks all over the matrix.

Conducting a first conversation that responds to all these questions about your new acquaintance, however, is the basic, most critical skill for networking, because only by asking questions can you get information. Only by obtaining information can you find ways to offer something of value to the person you just met, and only if you are able to provide a clear added value can you begin to earn his or her trust.

It's the virtuous circle of networking: information, value and trust. And it's universal. Around the world, across any historical period, bearing gifts is a cross-cultural signal of good will that starts an exchange of trust.

As you earn greater trust you get the right to ask more precise questions, obtaining more specific information to, in turn, help out your new contact in your very own personal way. This will make you memorable and unique among the thousands of names on this person's contact list. Even if he can't pronounce your name as he reads it, your face will come up in his mind.

So, if you bought this book thinking that networking was just an opportunistic way of getting free favors, I hope you've learned your first important lesson. Networking is the art of building and cultivating win–win relationships with diverse individuals in a strategic way. Human bonds are made up of trust, and you can only build trust by offering something valuable.

Just think about it: when a stranger comes up to you to ask you for something, does he come across as reliable or do you feel like stepping back and protecting yourself. Sometimes even people trying to help you can appear dishonest, or just plain cheeky.

To put it plainly, your networking will yield quick results if you do three things:

(a) Understand the essence of what you're doing;
(b) Incorporate new methods and tools to optimize your time and discipline yourself to plant seeds of trust frequently;
(c) Invest some effort into improving your emotional and unconscious reponses, in order to better choose your friends and get more out of new occasions.

1.5 A FRAMEWORK FOR AUTHENTICITY

It may seem to many that building strong connections is something you can push and shove. But the intentional part of human relationships is only the smallest tip of an enormous iceberg of unimaginable details.

Yes, we will talk about what you need to do, the questions you need to ask, how you should behave. But we will talk a lot more about how important it is to let chemistry flow; to respect the way you feel even when it goes against your interests and plans.

The wonderful thing about networking is that you never know when a person will surprise you. It's a little bit like choosing a doughnut to eat with your coffee. No matter how much you analyze the appearance of the different options in the window, how many times you alternate the possible strategic choices in your mind, you won't know which one has the best filling until you try it. And then it will be your taste buds which will tell you it was really, really delicious, not your intentional mind.

Believe me when I tell you I am laughing to myself as I bring you this framework. It's a doughnut! A doughnut with a very rich, authentic filling that makes it unique and irresistible to any reader's palate. A meaningful human connection is all about the secret ingredients that you can't put into words or see from the outside.

As I will later discuss in Chapter 10, human behavior is the external layer we can see and analyze. It responds to a second layer made of our thinking and the strategies we choose to pursue. The core is emotional in nature, driving every thought and every reaction to the environment.

Our emotions are difficult to harness. We try to control them while it is often they who control us. Like Dexter often describes on the popular TV show of the life of a serial killer, our very own dark passengers take over our actions when we least expect it. This is why I place feelings and emotion at the core of all my frameworks to describe executive actions.

Emotions are the archaic language of the deepest and oldest part of our minds. The part of the human body that we inherited from mammalian ancestors, it speaks to us through fear, alertness, joy and irresistible attraction to certain persons we meet. This is the authentic part of interpersonal chemistry you can't fake, copy or pull apart. It's the part of the iceberg that sits under the water, the core filling of the doughnut that makes it so mouth-watering.

GRAPH 1.2

The doughnut of networking is made up of these three layers: emotion (e), strategy (s), behavior (b). Each phase of the method I offer you in these pages can help you analyze all three layers.

Review your present: Chapter 2 will provide an exercise to analyze your current network with the POTENCIA® methodology. The present is always a result of the paths we've followed in the past.

Plan your future: Chapter 6 follows the thinking you need to do in order to organize your goals, your budget, your time allocation. You will think about playing on your strengths and choosing the situations and tactics that downplay your weaknesses.

New contacts: Chapter 7 will help you choose events and places to meet new people. You will reflect on the way you approach first conversations and whether you follow up on them in the best fashion.

Better contacts: Chapter 8 will help you look at how you take relationships to their highest potential. What you do and what you don't do to build on the trust, drive more content, and make time spent with your contacts more meaningful to both you and them.

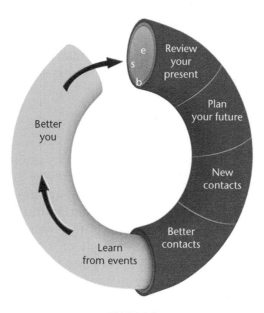

GRAPH 1.3

As you can see, this is the easiest part of the doughnut. The obvious, intentional process you can learn a lot from. You will very probably get a lot better at networking than you are today by just pushing through these phases. But the authentic part of your networking will need lots more work.

A better you: the emotional filling of the doughnut must be developed and worked on as well. Learning from events will help you build a better you. Because if you stop to listen to the details you ignored in a first conversation, if you notice the mistakes you repeat once and again with certain people or in certain situations, you will have the chance to change the way you respond in the future.

Chapters 3, 4 and 5 will provide a lot of tools and information about why people react the way they do, what human trust is all about and why networks are a very basic pattern that appears once and again in everything around us.

Whether you refer to it as executive development or as personal growth, it all boils down to acknowledging the fact that your body has very good reasons for reacting the way it does. The time and effort you invest in training yourself to react in new ways to the same problems is the most effective and worthwhile change you can apply to your networking skills, and to any other soft skill you would like to improve.

As you become a better you, you will attract better people towards you. You will run into fewer conflicts, suffer fewer disappointments, and build harmonious, valuable relationships around you. You will be a more effective manager and you will lead many others to follow your example. The best of it all is…you will be a lot happier too.

1.6   AND A LITTLE TOUCH OF INSPIRATION

I always recommend friends to start my books by reading the personal interviews at the end of each chapter. We have a very international and diverse array of successful networking styles to inspire your actions and provoke your thinking. Their generous contribution makes this book better for all those who will come into contact with it.

The book thus becomes a great example of something I've started to call the "win–win–win strategy". They win, I win and you win. By collaborating in a trusting way, we all created more value for everyone involved in *Success in Six Cups of Coffee*. Good networking is truly about making everybody win. And it's so much fun to make it happen!

1.7   JAVIER GOYENECHE, FOUNDER AND CEO OF ECOALF

Ecoalf is the center of a growing network of 18 companies in Spain, France, Taiwan, Japan and Korea. They are all working to create new solutions that offer design and fashion to the world in a sustainable way. In this interview the creator and leader of Ecoalf's quest shares his passion for green fashion with us.

Javier Goyeneche could have chosen an easier path for himself. Son of a well-respected Spanish businessman, he probably could have sailed placidly along on an easy tide of corporate jobs in his home country. He could have fulfilled a successful career without ever worrying about what happens out there in the big, wide world.

But there's nothing Javier likes more than a challenge, as his third business venture shows. His company Ecoalf integrates design, innovation and environmental respect to create beautiful bags, coats, or even electric bicycles.

Ecoalf has created an innovation network of 18 joint ventures to create fabrics that are 100% recycled and 100% recyclable from polyethylene terephthalate (PET) bottles and discarded fishing nets. "Everybody told me it wasn't possible. Now we have more than 50 fabrics. About half of these look cool and feel great!" he exclaims. "They have similar textures and the same technical properties of other non-recycled fabrics. That's the whole point of Ecoalf!"

Ecoalf's very mission statement speaks of high ideals and noble ambitions: "Companies hope to find answers for the fast, uncontrolled changes taking place in society nowadays. I aim to achieve even more. I want to include emotions in the rational equation. I want to grab the future and bring it to the present without jeopardizing the times to come. OUR times to come."

The whole concept was born out of the perils of Javier's other business, Fun & Basics. Specialized in making and selling "simple and colourful items with a touch of fun," it ran into trouble in the midst of an aggressive expansion plan. While large city stores worked very well, shops located in smaller cities lagged dangerously behind in sales.

Fun & Basics commissioned a rigorous market study to find out why. That brand awareness was a lot lower once you travelled away from urban centers was no surprise. "But what did catch us off guard was our clients' purchasing motivation: they bought our products because of their functionality and innovative fabrics."

Javier turned around and said to his partners: "if people like us because they think we are innovative in our fabrics, why don't we take our innovation even further?" arguing that real innovation must be anchored on sustainability. A few months of research on the internet and specialized journals on ecologic fabrics gave him a list of 17 addresses to visit.

Once the exhausting Christmas and sales campaigns were over, Javier hopped on an airplane to go look for recycled fabrics around the world. "But I was very disappointed with what I found. The fabrics I saw were only partly recycled. They looked and felt too rough to the touch. Just too stiff and sturdy to be fashionable."

A few weeks went by before the owner of one of the factories he had visited in Taiwan called him up. "Anita had a rather small facility that serviced local needs. She had managed to make carpets from recycled PET bottles before. She said she wanted to develop better fabrics if somebody shared the risk and cost with her to help her create the right textures."

The crucial factor with Anita was, in Javier's own words, that "she was a lot more excited and optimistic about trying than any of the multinational firms I had talked to before."

That's how emails, phone calls, and lots of Fedex packages carrying trial tissues gave way to many mistakes, but ultimately a beautiful, soft, fully recycled polyester fabric was produced. "At this point Ecoalf was only supposed to be a provider of fabrics to Fun & Basics. But once we got creating sustainable solutions, we couldn't stop!"

Substituting PVC with PET as the hard material to armour luggage took another alliance with a company from Taipei. "PET is a lot more ecological than PVC because it relies on carbon dioxide and water. When it burns it doesn't pollute the environment."

Hours of discussions on online chats led Javier to "Max, a guy from Korea who was recycling fishing nets," he tells us, just before he calls attention to his shoes. "Look at these sneakers, for instance. I'm wearing them to test them before we launch them next month," he says, as he walks around the office showing off his trendy footwear.

The sleek green and white lace-up sneakers are more than 60% recycled. "Shoe skin is entirely made of recycled nylon fishing nets. No chrome has been used when treating the leather, and the laces are made of recycled cotton. The only thing that is not fully recycled is the rubber sole. But we have an alliance to solve that!" Javier affirms with a determined look.

Goyeneche's networking style is obviously not one of small talk. The portfolio of growing worldwide alliances he is building around Ecoalf is driven by the pursuit of new solutions. "Yesterday I was in Paris, for example. The offer of recycled materials was a lot smaller in this edition than other years."

Financial setbacks seem to have decimated entrepreneurial efforts in the green fashion industry as well. The people Javier met there told him that "at the end of the day, people want a nylon of 2.5 or 2.6 dollars and nobody wants to pay 5 or 6 dollars for a recycled nylon. We have no client!"

A little resistance is no match for Javier's conviction, however: "I think these guys like ecologic innovation in fabrics, but you have to work with them. At the beginning we had quite some trouble convincing them," he explains. Since then, Ecoalf's presence in international retail hotspots like Le Bon Marché in Paris, K11 in Hong Kong or Fred Segal in California has changed their minds.

This last visit to the Premier Vision fair in Paris offered the opportunity for a new innovative fabric challenge. "I met a guy from North Korea that has wonderfully combined cotton, corn and polyester into the most amazing textiles."

"I chose three fabrics from his stand and I asked him to make them for me with different materials. I instructed him to use organic cotton, corn and recycled polyester," he explains. He continues to tell us what he negotiated: "I will pay you for the samples you produce. If I like the result I will buy between five and ten thousand yards per season."

Javier's first approach to any relationship is full of content and meaning. It may even turn into a transaction if he finds the right elements and enough motivation from his counterpart.

"For me the key to establish trust is to see the other person as excited about sustainable innovation as I am," explains the entrepreneur. Another example is the small architecture and industrial design firm based in France: "An Australian, and English man and a French man got together to create Cigue. They are helping us develop stylish furniture accessories. We also have an alliance with Mormedi, who is working on an electric bicycle with a very high percentage of recycled materials."

Yes, this entrepreneur has a very determined way of building relationships. There's no time to lose when you are reinventing the way people buy fashion and saving the world from unnecessary pollution in the process.

"I believe that networks will be absolutely key to the success of Ecoalf going forward," claims the entrepreneur. "You see, if I don't tell you our fabrics are recycled you would never know. This is what Ecoalf is all about," he claims.

"Word of mouth from real life buyers to their friends will be necessary if we want to attract worldwide markets to the hidden innovative value behind the fashionable design of our products." But this isn't the only reason why word of mouth is key.

Ecoalf's business model doesn't completely follow the typical celebrity-driven economics of the fashion world. "The inspirational motivation that is pulling consumers towards our brand comes from people's real wish to participate in environmental protection," he says.

Yes. Nothing spreads faster than noble ambitions and high ideals. If Ecoalf is to become a global epidemic of green fashion, it will need a very sticky message to deserve buyers' recommendations; a strong emotional bond that drives a buyer to "wear his new sneakers to a party and tell his friends why he bought them. This is a lot more powerful than a celebrity ad!"

Javier reminds us that Ecoalf is open to share its innovative fabrics with those who want to use them in their product lines. If more companies use Ecoalf fabrics, the potential for environmental protection multiplies. "We are now recycling 300,000 PET bottles a month. We just ordered 10,000 kilos of fabrics made from recycled fishing nets. This means we have reduced the same CO_2 emissions a car would produce by driving 100,000 kilometers. Imagine what could be done if more companies followed our lead."

Javier Goyeneche is inviting the whole world to share his company's passion for innovation, sustainability and design. A global network of joint ventures drives the necessary innovation. Now it's up to you to spread the word. You CAN look great in a way that feels good to the planet as well.

CHAPTER 2

YOUR PRESENT: THE POTENTIAL OF YOUR CURRENT NETWORK

My good friend Claudio is from Corsica. Living in Rome, he told me he was interviewing for a job at a Spanish hotel chain. That same morning I had received a thoughtful happy birthday email from my friend Samir, another wonderful friend from Jordan who lives in Madrid and works at the same hotel chain.

Claudio's network already included a key decision maker for his interview process. He just didn't know it did. We all have networks full of potential. It's a fact of life.

So, we're getting into the substance of things

Begin by fully understanding the network you already have. Over time, your network has grown, including each new friend, peers at school, and colleagues from work.

You have already invested many hours keeping this network alive, reaping diverse benefits and satisfactions, as well. You've enjoyed parties, football matches, and dinner outings with friends. Professional opportunities like conferences, seminars, and meetings with work colleagues brought you closer to your ambitions.

2.1 WHY IS YOUR NETWORK THE WAY IT IS?

Usually, your network is a result of accidents, luck, or a series of coincidences bringing you close to some people and pushing others away. Think of the 2000 movie *Cast Away*, for example. Tom Hanks landed accidentally on an island in the middle of nowhere. He couldn't be found. His accidental and absurd "network" is a battered football with a happy face.

Your own character, personality, and temperament profoundly influence the development of your network as well. Do you feel better in the company of others, or are you very independent? If you prefer the first option, when luck or accidents introduce you to new people, you will choose to stop, talk to them, and even try to set up another meeting. If your own company or a few special friends suit you better, however, you will likely limit new encounters, even to the point of avoiding newcomers before they see you.

In the same way, a very personal chemistry influences all new encounters, making you feel comfortable with some people but not with others. This chemistry can inspire you to forge new links and discard others. Love at first sight is an extreme, but perfect, example of personal chemistry at work. We will take unusual measures to be near someone who makes us feel that special attraction.

The last and most important factor to play a key role in shaping your current personal network is, of course, your strategy. A shy, introverted executive can boast a large, multicultural, and powerful network because, at a very early age, he or she chose to actively grow their networks. And it's never too late to begin.

Analyze your current network's key generators

Let's do some work, shall we? Being more aware of what has shaped your network to date will help you separate the parts that depend on you from the parts that don't. More importantly, you will consider how to influence your network's evolution. The exercise is designed to help you respond to this question: why is your network the way it is?

So, draw a circle and divide it into four quadrants, according to the influence various factors have played in your relationship-building. The four factors you need to place on the diagram are: Accident or Luck, Personal Preference for Socializing, Chemistry with New Contacts, and Personal Will or Strategy.

In the following diagram we can see Rob's responses. His personal network is, above all, a product of Accident or Luck. Effort and personal strategy have had a minor influence, probably because he'd never really thought of how he could shape his own network. The second most important factor is his Chemistry with certain people. He says his shyness and a tendency to cover his discomfort with excessive talk "have probably made me sabotage opportunities for new business deals or relationships."

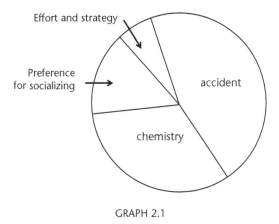

GRAPH 2.1

Lastly, Rob also admits his low preference for Socializing has played a role in his network. If he has to choose between a party and watching a movie at home with his family, he's very probably going to do the latter.

Now think about each of the generators of your own circle and answer the following questions. Better than just thinking, you should write down your answers to make sure that you don't skim the surface of your responses.

(1) Has each factor influenced your network in a positive or in a negative way? Describe the details and symptoms.
(2) Why didn't each factor have a greater influence? And from now on, do you want to be more important or less decisive?
(3) What's the relationship between each factor and the rest of your life (family, friends, culture, elderly models, etc.)?
(4) What can you do to influence each factor instead of being influenced by them?

If you've taken the time to analyze all these elements, you now have a better understanding of your own past, your personality, and how you interact with your environment to spur the events in your life. This kind of thinking is fundamental to enable learning and personal growth to improve networking capabilities. It will help you put your finger on involuntary reflexes and behavior patterns that may be limiting your achievements.

Be patient, though! Sometimes these introspection exercises don't yield immediate results, but delay the sought-for answers several hours or days. You may then jot down this new answer near your initial thoughts to help you respond to the key question: why is your network the way it is?

2.2   STRATEGIC FIT

Understanding how your network came to be is a first step, but the bigger question is whether your current relationships leverage your efforts to develop personally and professionally, or, on the contrary, consume your energy and your time.

I developed a methodology acronym I call POTENCIA, the Spanish word for potential. It focuses on eight fundamental parameters that describe your network today, represented by each of these eight letters.

This method was inspired by several sociology models and analytic tools that study social networks. Selecting and combining these approaches to provide a pragmatic understanding of personal networks was a first step, followed by research and ongoing testing in seminars with hundreds of executives and businessmen.

The primary goal we're pursuing is to establish whether the network generated by all the elements previously discussed is the network you want to have.

2.3   SELECTING THE SAMPLE

An exhaustive analysis of your network, including the names of each and every person you've met, could consume lots of time, and we might get lost in analysis paralysis. It's more practical to select a representative sample of your closest bonds.

Most sociological tests recommend this approach, justifying it with the idea that when you analyze your closest friends and associates, those who make up the foundation of the whole structure, you will identify patterns and trends that replicate across the entire network.

A frequent question around selecting the sample is whether to include family and friends, or keep it strictly work-oriented. But if we maintain the integral perspective presented in the previous chapter, we can consider a pleasant chat with family as a private goal that everyone will have in order to get a good rest from work and to nurture emotional needs. It makes sense, then, to include the personal part of your relationships in the sample.

You may choose to draw your sample either way, but here I will describe a professionally oriented method, as I am assuming that most of your private or emotional needs are more or less covered intuitively. The professional arena usually demands greater attention, presents larger challenges, and elicits critical doubts when pursuing tangible business goals.

Start by preparing a list of no more than 25 names to represent your nuclear business environment. The list should include people from your job, your studies, and friends involved in your professional life. To help you build the sample, here are a few triggers you can use:

(1) People with whom you discuss business problems and delicate professional concerns.
(2) People you interact with most often in order to get your job done (e.g. you meet, exchange emails, or call them every week).
(3) People you go to in order to unblock work issues, get advice on complex situations, or whose experience and organizational role make them special and in a position to add value.
(4) People you come to when you want to get your CV out there, or get sensitive information about companies, markets, and countries.
(5) People you run into often at events and professional gatherings like fairs, conferences, golf, and cocktail parties.
(6) People who have sent you lots of emails concerning business, or have called you on your mobile more frequently in the last month.

Make sure your list contains at least 20 names and 25 at most, prioritizing the first people who come to mind. The same person may come up more than once in response to the triggers, but if it's already on the list, don't repeat it.

Remember that the presence on this list of family and friends is not a problem or a surprise, really. It makes sense to include your closest ties in your business concerns and challenges, and they will naturally worry about your problems.

In the case of young consultants, lawyers, family business owners, or executives who have moved recently, the people on the list will very probably coincide with your key emotional bonds. Long work hours and the very nature of work may facilitate the formation of deep bonds of affection in order to deal with pressure, or simply to help grow new roots in a new city.

2.4 YOUR NETWORK'S POTENTIAL OR, IN SPANISH, POTENCIA

Here we go then! The acronym will guide us to discovery.

P for Profound

Write the 25 names in a vertical list along the left margin of a white piece of paper. Look at the example below, setting the sheet of paper horizontally. As we complete the exercise, we will create several columns to the right of the names, one for each parameter.

The first way we're going to look at your network is in terms of its Profundity, "P," that is, how profound and strong the ties are between you and your close ones. Draw a second column to the right of the names and assign a score to each item on the list to define the level of trust existing between you and that person.

Score those who represent the maximum possible trust and close-ness with a three, and then adapt the successive scores of two, one, zero to the rest of the names in a proportionate way.

ROB'S NETWORK POTENTIAL					
Contacts	P	O	T	E	
Frank	3				
Silvia	2				
Tim G	2				
Steve A	0				
George W	1				
Samira S	2				
					PAGE 1

GRAPH 2.2

What we want to do is differentiate three levels among your 25 closest ties. Obviously all of them have an important level of trust with you, but this analysis needs to establish differences among them, so that, ideally, you should have one or more persons in each level.

Now you need to get another piece of white paper and set it horizontally, following the example below. Draw a small circle in the center of the page and write your name inside. Then draw another three circles around this first one to represent the three levels of depth in your nuclear relationships. It will look a bit like a topographic map of a mountain or a lake. Now you can space out the 25 names as dots, as shown in Graph 2.3.

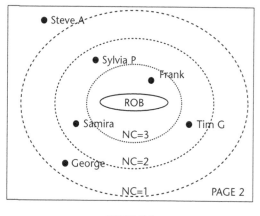

GRAPH 2.3

What does all of this mean? There are two theoretical extremes that could result from this exercise: a totally profound network, in which all the nodes are level three, or a mostly superficial network, with all nodes on level one. These are only abstract possibilities that wouldn't really come up as your response. Your analysis should fall somewhere in between these two.

Each of these abstracts represents a number of opportunities and threats, however, and neither is better than the other. When a network is profound, most of the nodes will show up in the smaller circle of the diagram, just around your name. It's a close, compact, strong beehive of connections.

Its main advantages would include comfort and companionship at all times, keeping you away from solitude and making it easy to find allies without a lot of effort. This kind of network circulates information at great speed and reacts rapidly to any of your needs.

On the downside, a profound network generates a lot of hard work. A high number of engagements and demands test your loyalty often, while connections with the outside world are very limited. High-trust communication rapidly tunes ideas, expressions, habits, and beliefs. One's attention can be diverted from a different, uncomfortable exterior, missing out on news and surprises.

A superficial network, where all nodes are placed in the outer circle of lower trust levels, is a network of acquaintances who may reach all sorts of environments, markets, and information channels, providing you with novelties and varied chances all the time.

Mark Granovetter is an American sociologist who's contributed significantly to social network theory with his studies on weak and strong ties, which could correspond to what we're calling superficial and profound connections.

Granovetter's research[1] shows that job hunting was more likely to produce results and better-quality information through weak ties than through strong connections. Weaker links turned out to have important value because they acted as bridges to other environments, providing new data that wouldn't be available through one's closer ties. These tend to have the same type of information and access points as their job-hunter friend because they frequently synchronize their interests, agendas and tastes.

The superficial network becomes less appealing when we look at its slow response to your demands or its low awareness of your needs and rhythms. Suppose you're organizing a dinner party at home. You will have to contact every guest at least once to get their confirmation, make sure they don't forget to come, have the address details. Seeing that these guests would not be your closest friends, either, they can easily have other engagements they prefer to yours.

What you need to think about isn't really whether your network is more or less profound, but how profound it needs to be to optimize your personal and professional development. In other words, what we want to analyze is the fit between your network and your personal strategy.

Rob, our guinea pig, happens to be a freelance photographer. We could imagine that his sales are in line with his financial needs, and suddenly they begin to grow significantly. Rob does the numbers and discovers he will need some kind of loan next year. He'll go round several banks to inquire on the types of financing he can opt for and the payment conditions.

When Rob goes down to the local pub and shares his troubles with his close friends, however, he is lucky enough to get an offer for a loan from two of them who don't require interest. One other friend offers to invest in Rob's business in exchange for the loan.

For this goal, as we can see, the mostly profound structure of Rob's network becomes a great asset. Rob didn't think of going to ask his friends for money. On the contrary, he went to see the banks and then found himself sharing a problem with them that wasn't urgent yet. This lack of urgency, coupled with Rob's relaxed attitude and a good dose of friendship, has allowed for three people to voluntarily jump in with help.

If his network was the opposite kind, that is, a more superficial web, Rob wouldn't have discussed such a delicate problem with his friends in the first place. But even if he had, the most he could have hoped for would be vague information about this bank or that other.

So when you think about the type of needs and goals you have mid term, what level of trust do you need to have in your network to make it work for you?

O for Objectives

Many executives give funny answers when they're asked how they evaluate their networks. They say it's related to network size!

But a larger network makes for harder work, demanding more exchanges of information and favors, more relationship-building. An executive's resources are limited, so good contact management doesn't necessarily translate into lots of contacts, but into smart investment of the resources he does have to achieve his goals. The "O" parameter looks at how every executive's network supports or obstructs his achievements.

Start by choosing two different goals you are currently pursuing – a possible promotion in your job, learning a new language, or finding an attic to rent in the city center, for example. Write a complete sentence to specify each of these goals.

Now, go back to your list of names and create a new column for the first goal. Assign each person a score to signify his or her capability to help you achieve this objective. Use three points for those who can really make a difference in your results, and one point for people who can help only slightly. If a given friend has no relation at all to the goal, then assign zero points.

Draw a new column for the second goal you specified and repeat the same scoring exercise. Each contact's capacity to help is going to depend on his or her knowledge of the subject, the accumulation of similar experiences in the past to strengthen their advice on the challenge, a number of contacts in sectors relevant to the objective, and privileged access to the resources you don't have.

Once you've assigned each of the 20 names a score, add up the total for each column to discover the value of this sample network. It becomes obvious that your network's value depends a lot on the goal you are pursuing. The very same network can be invaluable for some of your challenges in life, but ineffective in the face of others.

Let's look back at Rob's example to interpret his results. His two objectives are:

O1 Finance my company's operations for the next 12 months.
O2 Move my company to a more central location, with larger offices and great views to impress clients.

As you can see in the following diagram, Rob's network is more valuable when we measure it against his second goal. His closer bonds can't do much to get proper financing, but because some of them work as real estate agents, or because they themselves have recently moved, they can provide information, advice, and good references to help Rob engage the best agent for his move.

ROB'S NETWORK POTENTIAL					
Contacts	P	O1	O2		
Frank	3	1	2		
Silvia	2	0	2		
Tim G	2	0	2		
Steve A	0	1	0		
George W	1	2	1		
Samira S	2	2	2		
		O1=6	O2=9		
					PAGE 1

GRAPH 2.4

It's also important to think about the evolution of our goals over time, as we sail out of one professional phase into another. Our network's value isn't anything absolute and timeless; instead, its strength ebbs and flows as our goals vary, over time.

T for Transaction

Another characteristic of your network is the intensity of activity that pours through its veins, completing more and better transactions. The key advantage of any type of network is precisely the mobility it provides for valuable resources, enabling their flow to the spot where they are most needed. Bonds and nodes that don't close transactions will tend to block this natural flow, however.

Graph theory, the science that studies the composition and behaviour of networks, would refer to this overall mobility as intensity or traffic volume. We are used to hearing about it when discussing road traffic in cities, or even referring to the railroad network and the critical point beyond which a collision becomes highly probable. Each network has its own critical point, and in social networks it will depend both on quantity and on quality of the flow.

Suppose you're planning investments on roads in a rural area. You will need to look at how often people travel from one town to another, so you won't spend your money on improving a road that is seldom used. Transfer this notion to an executive's network and a provocative question arises: should our busy manager continue to spend time and money on the paths of his network that seldom transport information or value, or should he allocate his resources elsewhere? Would that bond become useful and busy if more resources were invested in it?

There's a limit to this logic, though. How many extremely busy bonds can come together in a cross-section (that would be you) without saturating it, or in other words, without driving you crazy? Beyond this critical activity level, the probability of making mistakes and telling one person what you were going to tell another person very confidentially becomes alarmingly high. Picture a stressed-out executive, running late all the time, and doing a dozen things at once...the risk of error with a stray short messages (sms) or email gets even worse.

What we're going to do is establish an indicator to estimate the level and importance of transactions going through each of the bonds in your sample network. Draw two new columns on your work page, and use the first to establish frequency and the second, quality. Frequency will refer to the number of emails, calls, and short messages you exchange with each contact. Quality will estimate the value added by these exchanges. Once more, this is not about being exact, but about differentiating the relationships you have with the people in your sample network.

Using our now typical one-two-three scale, assign threes in the frequency column to the people you talk to daily and ones to the people you interact with less often. Then use the scale to score those cases where the value added up to now has been extremely high with a three. Assign a one to those whose value has been negligible. If you find someone on your list that has never helped you in any way, someone you haven't assisted either, you may assign a zero. I'll leave it to you to play with negative scores if you really need them.

Draw a third column to represent the total value of T, Transaction. Multiply the numbers assigned for frequency and quality for each name on the list to obtain the total value exchange that you perceive in that relationship.

ROB'S NETWORK POTENTIAL						
Contacts	P	O	F	Q	T=F x Q	
Frank			1	3	3	
Silvia			2	0	0	
Tim G			3	3	9	
Steve A			0	1	0	
George W			3	0	0	
Samira S			2	0	0	
						PAGE 1

GRAPH 2.5

Rob remembers how his friend Frank, a Wall Street broker, gave him a hot tip on an acquisition that would probably affect Rob's investments in the stock market, maybe even grazing legal limits and his firm's policy. Rob valued this action enormously, not only because Frank's tip turned out to be right on track, protecting Rob's portfolio, but also because Frank had assumed a significant risk by telling his friend.

Beware, dear readers, I'm not suggesting that anyone turn to illegal brokering all of a sudden! I'm just illustrating small exchanges that go on daily and that nobody confesses to openly, but that constitute a very valuable currency in terms of trust and friendship.

A friend who once lent Rob money and another one who risked her own position in her boss's eyes to recommend Rob for a job represent highly productive bonds in Rob's perception, even if they don't speak very often.

Note that when Rob multiplied frequency and quality of his bond transactions, his network seems to have reduced. Maybe he's been a bit severe assigning scores today, and if he repeats the exercise tomorrow he may come up with no zeros. Still, we're more interested in what the score represents than in its absolute value.

Silvia is a friend he sees quite often, but there is no value exchange between them. It may be a relationship that is kind of forced by working in the same team or because she may be the close friend of another of Rob's closer ties. The environment makes them come together often, but they don't exchange anything useful, so Rob should take note of this fact and act accordingly.

In future chapters, when we talk about the nature of human bonds, we'll show how building a relationship is a task you share with the other. If Silvia shows no interest in exchanging anything other than "Hi, how are you?" every day, she will never become a meaningful person in Rob's network, no matter how much Rob would like her to be.

Steve has practically no interactions with Rob, but he's adding value in some way. He might be doing an MBA abroad or lack the time to write, but Rob has scored him as relevant. There must be something in their past that doesn't erase over time. Rob smiles when he thinks of Steve, even if right now there isn't much contribution to the general intensity of the network from him.

This parameter is very useful when evaluating new contacts, so that if you don't observe any real offerings to the network, or these contacts do nothing whatsoever to build stuff with you, it will show you that they're not really into networking, and don't think it a worthy use of their time. There are lots of people who live as if social networks don't exist or are totally irrelevant to them. In these cases you risk investing yourself in a relationship that won't evolve with time, instead of choosing another acquaintance that will reciprocate your efforts. It's a cost of opportunity that only you can measure, but make sure it's you who decides, and not chance.

E for Extension

Extension alludes to the mixture of people that blend together in your network. As discussed in the section on objectives, it's not the size of the network that counts. High extension means there are several angles of diversity among nodes, which in turn connect you with new environments and ways of life that can enrich yours. If our friend Rob relates to only Spanish men of the same age, similar political views and religious beliefs, and they're all crazy about football, we could say the extension of his network would be minimal.

If, on the contrary, Rob includes among his closest ties other men ten years his senior and others who are ten years younger than he, he'd be able to look at his financial challenges through both a more traditional perspective when discussing them with his older friends, and a more "hip," optimistic angle over beers with the others. These conversations will provide new ideas or questions he hadn't thought about, as well as connecting him to new people and sources of information that aren't accessible from Rob's position. It's just impossible to keep up with everything that goes on around you!

Age is one of the variables you can study, but also gender, industry, college background, geography, and any trait that defines a person. The more degrees of diversity, the greater is the extension of Rob's network.

Now, here's the catch: human nature. Apparently we tend to get together with people who share our interests and values. You must have felt suddenly lazy about all this just reading the last paragraph and planning all the uncomfortable things you'll have to do to increase your network's extension, right?

It's easy to make friends at work who are the same age, go to the same gym, and live close to you. The probability of actually building a relationship with someone who doesn't match all these traits is, frankly, minor.

Evolutionary psychology tells us that human evolution is to blame for this preference. The first hominids learned to distrust members from other tribes and to stay alert if they encountered any, identifying them quickly because of their different attire and peculiar habits. A harsh environment made tribes compete violently with one another in order to secure the best caves in the right places, with superior hunting opportunities, the most desirable mates, and other luxuries like easy access to water and food. In the fight for survival a member from another tribe could easily mean death.

There can be great advantages to mingling with diverse crowds, though, opening doors to other worlds currently out of your reach. The best part of maintaining a diverse network is that each member sees and interprets reality in a completely different way, increasing the variety of suggestions and reactions you receive from interacting with them.

The ability to interpret a challenge from several angles is the first requisite to reach truly innovative approaches. It also helps you control the gravity of your problems by making you aware of what happens around you. Sometimes you even get an unexpected surprise by navigating the sub-networks of these diverse relationships.

If Rob had discussed his financial troubles with his group of clone friends, they might have been very negative about the problem and pessimistic about possible bank loans, leaving Rob unsettled and worried. If he goes out to lunch with his diverse friends instead, his older colleague's experience may point him to other sources of funding. He may mention a private investor friend of his who could provide a few tips, explain what the best negotiation tactics are, and how to present his company in a compelling manner.

So, getting back to you, I suggest you return to your work page and draw three new columns. You can choose to use the three parameters we are proposing, or just focus on three of your own.

The first column will describe age range: those whose age is no more than three years from yours can receive an equals sign (=). Those who are more than three years your senior can be marked with (>me), and the people who are more than three years younger can be marked with (<me).

The second column will show nationality, and the third column will refer to sector of activity. Let's look at Rob's work table:

ROB'S NETWORK POTENTIAL					
Contacts	...	Age	Nat	Sectr	
Frank		=	SP.	law	
Silvia		<R	SP.	Law	
Tim G		=	SP.	law	
Steve A		=	SP.	Energ	
George W		>R	AM.	law	
Samira S		=	Jord	bank	
					PAGE 1

GRAPH 2.6

Four of Rob's ties are the same age, four are Spanish, and there are more lawyers than anybody in his network. There are some international contacts, an American and a Jordanian woman, two friends in different age ranges, and two people who know nothing about law. In this reduced sample of six, diverse people make up one-third of Rob's entire list, which is not negligible.

31

If we go through the whole 30 names and find a lot of Spanish lawyers, however, we'd be talking of a pretty limited extension.

Once you've completed your columns, take a broad look at each one and identify general patterns. We're not trying to perform a detailed statistic study that won't yield any conclusions. What we want is to decide whether each column is diversified or homogeneous, instead of counting exact numbers of responses this way or that way.

Take the most frequent answer. If it appears in more than 18 or 20 names, you can qualify your network as flat in this parameter. If there is no value that repeats itself more than ten times, you can qualify it as diverse. When looking at the ensemble of parameters, how would you qualify the extension of your network?

N for Nature

The nature of your bonds is also something to look into. In Chapter 4 we'll discuss how human bonds are like walls made up of bricks of trust, but trust can be separated into two kinds: cognitive and emotional.

Cognitive trust is the kind we typically establish with a new boss or work colleague. It's based on our belief in the other person's promises and trust that he or she will honor engagements. He'll show up for work every day, efficiently finish any task we ask of him, and correctly answer any questions we have on the topic he says he's so good at.

Affective or emotional trust, on the other hand, is what we have in our parents and siblings. It's based on a strong feeling of affinity with the other person, for reasons we can't explain, but which are abundantly clear in our gut. When we enjoy another person's company, we look for more occasions to relish our good times together.

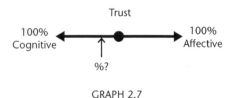

GRAPH 2.7

Each one of us tends to build bonds with a mixture of both components, resulting in a different nature of trust. The way we say hello, the subjects we choose to talk about, and the locations we prefer for the following meetings define whether we move on the right or on the left of this graph.

This also selects the types of people that connect to us, as they will feel uncomfortable if the nature of their trust, understood as their preferred mix of trust types, is very different from ours, making it less easy for the relationship to consolidate.

For example, Luc was the director of online training at a large company for a number of years. He obviously received many visits from HR consultants, one of whom was a woman who, in his words, "kept touching" him throughout the entire meeting. He hated her. He was so put off by this incident that he told and retold the story of her visit many times, clearly uncomfortable with the whole thing.

Probably what happened was that this woman was very physical in her expression of trust, and pretty fast at feeling at ease with others, using physical touch as a way to build bonds with them. What she didn't notice was Luc's preference for cognitive bonds, at least in professional settings and office meetings.

You've probably encountered someone you found to be cold, or an office colleague who never comes out for drinks with everyone else on Thursdays. Maybe he prefers to keep his work connections on the cognitive side of trust.

What are your connections like, then? Let's draw two more columns on your work page, and distribute five score points among both columns for each name. The first column will represent cognitive trust and the second one emotional trust. The sum of points assigned to both columns for each name must be exactly five. No more and no less.

ROB'S NETWORK POTENTIAL				
Contacts	...	Cog	Afec	...
Frank		1	4	
Silvia		5	0	
Tim G		4	1	
Steve A		4	1	
George W		3	2	
Samira S		5	0	
				PAGE 1

GRAPH 2.8

We can see that Rob's relationships are mostly cognitive. Except for Frank, with whom he seems to have a profound friendship far from professional or transactional aspects, the rest of his ties seem to be more connected to him by non-emotional elements.

This graph is telling us that Rob prefers to define an objective base line to his personal relationships, probably maintaining a well-polished attitude and refraining from too much touching and physicality in most bonds.

But what type of people should he be interacting with regularly? Does he work in finance, a conservative and cool environment? Or is it something more demonstrative, like fashion models bringing their little dogs to the catwalk and telling everybody all the quirky details of their latest love story?

It's the strategic fit between Rob's preferred trust mix and his professional environment's customs that we're interested in. This will determine whether Rob should consider shifting his preferences, or changing his career plans if necessary. Even if this is something quite hard to change in an adult, it still is another piece of information to help us understand the whys and why nots of Rob's success in life.

Look at your own answers and think about the nature of the bonds that are more abundant in your sample. Compare your observations with what you perceive in other people around you and notice how this helps or hinders your networking efforts.

Don't worry if you're beginning to think of your sample as the 'anti-network'! We're only performing a preliminary, detailed exam to help you process all the different notions that come into play, but none of these parameters is crucial on its own. We must complete the POTENCIA method in order to test all the information and extract global conclusions about you and your network.

C for Credit

This is where our Spanish anagram, POTENCIA, diverges from the English word POTENTIAL, so instead of a T we have a C. You even learn a tidbit of Spanish while focusing on networking today!

The law of reciprocity is pretty well known to all of us, but it's a lot more complex than you would think and it's especially relevant to our topic.

The worldwide law predicates equality between what we give and what we receive, explaining why we feel the need to give something back when someone has been generous to us in some way; just another obvious idea that's never as easy to interpret in reality as it should be, right?

This law is not exclusive to the human species, and may be observed among other mammals as well. Some experts argue that the instinct to reciprocate appeared in evolution as a way to spread limited resources as much as possible through group sharing.

From time to time a marketing expert manipulates this law to convince companies that a fast way to seduce customers is to offer them a gift first, sparking their need to reciprocate by buying the company's service. I'm not saying it doesn't work, but this interpretation is far from the principles of networking we are covering in this book. For better or for worse, networking tools, and emotional skills at large, are at everyone's disposal, whatever ethical spirit is guiding them.

One example is those cosmetic samples we get in shops after buying an expensive cream. Does this gesture make you feel obliged to shop at that store or consume that brand? Hardly! And the reason is simple: it's not authentic. We know perfectly well that it's an impersonal selling trick, to the point that we might choose not to take the samples. If only we could get a discount on our purchase instead!

There is a very fine line between authenticity and interest, and there doesn't seem to be an infallible test to distinguish them. But the generous offering of help or added value, as proven with the little exercise we did in Chapter 1, is the very essence of networking.

So, yes – offering something freely, without an ulterior motive, is the beginning of every bond of trust, a universal custom. In millions of instances of our history as a species, new neighbors have brought gifts with them to represent good faith, peaceful wishes, and a will to become friendly. They've also been used to fool the naïve, by using a giant wooden horse to infiltrate Troy secretly, for example.

We agreed also that in order to add value to someone we needed to get information. Our offering must be authentic, but also customized to each individual we meet. It is the receiver who determines its value, no matter how much we think it's worth.

To give away diamonds might seem like a great tactic to some, but to those who have thousands of diamonds it means little or nothing. Those who are against the trade of diamonds and its obscure shadows of exploitation might require a certificate to clarify its origin, and others, who've never seen a real diamond, might try to bite it or even sell it, because it's completely useless where they come from.

Standardized gifts like diamonds or luxuriously printed corporate greeting cards with nothing but a business card inside are not the builders of trust they're made out to be. They don't require a personal effort, and this is something the receiver perceives intuitively and immediately. This little detail is stored subconsciously and used to evaluate us later on.

The law of reciprocity has been playing a key role in every relationship you've established up to now, even if it doesn't show. Often we fall into a lack of reciprocity because we aren't paying attention.

Let's take a look at your state of reciprocity, or, as we've called it here, the credit available in your network, shall we?

The credit in your network alludes to the disposition of your contacts to help you out spontaneously in case of need. It is directly proportional to how much you have done for each one of them in the past. And yep, we're going to need another column!

This time we will score each name as if it were the statement of an imaginary bank account where you've been saving money with each past interaction. If you've helped a given contact more than he or she has helped you, you have credit available for future spending. If, on the contrary, you've been living the life and enjoying lavish attentions from your friend, or if you happened to ask a big favor recently, then your account is in the red.

ROB'S NETWORK POTENTIAL			
Contacts	...	Credit	...
Frank		1	
Silvia		–10	
Tim G		0	
Steve A		10	
George W		5	
Samira S		–5	
			PAGE 1

GRAPH 2.9

On this occasion you can assign up to 10 points of credit, or as much as –10 points to signify debt. Using this scale, a zero means you are in perfect balance with your contact because you've both reciprocated regularly along time, or you simply haven't done anything for each other. Needless to say, if you score your friend with a –10, you have a lot of catching up to do!

Rob's scores are shown on this graph, and if we add up all the scores in his column, we get a total of one point. Is this good or bad? On one hand its good because it means that on a global level there is good reciprocity between Rob and his network. But on the other hand it's also bad because Rob isn't taking good care of his friends, or cultivating the credit he might need in the future.

A network with a total sum score near zero or negative is telling us that we've lost track of our credit situation and have let our network take good care of our needs without thinking of giving back, or simply sticking to minimum effort reciprocity.

If we find ourselves needing a fast response, we might be left standing. Our network doesn't feel significant debt towards us, lacking an inner impulse to run to our rescue. Our close ties will respond eventually, but probably more slowly and with less enthusiasm.

This parameter points clearly to the limitations of network size imposed by our own ability to manage it adequately, watering it regularly with help and well thought-out services.

No matter what your current work environment is like, you need to cultivate the credit in your network. A network without credit cannot support any personal growth strategy. It could happen that the standard in your business sector is one of dried-out networks, lacking credit, but in such a case the whole industry would be riddled with issues of distrust, probably moved more by aggressive competition and selfish power struggles.

I for Intermediation

An import agent's address book or database is a network of intermediation. A match-maker's network would be too, whether she be an online web community manager or a real-life head hunter. Other daily examples include travel agents or international brokers.

All these persons or entities are the centric node surrounded by a network of people who interact with it to do business. An intermediation network is shaped like a star, as illustrated in Graph 2.10.

All the members of this network need to go through you to interact with the others. This configuration became a popular business model through the ages when the central node decided to charge a fee in exchange for opening the connection between two parties.

A travel agent connects tourists to hotel managers and to airlines, charging a commission for her service.

Such a service can be enriched if the central node chooses to assume the risks involved, if he can provide additional information to help his

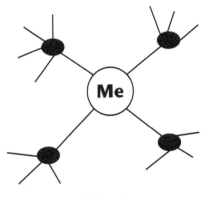

GRAPH 2.10

customers achieve their goals, or even advising them professionally on how to complete their transactions. The intermediary may do it for free also, funding his activities through publicity.

The other extreme is a cohesive network, illustrated in this other graph, where all the nodes are connected to all the other nodes. Does it remind you of anyone? How about your family? Most families respond to this pattern.

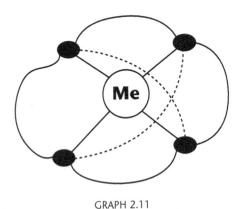

GRAPH 2.11

No money is to be made here, as you can see, unless everyone fought and needed an external mediator to help them negotiate, as happens all too frequently today.

Our next question is whether your network is closer to cohesion or to intermediation, and what advantages you can reap in either case.

Take a look at your second work page, the one with the concentric circles. Draw a black arrow between every two nodes that know each other. It's up to you whether to assign arrows to those who've only seen each other a couple of times or keep them for connections that are closer to each other. Do whatever works better for you.

A cohesive network has 100% density, a parameter used frequently in graph theory, and calculated by dividing the number of black arrows in the network by the total possible number of connections you could establish.

We're going to simplify calculations and just focus on the visual impression you get by looking at your diagram to decide whether it looks more like one extreme or the other. Look at Rob's exercise on the next page in Graph 2.12.

Although George seems to be connected to quite a few people, and Silvia and Steve are connected to each other, Rob's sample looks like an intermediation network. The key advantage he has is what researcher Ronal Burt had named a "structural hole," which will allow him to create value for his peers easily.

Obviously Rob's job is to manage affairs for his company and he's not going to start charging his friends a commission before he introduces them to each other. But just by fixing them up he's adding value to both of them.

Burt's structural holes[2] are the spaces without bonds that are left in Rob's network, representing an opportunity to build trust by joining people who can benefit from knowing one another. According to his vast research, executives who have structural holes in their networks achieve better results and increase their leadership.

An intermediation network, riddled with structural holes, is a land ripe for growing value with ease, helping people fulfill their individual needs once they are introduced to one another. How much do you appreciate the person who introduced you to your current wife or husband? You probably both think of this person with appreciation. How about the friend who connected you with your current boss? Well...that would depend on how good or bad your relationship with him is, right?

But there are more advantages to intermediation structures: information from all sorts of origins can reach you, enabling constant innovation and creative thinking, even accessing the most sensitive information before others do. And you're probably invited to lots of parties!

The catches would involve work-load issues and the difficulty to mobilize your network towards your goals and ideas. Members don't know each other, so they need you to push information around to each

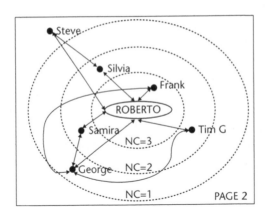

GRAPH 2.12

of them. If you're the one organizing a party, you will have to call each friend several times, as each of them belongs to other more cohesive networks that consume their attention and also organize cool parties.

It's a bit like sitting at the middle section of a long table with many guests. You can talk to all of them pretty easily, choosing the best conversations to blend into, but you have to pass the oil and vinegar, the wine, the drinks, from one side to the other, all the time.

A cohesive network's key advantage is comfort and easy management. You don't need to plan or think out who you will call and why. You meet them constantly at cocktails and events they all attend. With this crowd a party's a cinch; all you have to do is call one or two of them and they'll tell all the others.

Communication in these networks is redundant because any piece of gossip can travel many paths simultaneously to reach other nodes. Picture the birth of the newest family baby, for example, and how the news travels through parallel emails and telephone calls, reaching each family member several times from different sources. This turns inconvenient when you're trying to do something discreetly in a small town where everybody knows everybody. It's almost impossible to do anything without the whole town finding out about it.

Cohesive networks can create important peer pressure on their individual members, and may even obstruct innovation. Independent thinking and individuality are not looked upon as good things, but rather signs of disloyalty to the group. Group thinking tends to align perspectives, brushing off or simply ignoring ideas that come from the outside. Conversation tends to close doors to external news and focus on problems closer to home and the members of the network.

If one of the group members starts thinking about a professional change, or feels his sentimental relationship might be over, the rest of the group will try to talk him out of these outlandish ideas. The group needs him to stay the same and avoid change. It's cozy and familiar for everybody, and changes will only disrupt that close balance they share. It's better to stop members from straying into other interests and hobbies.

Latin social networks tend to be pretty cohesive, as a matter of fact. Family ties are very strong, to the point of flooding individual agendas with plenty of family gatherings and celebrations. It can be very difficult to find time for non-family related friends.

Family circles extend to friendships across generations, breeding forty-something executives who are proud of their weekly dinner with kindergarten peers. In certain cities or city areas it's impossible to access these close-knit networks unless you're born there, unfortunately isolating newcomers.

These networks are very resistant, with strong ties reinforced by shared memories and anecdotes. They lack structural holes, however. Even if they do love their members dearly, they shy away from novelty, penalizing exploration initiatives and criticizing anyone who plans to leave everything to set up a bar on the beach.

Once again, focus on your needs and mid-term objectives to decide on the most appropriate configuration for you. When you're single, intermediation networks keep your social life interesting, making sure you don't rot at home. But once you've settled down and have children, there's nothing better than a close-knit network of loving family members and friends eager to take the children from you.

A for Acquirement

Acquirement is the unlikely noun derived from the act of acquiring a certain skill or trait, and I'm choosing it as the best noun in English to define the A parameter of POTENCIA, the Spanish word for "potential."

This parameter looks at your network's capacity to evolve and develop new properties with time, something that occurs through the entry of new contacts. In acquirement we will measure the number of new people who enter your network, because only through them can your network evolve to follow your personal and professional growth.

A closed network has no opportunity of renovation. Even if your current figure of concentric circles looks great and up to date right now, there are many factors that could distance your friends from you.

They might move to a new city, start dating someone who dislikes you, or disappear to Natal in Brazil to start a bar on the beach and never come back.

The ugly truth is that you can't control these factors, so you have no alternative but to admit that the current comfort of your entourage hangs on a delicate balance that may break any day, for a reason as insignificant as small quarrel between your two best friends. All you can do is make sure your network is nourished by new contacts, constantly.

Only a network open to acquirement can bring you surprises and new business practices by incorporating new people. Cultivating your network, therefore, consists of making sure that new contacts blend in regularly. Nourish each new bond to bring it to new levels of trust and intimacy, until one of them becomes an excellent business associate or a truly wonderful friend.

Let's analyze it as follows. Draw the last column on your work page and assign each name on the list one of these three categories:

(a) If he or she has been in your network for less than a year.
(b) If you met him or her more than a year ago but less than five years ago.
(c) If you met more than five years ago.

A simple look at the column should be enough to determine whether your network is acquiring new skills or not. In Rob's (Graph 2.13) we can see that he's kind of sitting on his comforts.

2.5   INTERPRET YOUR NETWORK POTENTIAL

If your head is spinning and you're creeping up the walls with unease about your network, this is the part of the exercise that will help you come back to your senses. Our last analysis will help you weigh up all the information and filter it into two or three improvement goals.

This exercise is a tool coaches often use, and it will help us prioritize all these conclusions instead of drowning in the details. Take a new piece of paper and write the acronym POTENCIA in capital letters down the left margin as shown in Graph 2.14, with two columns to the right.

ROB'S NETWORK POTENTIAL									
Contacts	P	O	T	E	N	C	I	A	
Frank								C	
Silvia								C	
Tim G								B	
Steve A								B	
George W								C	
Samira S								C	
								PAGE 1	

GRAPH 2.13

The first column will signify your level of satisfaction with your network in the corresponding parameter. If you are very happy with it, you can assign a score of five points, and if you are completely unsatisfied, assign a zero. Rob seems to be just as unsatisfied with the credit of his network, as you can see.

	level of satisfaction	level of importance	
P	4	1	
O	3	7	
T	3	5	
E	5	2	
N	1	3	
C	0	4	
I	2	6	
A	4	8 ←	

GRAPH 2.14

Given that your resources are, after all, limited, you need to identify a maximum of two or three development goals to focus your energy. This is what the second column is for: a ranking where you will assign a score between one and eight to establish each parameter's importance in your current life strategy. Remember it's a ranking system; you can only use each score once, so that the most important parameter will be the eight and the least important one will be the one.

With these two perspectives you can choose the two or three parameters most important to you and needing improvement. Rob's example shows that his acquirement is the most important one, but it's performing pretty well, so he's ranked Objectives, Transaction, and Intermediation, instead, as the next three important parameters, with medium to low satisfaction levels.

Rob's development strategy is going to focus on shifting his network configuration away from cohesive structures, develop new contacts related to his future goals, and improve the frequency and quality of interactions with his network nodes.

Take a few minutes to write down the changes you are looking for in the three parameters you've chosen, clearly stating what development goals you want to achieve in the next 12 to 15 months.

As we will insist on once and again throughout the book, networking is an art that takes time, care, and patience. Immediate goals can no longer be achieved through your current network. It's too late. Look towards the future and keep reading to make sure that the next time you need something, you and your network have become perfect allies.

2.6 ERIK WACHTMEISTER, FOUNDER OF "A SMALL WORLD" AND "BEST OF ALL WORLDS"

A Swedish entrepreneur who constantly travels around the world to do business and meet new friends, Erik Wachtmeister was among the first to imagine what intimacy would look like on the internet. Creator of the exclusive online community "A Small World," he now tells us how the idea came to be, and why he's working on a new venture to bring the "Best of All Worlds" to each and every one of us.

Today's world has been made a lot smaller with the emergence of online social networks. Still, the question everybody is asking is how the art of building human relationships will be changed by internet-driven connectivity. How does human trust develop over keypads and screens?

Over a warm cup of coffee, Erik Wachtmeister, a very global citizen in every way, shares with us his unique perspective on this phenomenon. A Small World, his first venture in social networks, fast became one of the hottest invitation-only online communities in the last decade.

Founded in April 2004, the community has 700,000 users and has been labelled "MySpace for millionaires" by *The Wall Street Journal*, as well as "Facebook for the few" by *The New York Times*.

Drawing on the lessons learned from this first experience, Erik is now fully engaged on the launch of his new online community: Best of All

Worlds.com, where he wants to provide the latest technology-enabled services to global niche groups such as Entrepreneurs, New Mothers, Golf, Hunting, Luxury Industry, McKinsey Alumni, etc.

This incurable entrepreneur is Swedish, born into a diplomatic family that provided a very unique education, divided between Moscow, North Africa, Washington DC, London, Paris and New York City, to name just a few residences. From a very early age he was exposed to different cultures, languages and protocols of human interaction, nurturing in him a strong passion for international social connectivity.

His career as an international corporate finance banker furthered a lifestyle made up of constant travel and sharing of common interests with citizens from remote cultures. "It became increasingly clear to me that there was a global network of like minded individuals who met each other at several social hotspots in key cities around the world... they were already connected!" he remembers.

By 1997 Erik had his first business vision of an online tool to help all his friends and acquaintances keep in touch, share information and exchange useful recommendations to cover both business and leisure needs. "I kept running into friends who needed contact details for a shared contact, had forgotten the name of the delicious little restaurant hidden away behind touristic streets of Paris or needed a recommendation to get into the V.I.P list for a sumptuous new ski resort in the Alps."

Erik reflects, "It was never about excluding anybody. On the contrary, my idea had to do with creating an intimate environment where you could let your hair down and feel at ease when interacting with other people," he specifies.

Pulled on by his profession, Erik started a small venture fund, Viking Internet PLC, which he managed to take public in only 90 days on the London Stock Exchange. It would be a few years before he put together a questionnaire to ask his network what they thought of such a community in 2003, thus placing the first stone of the acclaimed virtual hotspot.

By and large, Wachtmeister initiated a trend that may only grow stronger in the years to come. The problem we all experience with enormous open networks like Facebook is that they resemble busy city center squares in Rio de Janeiro, Moscow or New York; open spaces swarming with busy people pursuing their own needs, competing to grab the first taxi cab and avoiding dangerous strangers. It's tough to find and make friends in a place like this.

Erik asked himself the question, "If the world has six billion people, could there be a smaller group of three million with whom you share enough to build a friendship, where you are only three degrees apart from everybody else?"

One of the key drivers of his success was probably his wide and diverse network in real life. Seven hundred people received the survey he sent out to get feedback on the features and services this community would appreciate, what they would be willing to pay for, and what would make their lives easier or more enjoyable.

"We were global from the get go. The test run was pulled into live activity immediately. The first two thousand people I invited into the online community were exceptional networkers who connected to many others in their local markets. Very cool, great people that were soon organizing 10,000 events a year to spend time with others like them," he describes.

Erik compares these initial steps of the invitation-only group to one of those unforgettable wedding parties we have all had so much fun at. "It's typical at a wedding to meet people from very different walks of life who treat you as a friend instantly because there's already something important in common: the bride and groom."

Smaller online networks that can provide minimal guarantees are, in fact, a natural response to our human evolutionary design. Confronted with a stranger in the wild, uncertain habitats we evolved in, it was better to run for your life than to wait around to get your food stolen from you. We are programmed to be wary of strangers, unless we meet them in a secure setting.

Wachtmeister is especially proud of creating the opportunity to help people find what they were looking for: "many thousands of people have been getting together around the world to build new businesses, start wonderful friendships and learn from each other. We created an atmosphere where people became more open, and accommodated to treat strangers as friends. It's the kind of intimacy that doesn't exist in the World Wide Web!" Or in a busy underground station, I might add.

Like so many other new ventures, A Small World brought in financial investors who came with new visions and interests that didn't quite convince Erik: "There was a lot of debate through 2007 and 2008 about income models for small communities and how much advertising we should do. But for me it was all about giving our users the best possible service."

By 2010 Wachtmeister resigned from the board and decided to start a new online community: Best Of All Worlds. "I truly believe there is still a huge vacuum in social networks that ASW has failed to cover, and which has nothing to do with the 'collecting connections' approach of mass networks."

His vision is simple: "Constantly leveraging the best technology available will provide tailor measured services to niche interest communities who live and travel around the globe. Once again, it's about responding to a need that already exists...all great businesses do."

"Mass social networks provide an excellent way of indexing your relationships or reconnecting, but in Best of All Worlds we want to help people build their future relationships. By entering secure global communities that respond to their new interests, users are helped to grow and develop new relationships."

Erik insists on the importance of the "signal to noise ratio" in a World Wide Web with increasing information saturation. As more and more people upload videos, documents and photos on to the web, it's becoming harder and harder to find what we are looking for.

"By creating an intimate atmosphere of people you trust, the ratio naturally increases to help you find signals fast among the noise. It becomes a lot easier to find relevant, useful and unbiased information," he says.

Interestingly, the mammalian 'pack design' we still comply with today turns our networks of trusted contacts into the key filtering mechanism through which we find what we need, including information. We've been using trusted recommendations to make buying choices for almost every occasion for thousands of years. Why should it be any different on the internet?

Best of All Worlds is not a remake of his last venture, though. "Anybody will be able to join the platform, and then they will have to find their way into global private groups that will have defined their own membership rules...much the same as any real life club does today in most societies."

A supporting network of local ambassadors across geographic locations will be responsible for managing the consistency and careful growth of the groups. As Erik sees it, "you would be surprised at how many people are keen to help out in exchange for corresponding visibility and recognition. One out of every ten members tends to be extra active. Authority and dedicated expertise will be key to manage network proliferation successfully."

Wachtmeister confesses he's always been drawn to strong connectors with big, diverse networks and lots of different interests. It is that ability to relate on a range of different areas that lengthens and fills relationships. "If I had stuck to a network of bankers I would never have come up with these ventures. I strongly believe in creating a rich, diverse tapestry of relationships that join you in each of your own personal dimensions."

When asked about networking tips, Erik replies, "I would start by focusing on the network you already have. Get close to the people you are with, and enjoy sharing your passions and your friends."

Online social networks, he warns, "aren't standalone solutions. You may feel happy and connected because you have a thousand contacts on Facebook, but it may well be a false spell." And I can't agree more with him. Human relationships are built on trust, and as we've described along the book, there is an enormous part of trust that happens unconsciously in face-to-face interactions. Microsecond expressions and body signals drive good chemistry or alert us to danger.

Social networks are here to stay. They are changing the way we relate to each other in ways we cannot yet predict. This is true. But somehow emerging business models like Erik's are showing that the old rules still apply. We still need safe places where we can take our shoes off and feel at home, among global friends who expect nothing more of us.

CHAPTER 3

A BETTER YOU STARTS WITH A NEW UNDERSTANDING: WHY NETWORKS MATTER

Have you ever played a game of Go? This popular Asian game, called *baduk* in Korea, Go in Japan and weiqi in China, is over 4,000 years old. A board with black intersecting lines allows two players to manage the positions of their black or white stones in order to beat each other through the kind of elaborate strategy that comes with simple game rules.

If you have played, you could calculate your "Shusaku number" as the number of games separating you from the famous player Honinbo Shusaku. If you are a mathematician, you can calculate your "Erdós number" by counting the math papers that separate you from him. If you are an actor, your Bacon number will tell us the number of films between you and Kevin Bacon. The world seems to be made up of overlapping networks.

Until now you've looked at the world with nodal glasses. If anyone mentioned a group of people, you envisioned the individuals that composed it. When you looked at a map, you recognized the cities and mountains on the map. Any reality that entered your mind did so in the form of individual nodes that were more or less connected.

You only stopped noticing nodes when they were too small to see with the naked eye, and by then you'd be thinking of a unitary structure: a stone, a chair, or a planet.

Nature doesn't work in nodes, however, but through webs and meshes. Whereas man first looks at the nodes and then, through effort and dedication, sees the network, nature designs the network first, with nodes resulting from it. The individual nodes aren't essential, but are only pieces of a system that moves with its own laws to protect the ensemble in the event one of the nodes fails.

3.1 LIMITATIONS TO HUMAN INTELLECT: ISOLATED DOTS AND LINES

Graph theory, the first scientific discipline to study the nature and properties of networks, was applied to social studies by Paul Erdós and Alfred Rényi after the Second World War.[1] The origin of graph theory, however, is 200 years old: the Konigsberg problem[2] Euler described in the eighteenth century, later continued through G. R. Kirchoff and Francis Guthrie's work a century later.

Whatever starting point you take, the truth is that, after 200,000 years of *Homo Sapiens'* existence, we didn't started to look at networks untill 200 years ago. As several disciplines, including sociology, biology, physics, neurology, astrology, and even literary criticism advance independently in their understanding of the structure and impact of networks on the world we know today, they assert the sheer magnitude we still have to learn about networks.

This tendency to see things as isolated objects first, and fail to see connections among them until much later, has been reinforced by the development and popularity of the scientific method in the western world. Science has been the fundamental generator of enormous progress in our lives' quality, but science is also slave to the "cause–effect" principle.

Copernicus, Galileo, or Descartes were the fathers of the so-called "scientific revolution" that explains how we've come to set foot on the moon, build giant ski resorts in the desert, or keep us connected in real time with the other side of the world. It's also responsible, however, for our current disbelief in anything that hasn't been scientifically proven. It's the price we pay for science's beneficent advantages.

On the one hand, the scientist needed to observe the problem in conditions as close to those of a laboratory as possible. It's a way to eliminate all possible environment influences to infer a hypothesis or behaviour model. Such efforts at objectivity and decontamination of reality can make us lose experiences intrinsic to something real. For every effect there isn't one cause, but several causes acting independently, in their own measure, with variable strength. In other words, by being too scientific, too rational, we might lose the systemic vision that we are only beginning to recuperate in our research approaches.

It's true that the invention of computers has allowed science to develop multiple cause models, building mathematical formulas with N variables that reproduce the behaviour of the sea, volcanoes, or even subatomic particles. But even if our computers can process them, we still think one variable at a time, which is why so many technical "experts" make mistakes more often than not.

Why do meteorologists make incorrect predictions once every nine or ten days? Why do economists fail to anticipate events in global trade? Why do stock market analysts misread the future? No matter how much these technical experts know, and no matter how much experience they've accumulated, their predictions of multi-variable solutions entail huge helpings of intuition and imagination to sustain hypotheses.

The human mind seems to be designed for the linear and quantifiable. Maybe a few thousand years after the publication of this book, our species will have adapted its brain to the real multi-causal complexity of our curvy environment, but for the moment we're stuck with straight lines. After one cause comes one effect, and after a dot comes another dot, preferably aligned with the first one.

The world may be full of curves, but humans like to see straight lines. Everybody was deeply convinced that the world was flat because the segment of the horizon we could see from land looked flat. But Magellan demonstrated this line was only the edge of an enormous sphere.

Nature isn't made of straight lines, but of curvy ones. Most straight lines in the natural world come from accidents of man's hand. Take a walk around the islands on the blue route in south Turkey, or the snowy mountains of the Swiss Alps, or even the beautiful wild island of Fuerteventura. Count the number of straight lines you find in these landscapes that haven't been built by man. The ones created by Nature represent the smallest minority, and when you look closer, you begin to see they're not that straight after all.

To think of it, the first thing Nature does when man abandons one of his rectilinear edifices is to tear away little pieces from each contour and each beam. The process has concealed many architectural marvels. They have been discovered by sheer luck, hidden and devoured by jungles. Huge, ugly, and decaying real estate phantoms populate hundreds of sea-front landscapes because the builders didn't get the necessary permits before they started erasing the curves to draw straight lines with asphalt and iron.

The intellectual part of humans is so happy among dots and lines that since it created them it hasn't stopped improving them, multiplying them, adding them up. It's a lot easier to add up the length of two straight lines than that of two circles, not to mention irregular shapes.

Our evolving preference for straight lines can also be seen in the streets of our cities. The old centers tend to be more obedient to the laws of Nature, to its hills, and rivers, and winding paths. As soon as you find yourself in a newer city, however, there's little but squares, rectangles, and triangles. We've learned how to discipline rivers to make them more predictable, at least for the time being.

The Chinese have already started changing the course of one of their two most powerful rivers. The new course of the Yang Tse will oblige many thousands of people to move away from their homes and will certainly overwhelm the ecological balance of many areas. The scientists and officials behind this decision probably trusted complex computer calculations that judged social and ecological impacts as low. And the computer models used the variables they were given by the scientists themselves.

But who pays the scientists' salaries? We can assume this variable hasn't been positioned in the computer model, even when it could seriously skew the final results. It's just one of millions of possible examples of how we get things desperately wrong. We simplify, then lose sight of the systemic effect, when we express them in a linear model, comprehensible to scientific thinking.

So, what we're saying is that our imperfectly evolved mind tends to see straight lines, isolated dots, and one cause for every result. This wouldn't be a problem if it wasn't for another small detail: our mind loves to think it knows everything.

Whatever we can't see with our own eyes or comprehend with our own neurons doesn't exist, just as we ignore the 90% of our brain mass we can't utilize, even though it speaks to us in our dreams and exerts incalculable influence over our lives. Maybe this explains why it's taken us 199,803 years of Homo Sapiens maturity to begin studying networks.

3.2 A NEW WAY OF LOOKING AT THE WORLD

Listen up: nature thrives on irregularity and curviness in practically everything it does. It can't confine itself to isolated nodes. It creates holistic networks. Even the human species, the most intellectual, discipline-loving, straight-line-obsessed creature, is organized in curves and networks.

From the invisible ties that integrate or separate our neighbors, to the neurons that connect or disconnect thousands of times in our heads, we are anything but isolated, distinct beings. On the contrary, we are groups of cellular networks coming together in greater invisible webs. And out of loyalty to our linear intellectual limitations, we spend all day trying to create visible limits, like national frontiers, organizational walls, or family exclusions.

We've spent too much energy deciding the frontier lines defining who is a country and who isn't, or building and rebuilding walls like the one in Berlin or the North of Morocco. We've designed scores of ways to separate some from the rest, such as social classes, VIP areas, and ridiculous rules to keep people out of trendy places. Now we are getting nervous, however, about their usefulness in the face of globalization.

The greatest and most impressive network mankind has created, the World Wide Web, together with the growingly dense air transportation system, is making the invisible and spontaneous bonds between people closer and stronger every day.

3.3 NETWORKS EVERYWHERE

We live on the planet Earth, surrounded by the gyrating motion of a satellite, the Moon. We know our planet also travels around a star we call the Sun. Besides the Earth, there are another seven or eight planets turning around the Sun, as well, depending on whether we include Pluto in our list. These planets can have several satellites close to them, like the two moons of Mars or the 63 moons of Jupiter.

Our sun isn't the only star. We can see thousands of them in the sky at night, and there is already some talk of another four solar systems, stars with any number of orbiting planets.

We live in the Milky Way galaxy, and we've been able to assert the existence of other galaxies at variable distances from our own, which aggregate into cumulus, and these in turn integrate super cumulus.

It may seem at first sight that the sky offers us a huge collection of isolated nodes, but the truth is the positioning of each body depends on the gravitational forces generated between itself and every other celestial body around it. The apparently gigantic and disorderly group of galactic masses of varying sizes is really a network of networks: super cumuli made of cumuli of galaxies, each of which is made up of stars and solar systems like ours, with planets and moons.

Just because we can't see the ties that keep them close to each other doesn't mean they don't exist. Why isn't Mars closer to the Earth? And why are there nine planets in our solar system (as we think today) and not more?

This isn't a coincidence. The gravitational forces between all the different masses shape this universe as it is, configuring the exact places of each sphere and constituting the bonds of the network. Each attraction vector between a star and a planet, or between the planet and its moon, becomes a leash that compels it to travel around on its orbit without separating or getting closer. If we could build a vehicle powered by gravity, we could probably travel around the complete universe by jumping from one planet to another star and from one galaxy to another, leveraging the gravitational vector that keeps them apart.

In the other extreme of the three-dimensional spectrum, if we look at the smallest thing we know, we find networks of quarks and leptons. They make up atoms joined together by forces of attraction in repetitive patterns when they make up a crystal, or without any specific order, as in glass. Once more we find different types of networks whose behaviour is explained by the bonds between nodes.

What is a tree but a great network of leaves brought together by branches? Who denies that the human nervous system is a network of neurons and nerve cells sending each other electronic signals to process information and act?

And what about the movement of fish in shoals of thousands of individuals who change direction simultaneously, as if they were all part of a huge mesh? Today we still can't explain why fish form shoals and how they establish distance between one another, whether they use eyesight or not, whether it has to do with hydrodynamic properties in water or not. But we do realize there is something invisible between the fish that stops them from crashing into each other, keeping them together and articulating invisible paths from each fish in the shoal to all the others. Flocks of birds raise similar questions.

The fundamental structure of networks is present in practically every corner of the Universe. We're not only made up of networks and subnetworks of cells, but we ourselves shape invisible networks that connect some to others since we exist as a species.

No matter how much we like straight lines, we've also created, more or less intentionally, thousands of networks in our road maps, air carrier routes, and the very concept of the internet.

Some movies help illustrate the existence of social networks because they focus on that which connects characters who appear to be unrelated. An example of this was the movie *Crash*, which won an Oscar award in 2004, and illustrated social prejudice through an assortment of people from different countries who lived in Los Angeles. The coincidental crash of two vehicles in a city of more than four million people brings together a network of characters who have unknowingly interacted with each other in the previous 48 hours.

Another movie to illustrate the impact of social networks is *12 Monkeys*, in which Bruce Willis is a maniac in an asylum in a futuristic world that has been completely transformed by the action of one lab worker. He carried a highly contagious, deadly virus around the world, creating a global epidemic with just a few airplane trips to the largest cities in the world.

Imagine you are invited to a surprise party where nobody knows any of the other guests. The host hands everybody a hook to hang around their waist as they arrive at the party, with a ball of colored wool, each guest having a different color.

Our imaginary host asks each guest to join their strings of wool to each other's hooks each time they exchange more than ten words with any of the other guests. They then move on to their next acquaintance. What do you think the party would look like a couple of hours after it started? Can you guess at the number of colored wool strings crossing the room, and the amount of colored yarns you'll have around the hook at your waist line?

In real life, when you're late to a party you don't find a mass of colored yarn sprawling around the room, but you do guess that people have begun to mix. The noise is louder and there's more laughter and exclamations. You can't see them, but bonds have begun to build between the partygoers.

If the party is long enough, and the host makes sure nobody is left alone, a bond, whether stronger or weaker, is forming between every two people there. A pathway can then be drawn from each guest to any other guest, passing by the necessary intermediary connections.

Our society is far bigger and more complex than a party crowd, of course, but it still complies with this basic pattern of human relationships. It's a large network that connects its members, making pathways between every pair of individuals. This path may be invisible, but it's as real as the book you're reading.

A network is Mother Nature's preferred pattern. You could say networks are her very own signature. Just as Hitchcock took to appearing briefly in his own films and Klimt always used shiny textures in his paintings, designs 'made in Nature' are distinguishable because of their network structure. Consider this pattern as the fundamental fractal of the world we know, given that it's a basic shape repeated at all possible observation scales.

The successful pattern is used in the largest elements of our world, like the Universe of stars or the food chain in an ecosystem, and in the smallest elements we can't even see with the naked eye.

3.4 FREQUENT CHARACTERISTICS OF REAL NETWORKS

One of the funniest things about social networks is that their structure and behaviour are very similar to those in the rest of Nature. There's a series of characteristics that surprisingly repeat in several network types, and which, in the case of people, configure what we call the "small world effect" that makes networking such a worthwhile activity.

Erdós and Rényi,[3] two Hungarian mathematicians, looked into networks at the beginning of the twentieth century, reaching the conclusion that all social networks are random. It's an elegant way of saying they had no defined order, but spread equally in every direction.

The mathematicians observed that it was enough for each node to have one connection with any other node in order to build a giant network out of a group of smaller unrelated networks. Notwithstanding, it seemed Nature regularly assigned more ties than the one needed to enable the network. Nature tends to avoid risks, duplicating, tripling, and multiplying the basic needs in every way.

These supposedly random networks had very flat or regular structures; each node had a similar number of connections. If we tried to draw a typically regular network of six billion nodes – obviously when suffering from an acute case of incurable boredom – we would see a dark cloud of massive proportions, in a fairly flat shade of color, given that the distribution of dots would be endlessly repeated across the drawing.

Stanley Milgram's popular "small world" study[4] conducted in the 1960s and currently continued by Columbia University, however, showed otherwise. Their famous conclusion stipulated that between every two people in the world there is an average of six degrees of separation. For instance, if you were feeling especially whimsical one afternoon and wanted to have dinner with Paris Hilton or play golf with Barack Obama, you would have to call a friend who would text his cousin, who in turn would speak to a third person, and follow along two more human nodes to get a message to Hilton or Obama.

Think about the cloud of six billion dots you drew before and visualize each dot as a person. Mentally select three random dots to represent "Hilton," "Obama," and "me." Does it seem possible to connect these three dots with paths that pass through only six dots? Or twelve? Or eighteen?

How can the path between any two people among the six billion that populate our planet today be so short, if our network structure is regular? It's easy to see that the path from one extreme of the flat cloud can't be connected to the other edge with only six dots. Neither can it be done with ten dots or twenty. People clearly don't arrange themselves in flat, regular structures.

Albert-László Barabási's book, *Linked*,[5] accurately describes the story of hypotheses, correct guesses, and false conclusions reached in scarce sixty years of scientific study of networks. The book talks about different research teams and how they've discovered the characteristics that repeat time and again across all types of networks, including the ones fabricated by Nature and the ones made by the human hand. Malcom Gladwell's bestseller, *The Tipping Point*,[6] also discussed man-made web properties.

The first fascinating trait we come across is the irregularity of real networks. Gladwell talked about connectors, while other authors call them gatekeepers or hubs. A handful of privileged nodes are much better connected than the average node in real networks.

Think of a road map in Europe. It's an example of a network where cities and towns have roads coming in and heading out of them. Although more important cities tend to be better connected than the rest, you can't really conclude that they have more roads than the rest.

Now think of the typical map you find hidden among the last pages of any airline magazine, the type you read if you are once again dying of boredom, but this time sitting uncomfortably in a cramped seat several thousand meters above the ground. This map also shows a network, but in it there are a couple of nodes that cater to almost all the flights on the map. They are the selected airline's hubs.

"Hub" is the term IT experts use to describe the box that connects several cables coming from diverse computer terminals to the one network cable that supplies the signal. It's also the word used by American aviation to identify each airline's base station, connecting the majority of the flights they offer their clients.

A good example of a human hub or connector would be the famous banker, David Rockefeller. Sociologists who research the "reverse small world"[7] problem have tried to find out how many people a manager would know by mapping out all their weak ties. Estimates run between 3,000 and 10,000 contacts throughout their lives. But according to the video on the well-known banker done when he was at Chase Manhattan, his address-book had more than 50,000 names. Imagine the army of assistants he had to employ to keep all those contact details up to date at a time when there were no databases or personal digital assistants (PDA).

Another very publicized example of a connector would be Kevin Bacon, the actor, in relation to the rest of the actors in Hollywood. On a web page belonging to the University of Virginia, you can put his networking prowess to the test with what has been called "Kevin Bacon's Oracle."[8] This web page hosts a database containing all the movies this actor has participated in, including the name of all his collaborators in each film.

This web page is accessible by anyone, so when you enter the name of a certain actor, it brings back the number of degrees of separation that separate him or her from Kevin. Paco Martinez Soria, a popular Spanish actor you wouldn't know outside Spain, is only three degrees away, as is Dev Anand, a famous Indian actor. Finnish star Vesa-Matti Loiri is only two degrees away.

Kevin Bacon's oracle is talked about in most books and seminars about networking, but the truth is, he's far from being the best-connected actor in Hollywood, as Barabási's team has shown.[9] They ranked the best-connected actors in Hollywood scientifically, showing Rod Steiger as number one, and finding Bacon far down the list, below 850 other actors.

As it turned out, the Hollywood acting community has a maximum of three degrees of separation between any two actors. Kevin Bacon's fame as a connector was the lucky result of a number of coincidences, leading to a couple of bored students getting creative with a database after watching a program about Bacon.

The connector phenomenon is not exclusive to human social networks. Protein interaction within cells follows this pattern too, as most proteins interact with one or two other proteins, except for a small few which choose to annex themselves to a wide variety of others. The Yahoo! and Google portals are also examples of web pages with a lot more connections to other web pages than the average.

This phenomenon is commonly accepted under the name of the Pareto Principle,[10] which dictates that 20% of the causes are responsible for 80% of effects. In supermarkets, for instance, usually a small share of the assortment generates most of the shop's sales.

This unique understanding of the world and how it works is basic to any networker: global social networks articulate around a small number of hubs or connectors, acting as super-fast freeways to any contact in the world.

For one thing, hubs bring resilience to networks. An airplane, designed by brains that prefer straight lines, can fall out of the sky if one of its components fails, whereas the network of hardware servers around the world that support the World Wide Web requires simultaneous failure of all its large servers to go dead. The architects of the internet were obliged to overcome linear restrictions precisely to avoid an event of the sort.

Another wonderful example of resilience is Nature itself. In the giant ecosystem we call Earth there are between 3 million and 10 million species, and each year 3–10 whole species disappear, so why haven't we noticed great changes until the industrial era?

Natural designs tend to attach to networks whose backbone is made up of hubs, so the ensemble can continue to resist, even if some of the nodes fail.

On the other hand, the very structure that brings strength and resilience to networks is also its greatest vulnerability. If most hubs are attacked simultaneously, the network will break down.

Such has been the case of great epidemics, which were tightly linked to the enormous connectivity of their first victims. Once the virus appears it is equally likely to attack an unemployed youngster who never leaves home or a salesman who makes twenty personal calls a day. But the salesman is twenty times more likely to catch the virus each day through any of his visits, and he's also twenty times more likely to pass it on daily. Hubs are responsible for taking an ailment that only attacks a few and building it into a widespread epidemic. This phenomenon has been widely studied and is leveraged through viral marketing techniques.

This is why you need to think about this basic structure and recognize it in your own networks. To conquer any given group of people, you can greatly improve your chances of success if you start with the group's connectors. If you want to integrate existing networks in the company you've just started working for, the best strategy is to strike up a chat with one of the network's best-connected hubs.

A networker who can recruit and involve good connectors in his network will multiply his access capacity and quickly build his society's trust in him. By convincing one connector of his ideas, he is accelerating the persuasion of everyone connected to him.

We will examine two other common traits in most existing networks, but first let us look at what makes human networks different from the rest.

3.5 EVOLUTIONARY CURIOSITIES OF MAN AND HIS NETWORKS

In March 2008, *National Geographic* magazine[11] published a fascinating story about the growing similarities researchers were finding between the behavior and intelligence of humans and other mammals.

The large colored photos featured a parakeet, Alex, who could pronounce up to 100 words in English at 30 years of age, including his own invented word: ban-erry. Apparently he used this word to designate apples, which, according to his trainer Irene Pepperberg, looked like cherries but tasted like bananas. The story also discussed Betsy, a black and white Border Collie which could understand up to 340 different words and follow instructions to sort objects by color or shape. Betsy could even count.

The article argued that traditional barriers between humans and other mammals were slowly crumbling. Dolphins can cooperate with humans to execute certain tasks, and even imitate our body postures. Elephants are aware of themselves, as shown by tests in which they look at themselves in mirrors, and sheep can tell other sheep apart by looking at their faces, or even pictures of their faces.

These shared abilities show that a generous Nature seems to multiply resources much more than needed to make sure the results are successful. In order to achieve the most sophisticated species alive, the human race, Nature seems to have practiced several parallel improvements across a number of species. The systems appear to be closer to networking principles than to linearity, for sure. Empathy, reconciliation, and self-consciousness are manifested across several mammal species, until one of them dominates all the others.

While a number of scientists study animals to identify exactly what makes mankind different, others are developing an increasingly widespread perspective about the evolution of human psychology that is especially relevant to our subject.

Evolutionary psychology tries to explain the array of human behaviours, reactions, and beliefs we call human nature as the product of a series of evolving adaptations to the main problems in their environment. Perhaps one of the milestones was the ground-breaking book, *The Adapted Mind: Evolutionary Psychology and the Generation of Culture*[12] by Jerome Barkow, Leda Cosmides, and John Tooby.

According to this study, evolutionary psychology stems from five basic principles that show just how important it is to network in human society.

(1) The brain is a physical system. It works like a computer, with circuits which have evolved through thousands of years to generate appropriate responses to the circumstances in the environment.
(2) Current neuron circuits have evolved through natural selection mechanisms to solve the problems and limitations encountered by successive generations of *Homo Sapiens* ancestors.
(3) Our mind's consciousness is a very reduced part of the brain's content and processes. Our capacity to diagnose our own feelings and thoughts is much lower than we think it is, so that we really use only the tip of an iceberg whose profound structures were shaped by millions of years of evolution.
(4) The different neuron circuits are specialized to solve certain types of adaptation problems. To illustrate this principle we can focus on the circuitry of the occipital lobe, which regulates hunger, the search for food, and distinction of different foods. These circuits are much, much older than those found in the frontal lobe that regulates speech.
(5) Today's human skull still protects a mind created for stone-age environmental conditions.

These five principles may seem exaggerated when you enjoy an ivy-league education, you've earned one or two MBAs, and you feel totally satisfied with your tailored suit and your sleek sports car, but the time scale of human evolution sets the clock impossibly straight.

Trying to offer an accurate timeline of human evolution is a messy affair. Paleontologists argue over the meaning and implications of each new discovery, as shown in the cover story of the July 2001 *Time* magazine issue, entitled "One giant step for mankind".[13] You can read it online, at www.time.com, to hear how different teams defend the position that their own discovered remains are more relevant and credible than the rest.

But a general idea of things is helpful to my point, so please bear with me on the broad timeline at least. Some experts place the first primate, or proto-primate, around 85 million years ago.[14] *Hominidae*, or the family of great apes, appeared about 15 million years ago.[15] Great apes include humans, chimpanzees, bonobos, gorillas and orangutans. And *Homininae* didn't appear until eight million years ago. No more and no less than 75 million years of evolutionary adaptations were needed to convert the first ever primate into a Hominin, which still includes chimpanzees, bonobos and gorillas.

Homo specimens, that is, all the known species starting with the word *Homo*, are as old as 2.5 million years. Another six million years of minor genetic adaptations to improve walking and the use of tools extended the size of the brain and shaped communication.

There does seem to be general agreement around the idea that several species of Homos walked the Earth simultaneously. By so doing they proved whether their adaptation to the environment was better or worse with the gradual but incessant dwindling of numbers for every other version, except *Homo Sapiens*.

Homo Sapiens, the name defining humankind today, were born a mere 200,000 years ago,[16] after another two million years of slow evolution. Since then there have been only minor variations produced locally, such as skin and hair color. The main differences between regions are in fact diverging cultural development paths, creating our current confusion and surprise.

If we needed several steps along millions of years, does anybody really believe that we could have taken a significant evolutionary step in the last two hundred thousand years?

Our feeling of being more exceptionally sophisticated than the less refined prehistoric visitor, the first homo sapiens, is rooted somewhere else: in the colossal transformation of our environment.

Homo Sapiens is the first species to transform its natural habitat to the point of putting itself and the habitat in danger. Global warming, the extinction of marine and other species, the contamination of water, and similar problems of global magnitude are the result of *Homo Sapiens* actions.

Our evolutionary superiority complex comes from the dizziness we feel at being colossal in our relationship with the environment, much more so than from any mental adaptations.

There's a saying in Spanish: "The monkey can dress in satin, but she's still a monkey." Applying this saying to ourselves might bring us down from our mighty heights, but it also speaks to the crucial importance social networks still have in the ensemble of societies and markets that don't always work according to the rational logic.

Nigel Nicholson, professor of organizational behaviour at London Business School, published a book in which he examined the findings of evolutionary psychology and their effects on everyday business life.[17] He described an interesting classification of society models that slowly distanced us from the model we were designed to live in: nomadic groups of hunters and gatherers.

3.6 THE SOCIAL LIMITATION OF *HOMO SAPIENS* VERSION 1.0

The current version of human software was modeled and tested for hundreds of thousands of years in semi-nomadic communities of no more than 150 individuals who fed on only hunted and gathered food. This number, 150, is not casual, but a direct consequence of the size of the human brain, according to Robin Dunbar's work.[18] The "Dunbar number" is defined as the theoretical cognitive limit to the number of stable relationships an individual can maintain at any given time.

Dunbar thought that the single most important factor for survival of Hominins, the extended family that includes humans, chimpanzees, and gorillas, is life in a group where they compete and live with equals. In other words, we need to live inside a community to survive. Dunbar's research shows a strong correlation between the size of the neocortex – the "grey matter" – of several primate species and the average size of their communities. By applying this same relation to the size of the human neocortex and its neocortical processing capacity, the number obtained is approximately 150 people per clan.

Dunbar verified that the number 150 was consistent with the size of Neolithic tribes and settlements, Hutterite villages, and even the base unit of Roman troops. Nicholson also mentions organizational studies and examples that establish this number as optimal for human organization.

To keep a community of 150 people together, Dunbar argues, a very strong common motivation, like survival, is needed. Each member is estimated to dedicate about 42% of his time grooming social relationships with each of the other 149 individuals. The development of verbal language in humans would have been a way to economize efforts dedicated to social cohesion. With language you could happily gossip away with a friend while your hands were busy gathering fruit and nuts.

But then Homo Sapiens 1.0 did something no other species had thought of doing before him: he invented agriculture. Ten thousand years ago we learned to cultivate the land, favoring a more reliable source of food if we stayed in an agricultural village.

Liberated from the uncertainties of hunting, the new agricultural age allowed us to abandon our nomadic existence and strive for the accumulation of wealth for the first time. Easier access to food made populations larger, requiring progressive organization in the form of laws and rules to facilitate coexistence. Without such norms it would have proven impossible to live together.

In a sense, Dunbar's limit was stretched through the use of rules and pacts, but this meant that it was no longer trust that kept the communities together. The obligation and promise to obey these emerging society rules, under threat of exclusion or collective judgment, was the new glue of life. Living isolated in Nature wasn't, and still isn't, a viable alternative.

The unstoppable progress of human knowledge has directly influenced life conditions, shaping the first great civilizations and the succession of empires and wars that have sculpted today's commonly accepted standards: democracy and capitalism. Today we live in cities with tens of millions of people and we work in organizations made of hundreds of thousands, many of which we have never met face to face.

The emergence of the internet and the development of air transport has tightened the nut once more, making our world even smaller and helping isolated problems like the subprime crisis grow into global pandemics, bringing banks and markets across the world to their knees.

Our society pacts and life standards have evolved at a pace impossible to follow even by ourselves, creating generational gaps and incredulity among our elders. But we still have the same neocortical capacity, and we still settle into networks of about 150 people to whom we really feel connected.

I recently learned that LinkedIn social network limits the total connections a user can establish to 30,000. Apparently more than one user has already reached the limit. While some researchers say that we can associate up to 2,000 faces to their names, others assert we can recognize up to 5,000 people.[19, 20, 21, 22] But we have only 150 information spaces to store the set of gestures, data, and anecdotes that make each individual different to us, and without which we don't know how to behave towards him or her.

The Dunbar number entails a critical implication for every networker's strategy: resources are limited. You can retain emotional indicators for only about 150 different people, so you need to be choosey. Who will you include in these 150 and who will you leave outside?

3.7   SOCIAL RITUALS INHERITED FROM THE STONE AGE

Discovered in 1928, the bonobo is a variation of the common chimpanzee. Its DNA shares between 98% and 99.4% of similarities with human DNA, and it is believed that both species parted on different evolution lines about six million years ago. The chimpanzee and the bonobo are the two living species closest to human beings.

We're especially interested in bonobos here because they are sex fanatics. Sex is the solution to almost every relational problem they encounter, and this is an evolutionary adaptation many humans would have liked to keep, I'm sure!

Bonobos have a smaller head than the common chimpanzee, a black face with a wide brow, pink lips, and long hair on their heads. Females have larger breasts than chimpanzees, but smaller than humans, and they walk upright about 25% of their time. A bonobo's face differs from another bonobo's face much more than one chimpanzee's face differs from another's. This gives them an identity that can be recognized at a glance. Their bodies are long and thin. And they love sex. Frans de Waal is a highly respected primate biologist. In his own words, "bonobos are the hippies of the primate universe: they're pacific and sexy. They show low aggression and have lots of sex."[23]

Bonobos use sex to say hello, to make peace after a fight, to return favors, even in exchange for food. They are the only primates, besides humans, that take to every possible creative variation of sex: any gender and every area of the body is perfectly fun to explore. They are intimately connected to one another and they spend an enormous amount of energy keeping their social bonds strong and current.

Other primates are less generous when it comes to investing energy in the care of their communities' social cohesion. Even though they all need to live in groups, share tasks, and cooperate to survive in the face of environmental threats, most primates have sought more economic adaptations to the costs of living in a community.

The most common ritual among primates to become closer and make friends is scratching one another's skin – grooming. Take a trip to the zoo to see it with your own eyes: it goes on constantly. A chimpanzee will catch up with his best pal by giving him a good scratch and getting rid of annoying little bugs. Parents perform this practical and very pleasurable task for their young, or at least it is pleasurable for the recipients. Members of lower rank also do it for their more powerful colleagues, and everybody lives scratchily, happy ever after.

You can even see versions of this ritual in indigenous human populations today, in small villages and humble abodes in South America, for example. With a television set in their small adobe houses and munching on McDonald's hamburgers now and then, villagers will share a wonderful Sunday afternoon basking in the garden with their neighbors, joining in a circle where each massages the head of the next. We probably do plenty of this in Europe too, only we no longer let curious strangers look in at us while we do so.

In the world of primates a good scratch will get you empathy, friendly company, acceptance by peers, and sharing of joy. We humans have made this exchange a lot more economic by inventing verbal language. Without speech, according to Dunbar, the time we would have needed to stay on good terms with our colleagues would be much greater, reducing even more the size limit of our clans and sub-clans throughout history.

Homo Sapiens individuals, less hairy and more sophisticated than their primate cousins, use verbal language as the preferred vehicle for bonding with each other. We call it rumor or gossip, and it's a universal practice adored in cultures all around the world. There's nothing we like more than sharing gossip. In modern countries, gossip is a multimillion dollar entertainment industry.

3.8   THE SOPHISTICATION OF OUR RITUALS

What is gossip? What makes it different from other forms of communication, and why is it so important for the cohesion of human communities?

The 1932 photograph "Lunch atop a skyscraper" depicted a group of men having their lunch in mid air, suspended over the ceilings of New York. They were working on the construction site of the Rockefeller Center, and they were deep in conversation. Their fearless postures showed trusting attitudes and how much each individual conversation mattered more than the possibility of a deadly fall.

This photograph is testimony to something we do several times a day every day. We informally share information in combinations of verbal language and body signals that indicate a certain degree of complicity.

One glance at the picture makes it clear to anyone that the workmen know each other from previous occasions. It also shows that what they are talking about is not something they would share with others. The least important part of gossip is its informative content. It is the ensemble of emotional signals that accompany any piece of gossip that reinforces the interpersonal bond. These are the emotional tidbits that make rumors so addictive to the human species.

When you receive a juicy piece of gossip from a friend, there are many emotional implications that affect the bond you both share. The fact that we are recipients of that certain information tells us we are included in the sender's category of closer and more valuable people. The more delicate and confidential the information, the greater the intimacy needed to grant us access to the message.

The information comes with facial expressions, body postures, voice tone modulations, and anecdotes or adjectives, as well as colorful, near-poetic expressions. We derive an enriched sense of how our friend feels about having a private chat with us, how he got up this morning, and what he's worried about at this time. We can all guess the moods of our husband or wife by focusing on the informal cues in the comments about how their day went. We also react in a similar manner, depending on the emotions we received with the anecdote, the joke, or the story.

Gossip also contains the sender's emotional attitude towards the subject or recipient of the gossip. We can use a rumor to rapidly empathize or antagonize somebody we've just met. Imagine a conversation with a taxi driver from any given world capital city on any given day:

- "How can we have such terrible traffic at eleven in the morning on the main avenue? Don't people have to work?," says the impatient passenger, on his way to his lawyer's office.
- "There you have it. And just you wait. Unemployment will rise again with the twits we have in the government. Did you see the stats in the press today?," replies the stressed-out taxi driver.

This very brief exchange between two strangers in the city jungle contains a small act of gossip-fishing to detect the other person's attitude towards government officials. If the client responds with something like "Oh, yes, it's awful, isn't it? Aren't they embarrassed at their own uselessness?" he will emotionally tune in with the driver's attitude towards the politician discussed. This gives the driver a free card to continue issuing opinions, properly exaggerated with anecdotes and adjectives, to make his disgust as vivid as possible.

If, on the other hand, the client turns out to be an admirer of the politician the driver dislikes, he may choose not to answer, or keep to monosyllabic replies. The passenger may even decide to confront the driver: "Well, the press only writes about what suits them. I'm sure the government can't be blamed for slow traffic."

A hidden camera in this taxi would not be able to clarify how much unemployment there actually is, who is the terrible politician in charge, and what the press is getting out of publishing the numbers. But it would show pretty clearly whether these two people were getting friendly or beginning to dislike each other.

Maybe neither of them can repeat the exact unemployment rate they are arguing about, because that precision is a lot less relevant to them than their feelings about it.

Gossip is the strongest and most unmanageable means of communication in any organization. It's practically impossible to map out, and it is slave to the shared emotions in the company or market. As anxiety rises among the employees of a company or the financial analysts of a stock market, the more gossip becomes exaggerated with unrealistic interpretations of official events and press notes.

In other words, the volume of rumors in circulation is proportional to the level of collective excitement, both good and bad. The quantity of gossip increases with rising fever, but so do the emotionality and tall tales contained in each conversation.

Have you ever played the children's game, "Gossip," imagining a faulty telephone? Children sit in a circle and the first boy chooses a short message to whisper into the ear of the girl on his right. She repeats what she heard to the child on her right, followed by the rest, each child in the circle getting only a fraction of what was initially said. The children fill in their own details as they pass the message on, and in the end the message rarely has anything to do with what the first boy said.

Excitement accelerates rumors: "bad news travels fast." In an office with 500 employees there are scores of rumors circulating about what the president said in this meeting and what Mr. X replied to his boss in the middle of that corridor. But if any two executives are caught imitating bonobos to further strengthen their bond with a good ration of creative sex, this kind of news gets to absolutely every employee in record time!

After three or four days there isn't a soul who hasn't heard about it. What's more, the story has improved with spicy details, and its protagonists have gained new qualities and lost others. Any employee who gets to tell the story at the coffee machine will enjoy his momentary stardom, adding as much excitement to the tale as possible, even if it means slightly twisting the truth.

Ronald Burt,[24] professor at Chicago University, has extensively researched gossip, publishing several books and articles about the effects of gossip on organizational trust.

Burt explains why informal conversations can be so powerful that people forget their content may not be objective. People gossip more to manage their social bonds than to actually get proven data, so that they take this unintended sub-product as straightforward and accurate.

His research[25] shows that people tend to hang on to the data and anecdotes that confirm what they already felt about a third person. The absence of an official standard against which to check rumors aggravates the problem.

3.9 REPUTATION

200,000 years of social sophistication, refinement of our customs, and modernization of our vital habits have not dethroned the king of our daily routines. Gossip is still like savoury salt to our daily jobs, the main connection mechanism we use to maintain human relationships around us.

Rumor is also the single most significant factor in the construction of something we all fight to cultivate and protect: our reputation.

Here's another one of those indefinable concepts that describe emotional attributes and obey more or less rational laws that executives rarely think about explicitly. Reputation especially affects an executive's own perception of his personal value, as well as that of his equals.

Suppose a journalist has taken interest in you. He wants to write a feature about you in a magazine or newspaper. After a few meetings with you in your office and many questions about your career, your successes, values, and beliefs, he requests your permission to find out more about you from your colleagues at work.

Moreover, imagine that you smile confidently and give him the go ahead. You send an email to your colleagues to advise them that a journalist will be in touch with them to ask questions about you. At that moment, inebriated by the pleasure of having a journalist deeply interested in your ideas and achievements, you think of the names and faces of the colleagues who will corroborate your version of the events, and who will add color and flattering nuances to your account.

However, a few weeks later, the journalist tells you that due to a change of direction in terms of the newspaper's priorities, they have to change the article. The article will now feature you alongside other directors of competing companies. Instead of writing an article all about you, the journalist will include a photo of you with a brief, five-line paragraph describing your personality and talents.

Now try to write down in your notebook or a piece of paper what those five or ten lines would be.

Look at what you've written and think over the next questions:

- How certain are you that the journalist would print something that resembles what you just wrote?
- What do you think would justify the differences between your version and the journalist's?
- How was the reputation reflected in these five lines built up?

When managers in large multinationals are presented with this exercise and these questions are put to them, the majority tend to reply to the third question with a confident: "the facts constructed the reputation."

And although on the surface, logically, this may be true, the truth is that it is NOT. The reputation of an executive in his or her company, has more to do with others' impressions and perceptions of events than with the demonstrable facts.

It is one of the mechanisms of social order that we develop to maintain cohesion in human groups larger than the number of Dunbar (see p. 63). It has a direct impact on the selection of allies we choose to promote new projects or adventures, because their reputations provide us with a commonly accepted guarantee of their trustworthiness and seriousness. The threat of public embarrassment serves to promote respect in our agreements and sets down rules considered appropriate by the community.

That is what happens with lists of defaulters, for example. Most men and women in business, who find themselves in financial difficulty, will end up paying their debts when there is a real threat of being included in the public register of defaulters. If it happened, it would affect their future business opportunities with the members of the community.

A reputation can be described as the expected behaviour of the person with whom you establish a relationship or collaboration. It can also be defined as the public image of an individual in the community. Such a definition assumes assessment or judgment of the individual by the community.

Objective information does not circulate at the same speed or intensity as biased information. Objectivity does not contain emotions, nor does it entice the intense and pleasurable feelings of gossip. The latter is simply more exciting.

This fact of life, often ignored or underestimated by many executives, is what ultimately molds the opinion that others have of them, and molds public assessment of the individual when they are asked about him. Think of the ex-president of the United States, Bill Clinton. What just came to your mind?

It would be interesting to do a survey of the readers of this book to determine how many of them would respond with the words: "oval office," "Lewinsky," "womanizer," and similar variations. It would be even more graphic, if we asked the respondents what they actually know about Clinton's presidency.

This is the gravest aspect of the phenomenon of building a reputation. Everyone can make an independent judgment of an individual who is mentioned in a conversation, regardless of the actual knowledge they may have of him or her. Simply rolling one's eyes can communicate one's opinion of an individual who is not present in the group. All rumors count, whether spoken or gestured. Each one of them is a color to pixel that contributes to the communal photograph of the individual.

In order for you to have a reputation in a group, the group must have definite and relevant limits. In fact, you can have several reputations if you are a member of several unconnected communities or networks: your workplace, your family, your gym, your professional association, your university classmates, etc. Each collective has a certain cohesion in its structure to guarantee that information can circulate without diluting or disappearing along the way. You can have a different reputation in each one of them.

However, unless you are a public figure, you would hardly have a reputation in a city or a country. When you begin your professional career, you are nobody, but as you start to garner achievements and years of connections in your sector, people start to "know who you are," because your name comes up in multiple conversations, linking you to good and not so good events and stories.

This is how everything people say about you contributes to your reputation. A colleague in your company sees you from time to time, sees your name on the organizational chart, then sees you in association with this or that project. He also hears your name mentioned at public events and private chats in the cafeteria, with adjectives and descriptive terms not under your control. You are at the mercy of the person speaking at that moment.

A group's interpretation of the facts can vary enormously, as is often proven in the media, for example. One news item dissociates into several different versions, according to the different schools of thought and the political affinities of the media source.

All in all, the key to the success of a rumor is the juice. This is why juicy, exaggerated, colorful opinions, whether filled with positive admiration or destructive insults, are the most likely to persist in an organization. They are "sticky," as Malcolm Gladwell describes them in *The Tipping Point.*[26]

What you do only provokes the attention and interest of your extended community if it becomes theatrically relevant, be it for positive or negative reasons. In other words, the facts, I'm afraid, don't speak for themselves.

In the case of a gym or golf club, conceivably there are no political interests or power alliances to affect the spread of rumors, unless you are among those who are competing for leadership.

The executives of most companies are at ease in their places of leisure, unconcerned about what may be said about them, because at the golf club they play in a bubble of professional anonymity. They are known to be nice Bills or Bobs, who take spinning classes and are always in a hurry, or who are known to read the paper as they listlessly pedal their exercise bicycle. But probably they aren't even talked about in their gym.

Similarly, if one executive decides to change jobs, he or she will gain the great advantage of starting a new reputation from scratch in the new company. Nobody knows his or her past mistakes or embarrassments. Unfortunately, it's tough to be a nobody on trial until everybody has the chance to exchange comments and observations. Only then will they formulate a reputation to help them decide how they want to interact with the new colleague.

At the same time, they compete with their equals for leadership, or to impose their business vision inside their companies, becoming the focus of a great deal of gossip.

The executive's allies will transmit flattering accounts, which highlight his or her successes and confer on his or her significant leadership qualities. Meanwhile, competitors will frame their narrative of the same facts with disparaging adjectives and disdainful judgments, tarnishing the person's reputation.

Ron Burt has researched this subject extensively. As he shows, when a person hears gossip about something or somebody they know, that person will believe it if it matches what he or she already thought. If the description doesn't match earlier impressions, it will be discarded.

What he or she believes has been inferred from all the information received. His or her capacity to reject false rumors increases with proximity to the object of such rumors. Your closer friends will defend you better than distant ones.

The above leads us to a central idea of this book and of your professional career. Most of your work colleagues in your company have superficial knowledge of who you are; therefore, they are easy targets for false rumors. Only those who have interacted personally with you can reject false or inaccurate gossip, or even refute it. Your direct contacts are the only people whose opinions are fed straight from the source. They will counteract negative currents with greater conviction the more they like you and the better they know you.

We could say that an executive with larger and more carefully knit networks has his very own radio station, in charge of circulating flattering anecdotes and comments, as well as striking achievements to whoever wants to listen. His is a collective network prepared to publicly oppose those who criticize him.

Forming and developing a personal reputation is so complex it merits another book in its own right, but for the purpose of our discussion we will highlight the following two ideas:

(1) Reputation is a medium- and long-term concept. Tomorrow's good reputation is built with the flattering gossip that circulates today, and today's reputation is made up of what was said yesterday.
(2) Reputation is contagious. Your image is influenced by the people surrounding you, as much as by the company logo on your business card.

3.10   STICKINESS AND THE TIPPING POINT

Stickiness and the tipping point are the two characteristics common to the majority of the real networks which we have left aside in order to deal with the specific details of the human context; but they are also very interesting and completely relevant to our discussion.

The term 'stickiness' was adopted by Malcolm Gladwell, whom we have mentioned before. In his publications,[26] Gladwell defined the three factors which allow a local phenomenon to turn into a widespread epidemic.

The first factor is the part played by the connectors, which we shall describe later (see Chapter 8); the second factor is the context itself, which creates sets of circumstances at critical moments which especially favor transmission; and the third factor is the stickiness of the message, virus, or whatever else happened to be circulating.

Stickiness is a colorful term. It expresses the ease of transmission possessed by a certain rumor or message, which helps it to reach many more people quickly. This is the effect people are looking for in advertising slogans, like "Where's the beef?," from advertisements a few years ago, or the way certain summer songs work, such as the Spanish Macarena we've danced around the globe.

The stickiness of the rumors circulating about you and your successes will be the determining factor of the power of those rumors. If the stories you tell are exciting, they will be stickier, because they will arouse intense feelings in both the person spreading the gossip and the listener, too, which means the rumor about you will move faster and reach more people.

We can also use the term stickiness to talk about a manager's personality, so that a sticky, fun personality succeeds in attracting and contacting many more people than other personalities.

People investigating networks have also identified the stickiness factor in their research, although they may have given it different names. Albert-László Barabási calls it 'fitness', which suggests a level of health or physical ability, and he defines it as the ability of one node to attract the connections of other nodes.

Observers of traditional models of networks, who in the past had assumed that all nodes were equal, with the same average number of connections, were surprised to notice that the majority of networks were standard-free. In other words, a small number of nodes had many more connections than the rest.

Even in this model, researchers continued to assume that all the nodes were similar and that the reason why some had many more connections was that they had been part of the network for a longer period of time. Those in the network for longer had had more opportunities to make connections.

But in competitive contexts, which obviously include the social context, "fitness" or the individual power to attract possessed by each node gives that node a clear advantage. This factor explains why small, unknown companies suddenly turn into market leaders, overtaking the more dominant businesses: their ability to attract is greater because their product or service "fits," and so attracts more customers.

Competition between nodes to attract connections is a basic mechanism to be found everywhere in nature. Cells compete with one another to establish connections. Males compete with each other to connect with the maximum number of females, in many species. And businesses compete with each other to connect with the greatest number of customers.

The stickiness of a node, of a manager, depends on the content of the node, and on how well that node can sell itself. The better the content of a node, its service, its product, or its ideas, the more connections it will attract.

Stickiness based not on content, but on selling or communicating content, is what we call opportunism or one-upmanship. There is no doubt that a certain amount of mileage can be realized from it. Some managers base their entire careers on their ability to do and undo through chats around the water-cooler. They have little or no interest in cultivating their own ideas, but occasionally use some faceless flunky to do their work for them.

The managers with the best advantage, however, are those offering a different, innovative talent: they communicate in a sticky manner.

The other feature worthy of examination is the network tipping point. This term, invented by Gladwell, refers to the point at which a gas changes its state, or a magnetic pole changes from North to South.

This is the point at which a critical number of components of the network have aligned themselves so that the liquid becomes solid, certain metals become superconductors, or water starts to boil. It is the point at which an innovation strikes an entire company.

It is the tipping point which divides order from disorder, when materials or a group of elements, which were in motion and in connection in a chaotic way, reach a critical point and begin to obey what are known as exponential laws. When we put water in the freezer, we notice that before it freezes there are tiny fragments of ice floating in the liquid, and later it turns into the crystallized solid, which we put in our drinks.

An exponential law is fundamentally different because its distribution allocates a wealth of resources to a small number. This is often referred to as the "Pareto Principle," and lies behind a large number of business situations. We look for the 20% of the factors which explain 80% of the results.

In the case of the atoms of a compound which is about to change state, at certain temperatures the way in which the atoms connect is found to change, so that now the majority are trying to connect with a small number of atom groupings.

If exponential laws herald the appearance of organization and structure in materials, and the tipping point is the flag marking the frontier between chaos and order in our universe, it is hardly surprising that it will profoundly affect the way humans function.

This means that in order to inject order into a company, to structure it and provide it with shared laws, principles, and ideas, it will have to pass through the networks of a small number of individuals. These networks grow in richness and size until they reach a point at which, in order to continue to proceed, they must negotiate and come to an agreement. This is how humans move from anarchy to order, and this is how the changes and innovations are produced.

If you wish to transform an organization, a city, or even the whole world, your strategy will be the same as that of liquids striving to become solid and metals trying to become superconductors. This means joining up with those around you who are already aligned with your plan, and working to get the other groups and units around the innovators to synchronize themselves with you.

When there exists a critical number of individuals supporting the innovation, the spontaneous transformation of the whole will be triggered. This phenomenon explains the dynamics of the power and leadership struggles we have examined so carefully and been so amazed by in the history of humanity. In the final analysis, we are not as original as we thought.

And yet, when we try to analyze what constitutes the forces uniting or separating us, we find that our original evolutionary sophistication has given rise to the most complex mixture of elements: compounds which cannot really be classed as emotion, nor yet as the exclusive property of reason.

3.11 ALEXANDRE OKADA, CREATIVE DIRECTOR OF PUBLICIS SPAIN AND FORMER CREATIVE COORDINATOR OF THE 2010 DILMA ROUSSEFF PRESIDENTIAL CAMPAIGN

Alexandre Okada has just moved from São Paulo to Madrid to work as creative director of the Madrid Publicis office. When asked why he is here today, he responds that "all the people I've met in my life brought me here. I believe in cause and effect: all the people you meet and all the words you say push you ahead through life."

Half Japanese, half Brazilian and grown up in Florianopolis, Okada "never had a plan. I never thought about becoming a hotshot creative director...I just wanted to do better, I wanted to learn, keep moving, and at some point I realized I didn't have to do it alone."

Just as movies connect actors to each other and games of Go do the same for their players, publicity campaigns build the boundaries, curves and rapids of the river that connects the people in Alexandre's career. "I have done many campaigns that touched people's hearts. I know this because they told me so each time. But three campaigns touched me to the point of changing my life too," he starts.

At the age of 30 Okada was working in Lisbon for a small agency with scant resources and many difficulties, until they won the McDonald's international pitch that nobody ever expected them to win. "It was the start of a gold period. After that we became a beautiful agency. Some months later we moved from our cramped little office into a spectacular old palace in the best area of Lisbon, and we won many international awards. It was almost like a dream!," he remembers.

Alexandre is convinced they won that campaign because of one idea. An idea they kept for the very end of the formal presentation they delivered to the room full of high executives from the multinational food giant. McDonald's was supporting the national Portuguese team in the upcoming 2004 Eurocup. Research showed that Portugal had not had a lot of presence in international football cups, but Okada was impacted by the story of the 1966 football world cup when Portugal came in third after an epic game against North Korea.

"The whole world saw how Portugal was losing three to zero against Korea halfway through the game. How they went down to the dressing rooms in total silence. Nobody knows what was said there in those few minutes. But when they came out they won the match five to three," tells the executive. The concept for the campaign became clear in his mind: "sometimes all a team needs is a word of support." People would be asked to send a "Mc-message" of support to the Portuguese team.

"There was total silence in the room after I stopped talking. We were unable to tell whether they liked our pitch, but the following day we saw the Ronald McDonald clown walking into our office and we knew it had to mean something good!" The client later told him his colleagues had been so moved by the campaign concept that they had remained literally speechless.

Not quite unlike the epic silence the world experienced as they watched the Portuguese team walk in and out of the dressing room in the match of 1966. "We will never know what happened there," says Alexandre, "but we saw the effect. Words have power. You need to be careful with the words you use."

And no words move people like thank you, as Okada's campaign for Greenpeace would show a couple of years later. Based in Buenos Aires, his agency was selected to participate in the Greenpeace international whaling campaign. It was the first time all the international offices had joined together to do one global campaign with two sides, one for Europe and North America, and another side for Japan:

> I remember I was in a meeting room with 20 high level Greenpeace people pushing through a deck of hundreds of slides when one graph caught my attention. It showed that Japanese consumption of whale meat had been very high just after the war, but had later dropped. Nobody ate much whale meat anymore and the industry was subsidized by the Japanese government because it wasn't profitable. So I asked out loud why they kept hunting whales. Nobody could answer my question!

Whale meat had become the main source of protein for the Japanese population after the world war so it had become part of their tradition. When the highly experienced Greenpeace experts confessed they had never thought about Okada's question, it became clear to him that the main problem was they had been fighting the wrong crowd for 20 years: "Guys, you are not fighting whalers with your campaigns. You are attacking the Japanese as a whole, even people who have never eaten whale meat."

Okada continued, "Japan is a remote island with low exposure to international influence and a strong emphasis on honour and pride.

You are acting like westerners who attack everything they stand for. You need to change your strategy. Talk to them as if you were also Japanese!" At which point Greenpeace asked Alexandre to fly straight to Japan.

It was Okada's first time in Japan, and nobody in his agency wanted to work on this campaign because of the reputational impact of Greenpeace and whaling issues. Alexandre presented his campaign idea to the local office. "It appears to me that whales saved the Japanese population from starvation after the Second World War. Now it is time for the Japanese to save the whales in return." Everyone in the agency jumped to the challenge.

Alexandre even remembers how one young creative associate came up to him and said "Okada-san, I had a very different idea about whaling before this meeting. Now I feel deeply ashamed of eating whale meat." The resulting animation movie was directed by an outstanding Japanese director, and you can watch it at the link:

http://www.youtube.com/watch?v=ozx1fzzuXdE

So touching was the two-minute video, that social network activity gave way to an offer from Discovery Channel to run it for free in all Latin America and U.S.A. BBC 1 did a special report on the making of the piece. Alexandre's work was working for him before he decided to take a giant jump into total professional uncertainty.

Regional creative director for Latin America, he had been living in Miami and Chicago until 2007, when he felt the need to move back to his home country. "I decided to leave the company because I felt I had ended a cycle. I had a nice little apartment in São Paulo and I wanted to live in my own country for a while. I came back to Brazil without a job or any professional contacts in the Brazilian publicity industry."

The Bradesco Foundation, owner of the biggest bank in Brazil, had seen the Greenpeace whaling piece, and asked Alexandre for his first pitch flying solo against big ad agencies. He won the pitch and he found himself working on a huge production, filming all over the country from balloons and boats. Once more, Okada's capacity to connect with the client's heart produced another beautiful campaign that you can see at the link:

http://www.okme.com.br/#/eng/other_projects

A big contract with McCann Erickson soon followed, giving Alexandre the opportunity to touch the heart of the country he had grown up in with many other imaginative campaigns.

"As I said at the beginning, I just try to do my best. When I was younger I focussed on learning and evolving. After a while, it wasn't enough. I wanted to bring other people along with me to grow together," explains the creative director. "Now it's not enough anymore. I need to build things that won't disappear if I'm not around!"

Alluding to the dependency many creative executives create in their organizations, Okada has learned that "building things is better than doing things. Creating a common ideology and culture, and a healthy structure that can still produce good work when I am not around is a lot more powerful," reflects Okada.

"I hate agencies where people can't be replaced. It turns both the employees and the agency into hostages. Not even the boss can go on a holiday or get sick, lest the agency be completely lost. I work to be unnecessary. Maybe it's a little suicidal!" exclaims Okada, laughing at himself.

The decision to come to Madrid is connected to everything Alexandre believes in, all the things he has learned in his career, and more importantly, two men: Miguel Angel Furones and Richard Pinder. "It's wonderful to work with people you know, you trust and love. I really admire both of these men. I believe what they believe." And he goes on, "we have big ad brands all around, but what are we talking about? Each agency is as good as the people that work behind its brand."

Okada would like to be better at networking. From time to time he makes the effort to go out to lunches and coffees, but it's not something that comes naturally to him. He remembers the first big meeting he had at Leo Burnett, when Furones was the big boss and all the top executives hovered around him. The Brazilian was the youngest creative director there. "I didn't know anybody. All the guys seemed to be great friends with Furones, joking and laughing loudly. Suddenly Furones looked straight at me and told everybody that he loved this guy – meaning me – because I never called him!"

Alexandre strongly believes that "sometimes you just have a natural connection with some people." He didn't make a proactive effort of going up to the big boss to try to get his attention because "I never felt comfortable doing anything with a purpose." But the chemistry, the unconscious part of human interaction that perceives and chooses even before we utter our first word, flowed spontaneously between them to connect both men.

Okada admits he has two attitudes to networking: "when I don't feel comfortable, I'm really shy and quiet, Japanese style. But when I find my space, I'm very, very Brazilian!," laughs our friend. Somehow his Japanese mother and Brazilian father shine through Alexandre's approach to the world in each present interaction.

Alexandre Okada advises readers to "trust that things will happen for you. You can't interact with people using a hidden agenda. You need to be yourself and help people without expecting anything. Not even gratitude. Good actions, good words and good decisions come back to you. You don't need to find tricky ways to the top. This is what I believe."

A man of well-proved talent, lucid perspective and contagious trust in life, Alexandre Okada is a walking example of successful networking without an agenda. People's hearts do reach out to touch each other when we don't mess around with unnatural intentions, don't they?

CHAPTER 4

THE PART OF THE ICEBERG
THAT SITS UNDER THE WATER

The first time I noticed him, his intense gaze called my attention. He kept looking at me across the room with an intensity that seemed out of step. I felt a chill go up my spine. But I soon forgot it once he came up to me and explained we had many friends in common.

A few cups of coffee led to a business opportunity that went through long meetings and never seemed to get off the ground. Until I read about it in the paper. I had known from the very beginning I shouldn't trust this guy. But I ignored my own wisdom. Does this sound familiar?

4.1 FUNDAMENTAL COMPONENTS OF PERSONAL BONDS

Every personal bond between two individuals is like a specially-prepared recipe containing a mixture of five basic ingredients, each in its own quantity and proportion.

Power

Much has been written about power. Dilbert comic strips depict it all the time. Alvarez and Svejenova[1] define power as the capacity to do things, and locates it in the organizational context as "the potential to mobilise people's energy in such a way that their behaviour helps us to achieve what we want."

Power is like a bag of marbles. Someone can seek favors and mobilize others according to the number of marbles they have. But they mustn't be wasted. Power is a potential resource of more or less value, according to the social context. The CEO of a huge corporation has only to snap her fingers to find practically everyone in the company will come running. And they're not even going to expect a marble.

But when that same CEO is trying to find a cab in the middle of some huge city, she can snap her fingers all she wants and dance a fandango to boot, but the cabbies don't know who she is and so they don't assume she has any power. Worse still, if a number of managers are desperate to flag down a taxi, the power is in the hands of the taxi drivers.

The balance of power is soon established in a relationship. This balance shapes the bond for all time, and may end up anywhere between total domination by one party to absolute equality between them.

If it never becomes clear who has most power, the parties will not know how to behave, what liberties they can take, nor what risks exist. A marriage, a boss–subordinate relationship, a family, even a group which has come together in a "Big Brother" house – they all interact until the dominant personality emerges. Once this happens, everybody behaves accordingly.

Influence

Another confusing ingredient, influence is defined as the exercise of power, or offering someone one of your marbles, in return for a favor.

The person who has the greater power in the relationship automatically has more capacity for influencing the other, and affecting their actions, opinions and views. A child exercises influence over his parents because they adore him. They will waste half an hour acting the fool for a smile. But the child can also exercise influence because the parents are afraid of what he might do. The threat that the child might spend the entire night crying or throw a tantrum in public is often enough to ensure that the parents will do what the child wants.

And even though the words "power" and "influence" make a lot of people nervous, the fact is that they are to be found in absolutely every relationship we have.

Dependence

Dependence is defined as someone's – or something's – need to achieve an objective, with help. None of us likes the idea that we "depend" on others, but, once again, dependence is an integral part of the way we organize society.

Because of the way jobs are allocated in a company, some people need others in order to carry out their work. The division of resources and goods in a society means that some people need others to solve their everyday problems.

It's very difficult to organize your life in such a way that you depend on absolutely no one. It might happen on a desert island, but even there you still need sources of drinking water and food to survive.

The importance of dependence in a relationship is a reflection of the strength of the relationship. The closer a partner or friend, the more we need them to achieve our professional goals or personal well-being. The upshot is that we end up becoming accustomed to their availability. Giving them up will cost us dearly.

This component comes in many shades of grey, from total invalids who depend completely on their carers to survive, to close friends who manage to live in distant parts of the world, and only seek each other out on special occasions, or to satisfy very unusual needs.

This is where the interests of relationships fit in, since the interest lies precisely in your willingness to take advantage of the resource offered by the other to achieve your own ends. It arises from your need for this resource, and it is clearly difficult to find disinterested human relationships.

Fear

Fear is the perception of an imminent threat. As you become comfortable, accustomed to a relationship, the fear of losing a relationship increases proportionally.

Fear of losing things is a typical resource of influence, since others are swiftly mobilized by it. It is a feeling of anxiety which grows in proportion to the gravity and likelihood of the possible loss.

It is a component of human relationships and is often veiled, but even so, it is better to acknowledge it than to ignore it.

Trust

Trust is the most important ingredient in the mix, the best recognized, sought and accepted by all. Everyone intuitively measures the trust in others, and it is also a dimension we like to talk about in all aspects of our lives.

The trust of the investors, in public opinion, the trust inspired by an economy or a leader, are qualities both sought for and valued, because they are the opposite of fear or anxiety. It creates security.

Trust can be defined in a variety of ways, but for the moment, let us settle for this: when you trust somebody, you give them the power to influence your actions and thoughts.

This definition shows us that trust is our preferred way of reading power and influence. It is a concept which stands as the opposite of fear, since when you fear someone, you are obliged to yield to their influence because you depend on them.

You might say that each of these components of human relationships resembles one of the five facets of the same girder extending between one person and another. The girder looks very limited and fragile when the people hardly know each other, and then grows in strength and solidity as the relationship becomes firmer. And according to the angle at which you choose to study this girder, you will see trust, fear, influence, power or dependence. The reality is that the only people who know the exact proportion of each face of the pentagon are the two individuals in the relationship, although they will know this in an intuitive way that virtually defies explanation.

4.2 GENERATING TRUST

Trust mixes expectation, beliefs, feelings of certainty, and desire, all in the same bowl. It saturates every transaction or interaction in our lives, from beginning to end, and that's why sometimes they can be confusing.

It is an expectation, because when we place our trust in someone, we hope they will be worthy of it. We don't expect to be betrayed, deceived, or let down. We simply make positive our perception of what might happen.

It is a belief, because we chose to believe that the other person is trustworthy, that they will do what they promise, although believing is no guarantee. Indeed, there are times when we go on believing in someone's trustworthiness in the teeth of information and facts contradicting it. Belief filters out compromising information.

A sense of certainty leads us to act, to tell secrets, to take risks, often without thinking. We feel that the other person will do the best possible for us, and we feel it is unlikely and even impossible that they could act to our detriment.

Trust, too, is a similar act of will, a choice we make at a given moment and which determines how we feel, how we filter the information reaching us, and what we expect as possible outcomes. When we place our trust in somebody, we begin to reveal secrets, weaknesses, running the risk of disloyalty because we simply believe it won't happen.

In other words, trust is one of those mysteries we can't explain rationally, yet it is found in almost everything we do. Specifically, trust is the mystery which makes things happen, and when it is absent information stops flowing, deals are not closed, and the money never comes.

Quite simply, with no trust, there is no life. So how can trust be generated? Why does it seem that some people are quick to place their trust in others, while others are very slow?

We basically learn trust from our parents. A human baby is born in a condition of utter dependence on its parents, needing someone else to care for its hygiene, feeding, physical well-being, and its need for affection.

A baby seeks out its mother and recognizes her voice before anything else. The first months are spent in symbiosis between mother and child which has grown from the complete union of pregnancy to a state of organic separation in which both parties must find each other constantly in order to be together.

The growth and increasing maturity of the child means it will explore spaces ever more distant from its parents, getting ready for its independent life. During this long preparation the growing child's every interaction with those in its environment has an effect on its ability to trust in the future.

Some writers see this trust in parents as perfect trust. This is trust which does not recognize the possibility of deception or betrayal, and this is what the child feels towards its parents instinctively or simply by genetic conditioning.

Later, adolescents discover their parents are not perfect, that they are just human. At this time, the majority of children learn what is known as supported trust: trust which can, indeed, be betrayed and which needs support and care to survive.

Making friends with schoolmates, dabbling with love, and the social and emotional disappointments which are so much a part of the difficult adolescent decade are crucial to each individual's relationship learning curve. All these experiences modify and fine-tune the broad principles learned and copied from parents.

If the affection shown by a child's parents was uncertain, or if the child found that they were not to be trusted, this child is likely to distrust early in life, leaning more towards mistrust than to trust as an adult.

Supported trust is placed willingly by the adult, knowing that it can be betrayed at any time. Trust must be supported by both sides if it is to last.

This illustration shows how trust is built up with another person over time. Three phases can be distinguished (see Graph 4.1).

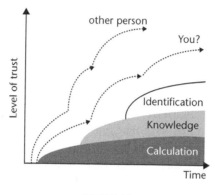

GRAPH 4.1

On the first meeting, you calculate how much trust you can initially place in the other person, basing your judgment on experience, on the impressions you gain from the conversation. You also decide according to completely subjective parameters, which may include their similarity to a much-loved family member, or gestures and laughs which resemble those of somebody else. In other words, in the initial phase you make a bet on that trust, which allows you to exchange information and make resources available to the other person.

As you continue to interact with the other person, maybe because you meet at the office or at leisure events, you talk on the phone or exchange emails, you move on to a second trust phase, and this one is based on acquaintance. Now you have an inventory of first-hand experiences. You have seen how the other person behaves, and now you trust them because you know them.

Some relationships never seem to gel, and only a few will reach the next stage, that of identification. In the identification phase, the two people now no longer need to speak to understand each other. They feel security, complicity, and personal equality.

What is interesting about this model is that it shows that confidence grows in a continuous manner, but that there are also qualitative leaps at various points in the relationship. But it also shows that every individual's curve is different. Some people reach identification quickly, but others need more time, more information, more interactions, while some will never reach this level.

These personal preferences to trust before or after the others are those we learn from our parents, from the values of our society, and which are ultimately affected by our experiences.

Children tend to trust one another spontaneously, until they learn to be careful at the suggestion of their elders. They learn not to talk to strangers, that dogs that bark don't bite, that if they assume the worst they will be right, that you can't trust people like this or like that. Children are handed a lengthy chain of beliefs and expectations which recommend caution and invite them to wait and do a little checking before they trust someone.

This means that all of us, throughout our lives, have collected a set of signals indicating caution or relaxation, which guide us to place our trust either sooner or later. None of us likes being rushed into placing our trust in a new acquaintance, and if we're pressed we're likely to feel overwhelmed and reject the contact until fresh information appears.

Oddly, however, most of us are in a hurry to have others place their trust in us. We try to keep the process moving, getting through the filters, signs, and time needed for them to feel comfortable. Paying attention to this is essential if you want to establish bonds of trust with others, since two-way trust is impossible if one party is unwilling.

Focusing attention on the trust dimension – an exercise

The following exercise will help you to understand how trust flows around you. Choose five people from your work environment, the five you feel closest to, for example, and put their names into the following table.

Now grade them between 1 and 10 according to the level of trust you have succeeded in generating with them, but do it in both directions. In the 'points given' column, assess the trust that you place in each one, and in the 'points received' column, estimate the level of trust you believe each has placed in you.

In the other two columns describe the actions, facts, and anecdotes which hinder the generation of trust with each colleague, and those which ease it.

Name	Points given	Points received	Hindrances	Facilitators

GRAPH 4.2

And, finally, give some thought to the hindrance actions you yourself perform without realizing it, and which trust facilitator behavior patterns will help you spread trust.

4.3 TYPES OF TRUST

The vaguer the concept, the more literature I seem to find about it, and the volume of opinions and categorization systems relating to trust is impressive.

Sandro Costaldo, from Bocconi University, makes a fairly complete summary of the various ways in which trust can be studied.[2] According to his report, the majority of existing classifications are based on the following criteria:

- What is the subject of the trust? Is the trust placed in organizations, in objects or people, or in other entities?
- What is the content of the trust? Here he compares the antecedents on which trust is based.
- What is the quality and consistency of the trust, ranging from fragile to complete?

There are many kinds of distinctions, but for the purposes of managing contacts, we will be most helped by the distinction already introduced in Chapter 2, between cognitive or conceptual trust, and affective or emotional trust.

To start with, this is a simple classification, easy to understand in a fairly intuitive way. The cognitive focus is based on rational and intellectual beliefs about the consistency between what an individual promises and what they do afterwards. The affective focus is based more on spontaneous, powerful feelings against which reason has little traction.

Some authors maintain that trust is an adaptive mechanism, critical to the survival of the mammals, and which acts through ancient mechanisms in the hypothalamus and the limbic system.

In other words, trust existed before the appearance of the neocortex, so that its roots are instinctive and can be seen in other mammal species, such as horses, dogs and dolphins, creatures with which man often forms a bond that is hard to explain in rational terms.

The defenders of Pet Assisted Therapy are using dolphins and horses to assist autistic children or children with social disabilities to overcome their relationship limitations, and many owners are convinced their pets understand them.

In the case of mammals, it is certain that emotional contagion occurs, which causes dogs to resemble their masters, and homes where anxiety or violence reigns tend to affect the pets which are resident there, as well as the poor neighbors.

Perhaps trust binds animals together, for example, helping dolphins to hunt as a group. But does trust mean they will sacrifice the security of the entire group to save one of its members? That is another issue. There are supporters for the theory that trust appeared as a survival mechanism with mammals, the first creatures to carry their young inside their bodies and which protected their young at birth rather than eating them.

And, lastly, it is interesting to highlight a series of terms related to trust which are often misunderstood, like the difference between a lack of trust and distrust.

- *Lack of trust.* A neutral attitude experienced by someone coming into contact with a stranger or a person with whom they have never interacted.
- *Innocence.* When trust is given without an understanding of the existence of betrayal, which happens with children, or when the risk of betrayal is deliberately ignored, which happens in the case of adults.
- *Supported or cautious trust.* This is trust which admits and accepts the risk of deceit.

- *Betrayal.* This is the act of deliberately breaching a confidence agreed to with another person. Some people believe that even considering the possibility is like a betrayal in thought.
- *Distrust.* This is defined by the existence of prejudices which exclude all possibility of closeness in the future. It may appear when betrayal has taken place between two individuals, but is also at the root of most expressions of racism and discrimination.
- *Fear.* This is an extreme degree of distrust of an individual, the result of the threat of a serious loss, whether by theft or violence.

Exercise on personal trust filters

In this exercise you are invited to consider the filters which affect your confidence curve, either pulling it back or pushing it forward. Write down the names of the three people whom you trust most, and describe what they're like in a couple of lines.

- Name 1:

- Name 2:

- Name 3:

Now write down the names of the three people whom you trust least, and, again, describe what they're like in a couple of lines.

- Name 1:

- Name 2:

- Name 3:

Read the descriptions you've just written down and pick out the physical, psychological, or other features which seem to be repeated in the persons you trust and those you don't.

Now see if you can fill out the table shown in Graph 4.3 with the elements and characteristics which make it easier for you to trust someone at a cognitive level, and those which hinder your trust. Use the elements which appeared in the lists of the names above to trigger the analysis process, but complete the list with other ideas which spring to mind.

	COGNITIVE	EMOTIONAL
FACILITATORS		
HINDRANCES		

GRAPH 4.3

4.4 EVERYTHING DEPENDS ON YOUR TRUST IN YOURSELF

As we've mentioned before, trust is initially learned from the parents, or from the adults who are responsible for the baby, and we go on adapting it or modifying it throughout our adult lives.

Although patterns and beliefs established in childhood exert a powerful influence, the rest of our experiences inject flexibility and expand the range of trust attitudes we are able to deploy.

When it comes to managing contacts, however, we observe the huge impact that this sequence of events has on the manager's personality and potential for professional, personal, and social success. This is produced through the manager's interpretation of the law of reciprocity.

The vast majority of adults find themselves at an intermediate point, located between two theoretical extremes. One extreme is total dependence, while the other is total anti-dependence. At a mid point equidistant from both extremes we find independence, where a transparent and real perception emerges of the interchange of value which is produced in relationships.

The extreme of total dependency converts an adult into a child who clings to those at his side or who cannot function without some substance or other. This is typical of those who have experienced traumatic events rife with injustice, and who seek reparation or compensation from others. The problem, of course, is that the others are in no position to compensate them, or to return what they have lost.

The extreme of anti-dependence is to be found in those very solitary adults who come to value self-sufficiency above all else, and who will not permit themselves to seek anything or anyone or to depend on anything or anyone. This is to be found in cases of serious betrayal of children by their parents, including deliberate desertion and violence.

At the extremes, self-confidence in the individual is very low. This is such that they either demand much more than they give in a vain effort to fill their inner void or they may also create a form of armour which protects them from accepting help because to do so would be shameful. They do not need and they do not accept.

Since the majority of managers lie slightly to the left or right of the mid point, they tend to accept more than they give, or they give more than they receive. This can be seen in the nature of their professional and personal networks.

If you find yourself frustrated by someone who gave you nothing in return for the significant help you gave them in the past, it may mean one of two things:

(1) That you're the one who needs to clean the lens on the reciprocity meter. You need to receive more than you give and so it turns out to be you who can't see the help that the other person has given you. You're a slightly dependent case, and you will have to work on your acceptance of the betrayal and "bad luck" of the past.

(2) Or that you do have an accurate perception of reality, and it really is this other person who is failing to value your contribution because

they need to fill their own emptiness. There aren't enough favors in the world to make up for what was taken away from them.

And if you give much more than you receive and aren't frustrated, surely it is because you tend a little towards the anti-dependent, and you feel uncomfortable when people help you, and you have to give away more to feel good again. In this case, it would help if you could accept things. It's very difficult to feel really close to someone who can't accept help and always looks perfect.

You must find your own locale in this spectrum of shades. Think about it and try to be as close as you can to the independent ideal, the person who knows how to move from an in-depth sharing experience with others, to allowing them complete freedom when they need it. Truly independent people know how to make their own way, but they're also comfortable with giving and receiving. Their reading of the law of reciprocity is crystal clear, and their networks generate value and build great things around them.

4.5   EMOTIONAL INTELLIGENCE IN THE NETWORK

Emotional intelligence is defined as a person's ability to measure and manage their own emotions and those of others. This implies:

- the ability to observe yourself and to objectively read what you are feeling;
- the art of managing your own emotions in order to produce the most effective reaction;
- reading the emotions of others, which includes understanding complex political contexts; and
- the ability to influence the specific political context in general, and the emotions expressed by some others in particular, in order to achieve a desired result.

The term began to be mentioned in the work of Wayne Payne, Stanley Greenspan, Peter Salovey and John Mayers, and eventually became the title of Goleman's well-known best-seller, *Emotional Intelligence*.[3]

Given that managing contacts acts directly on emotions and perceptions as deep-rooted as trust, it might be assumed that good contact managers would be bound to have a fairly high emotional intelligence coefficient, since they would be able to set aside their fears and brilliantly communicate their ideas. They can empathize with strangers, act creatively when the time comes to connect people and ideas with each other, accept risks, and manage conflicts. And they can do all this without losing the overall picture of what is happening in the broader network in which they are operating.

The widest framework of emotional skills is that shown in the EI Consortium website, based on the works of Daniel Goleman, which were published in his book *Working with Emotional Intelligence*. The final description of these skills in the context of networking will help you complete the self-analysis table on page 100.

Self-awareness

Emotional awareness. An individual's ability to recognize their own emotions helps them operate effectively in any networking situation, to realize when the impulse to speak or send an email is generated by mistaken emotions, to understand the extent to which they are being affected by the actions and words of others. They can adapt immediately, so they can make use of the moment instead of having to wait for the next chance.

Sound self-diagnosis. This is the degree of precision with which individuals can evaluate themselves, their readiness to accept and absorb constructive criticism, the reliability of their perception of their own weaknesses. It informs their contact management because their greater level of honesty with themselves helps them to set achievable goals, and to more satisfactorily adapt their strengths and weaknesses on first meetings. An objective assessment of yourself means you will be aware of the kind of people who will connect with you, and who will see you as inferior and uninteresting. Your planning will be more realistic and achievable, and hence the general output of the way you manage your contacts will be greater.

Self-confidence. Far from arrogant or overbearing attitudes, self-confidence shows itself in the warmth with which a person behaves. Managers who are at ease with themselves reveal a good sense of humour about their own defects and win allies precisely because of their honesty. And managers who are sure of their own worth will allow their contacts total freedom to stay or to remain, which is the best way of increasing their loyalty.

Managing and motivating yourself

Self-control.   This quality refers to managers' abilities to control their impulses and less-than-strategic reactions, and is vital in contact management. They sidestep any tendency they have to laziness, they attend business events and dinners, they overcome tiredness, defeat their own impatience and irritability with difficult individuals, and avoid tantrums when faced with the aggressive power-seeking tactics and moves to which we are all exposed.

Reliability.   "Walking the talk" means practicing what you preach. The term refers to a person's integrity and consistence. It is obvious that a personality founded on consistent values, revealed in actions and words, not to mention idle gossip and rumors, possesses a valuable advantage when it comes to managing contacts.

Exactly the opposite is what happens to the protagonists in the popular American series entitled *Damages*. In this series the ambitious lawyer Patty, her partner John and the young trainee Ellen, are remarkable for their lack of integrity and reliability, which also damages their own relationships.

Accountability.   This refers to willingness to take responsibility for your own output, and means correctly reading what has gone well and not so well in your interactions with others. There is no doubt that good contact managers have a lot to say about luck, but they never sit on their hands waiting for it to come of its own accord. Readiness to take the bull of your own destiny by the horns is clearly the first step in being ready to network.

Adaptability.   Flexibility in the face of change and unforeseen circumstances gives life its zest for good contact managers. Their reactions range from an ability to reveal different aspects of their personality depending on what their colleagues will be comfortable with, to riding with the blows and swift reactions when faced with a non-functional networking plan.

Adaptability is the ability to survive and succeed, par excellence. It separates successful species from losers in the evolutionary competition; still it leads some to success while turning its back on those who cannot build it into their lives.

Innovation.   Creativity is crucial in contact management, since a mind that reacts fast connects people and projects which at first sight don't match. The ability to create products, services, and new and different ideas is the best way to attract contacts, visibility and opportunities.

Perseverance with objectives.   The ability to be motivated by the sole idea of having reached the desired target is also fundamental for managers in order to find the time demanded by their networks and contacts.

Commitment.   People who are able to convert their objectives into the objectives of their organization or social framework and vice versa achieve the maximum commitment of their efforts, and this has direct repercussions on the output of their contact management. A typical error to avoid is a networking plan with objectives which either fail to match, or sometimes run counter to, the objectives of the social framework or organization in which networking is taking place.

Commitment to an end, an ideal, a company, a power group, is essential to take maximum advantage of the energy and efforts of others, and to achieve better results from each action or interaction.

Initiative.   Confidence and a willingness to get up and go are clearly an advantage in the contact management process. The ability to overcome stage fright and be brave enough to ask a favor or talk to someone we feel is unapproachable opens more opportunities and gives us a pleasant surprise from time to time.

Optimism.   Managers who see the glass as half full are disappointed much less than the rest, and you can see this in the way they walk, in their tone of voice and in the energy with which they defend their position with contacts and colleagues. And it is not this alone, since optimism and energy with regard to goals is often precisely what attracts attention.

When the going gets tough some people muster their strength to deal with the situation, and some people look for those who can muster their strength; they feel strong when they are close to them.

Reading the social context

Empathy.   This is the ability to feel what somebody else is feeling. It is a vital ability for effective communication in initial conversations, but also for sensing when to contact that person again, and how it should be done as the bond develops. It also helps you to perceive what is bothering your contacts, and that means that you can be of more help to them.

Service focus. This ability speaks for itself. Anticipating and recognizing your contacts' needs and concerns is the seed of good contact management.

The quest for diversity. This has already been discussed in Chapter 2, when the advantages for a network to contain a range of different people was analyzed. Reading diversity also presupposes better adaptation to the protocols and customs of different countries or companies, and is fundamental for the success of the interactions involved.

Reading the emotions of the context. Good contact managers can read an absolutely complete image of the networks surrounding them. They know who gets on well with whom, and why, and they know where to operate to influence the results of the discussion and decisions. They learn to interpret a social context through what the others say and through their own observations, and they are then able to adapt their own actions and choice of allies to the opportunities offered them by a given context.

Managing the social context

All the abilities listed above add power to social management skills. This is why this final part of the emotional intelligence skills framework consists of abilities more clearly associated with networking. These include influence, communication, leadership ability, change management, conflict management, bond building, collaboration, cooperation, and teamwork.

These skills or abilities are dealt with exhaustively throughout the book, so there is no need to cover them again in this section, with the exception of leadership and teamwork.

Leadership means the capacity to inspire others and to have them follow you, and although being a source of inspiration is not within everybody's reach, communicating confidence and consolidating a range of different individuals around a shared effort is, indeed, a frequent networking goal and is very valuable.

On the other hand, it is possible to see teamwork as developing a small, narrow network of contacts which cannot grow. In this case, development can be focused only on generating the maximum possible levels of confidence.

4.6   DIAGNOSING AND MANAGING EMOTIONAL INTELLIGENCE

The skills table focusing on the specific context of networking will provide you with an idea of the situation at any given time, allowing you to focus one part of your plan on developing between one and three specific skills to improve your contact management.

We have therefore set out Graph 4.4 overleaf, which includes all the abilities described, and they are set out in two columns. In the first column we suggest you give yourself a score between 1 and 5, with 5 being the maximum and 1 the minimum ability level.

In the other column, you should consider the current objectives of your contact management and choose the skills most important for the achievement of these objectives. So we suggest choosing the five which seem most important to you, and give them a position and ranking from A to E.

In this way, your table will show the maximum relevance for the skill which receives an A, then skill B, and so forth to E.

Then, looking only at the skills which have been marked with a letter in the ranking in respect of your objectives, and given your current output level, choose the three skills which should be prioritized for development.

You should do this exercise every three months, since the development of your network and the results arising from the way you manage it will cause some skills to become more relevant, and others less so, so you should adapt your emotional skills development plan to the shifting strategic objectives of your contact management.

4.7   ROSALIND E.J. GILMORE, AN EXEMPLARY REGULATOR WITH A KNACK FOR LEADER-BUILDING NETWORKS

Rosalind Gilmore is a fine English lady with a staggering wisdom of world affairs. Exemplary in almost everything she does, nobody ever really taught her that networking was important. In the interview we conducted in 2008 for the Spanish edition of the book, she generously shares with us how she discovered this.

Her fundamental contribution to the prestigious International Women's Forum has been helping many women around the world get closer to top leadership, including myself. I really couldn't be more grateful.

	EMOTIONAL INTELLIGENCE SKILLS	LEVEL	RELEVANCE
SELF-AWARENESS	Self-awareness		
	Sound self-diagnosis		
	Self-confidence		
SELF MANAGEMENT AND MOTIVATION	Auto control		
	Reliability		
	Accountability		
	Adaptability		
	Innovation		
	Perseverance with regard to objectives		
	Commitment		
	Initiative		
	Optimism		
READING THE SOCIAL CONTEXT	Empathy		
	Service focus		
	Quest for diversity		
	Reading the emotions of the context		
MANAGING THE SOCIAL CONTEXT	Influence		
	Communication		
	Leadership		
	Change management		
	Conflict management		
	Building bonds		
	Collaboration and cooperation		
	Teamwork		

GRAPH 4.4

Gilmore's career includes no less than 26 years in senior positions in the UK Treasury, where she became executive chairman and First Commissioner of the regulatory commission for the UK mortgage and savings industry.

"My most demanding job was as regulator for much of the UK mutual sector, which provided, amongst other things, 75% of residential mortgages and 50% of liquid personal savings during the first half of the 1990s when the housing market fell dramatically while interest rates and unemployment rose. Proactive regulation meant that no saver lost money and no taxpayer money was spent," explains Gilmore.

"The legislation we administered made the protection of ordinary people's savings the primary objective, and the prudent well-being of the industry our next duty. Both were achieved despite very difficult economic circumstances. This was, among other things, the time when the UK left the European Exchange Rate mechanism," details our friend.

At other times she was also director of the UK Securities and Investments Board, and a member of the Lloyds of London Regulatory Board and of the Banking Advisory Committee of the European Union. As if this wasn't enough, among other part-time directorships in the public, academic, and corporate sectors, she sat on the board of Zurich Financial Services for 10 years. In all she has been a member of around 20 boards, large and small, over the last 30 years.

You can imagine there weren't many other women around her in the early part of her career. "The men around us already had the right networks. They had been to school together and could always ring each other up for informal advice to help share their projects and proposals."

One of Rosalind's friends, a reputable journalist and writer in the 1980s, used to say that "at that time there were no more than 50 women you had ever heard of in the UK, and we all knew each other." Thus the basis of an interdisciplinary network already existed.

Several of these high-ranking women had established contact with a formal organization of female leaders based in New York. They decided to bring together about 35 women from very different professional backgrounds amidst a rather conventional society which had never intentionally considered organized networks. Men's networks in most modern countries had gradually emerged over several centuries as a spontaneous consequence of doing business and sharing leisure.

They started dining together six to seven times a year, drawing satisfaction not only from the company of other women, but especially from the diversity of backgrounds present in the group.

Reflecting on the succession of events, Rosalind argues: "there's a sort of networking people do all the time, and which one takes for granted. There is also a lot of informal networking done around work and business transactions, of course. But the structured women networks that emerged around that time were more supportive than I had expected."

The 1990s brought on the consolidation and formalization of the group. New generations increased the number of successful women so that the goal of the UK chapter evolved. Rosalind explains how "it had more to do with making you quicker. You had good friends in other business areas and countries, which made you feel like you had a broader vision of things". She soon became part of the governance structure of the international organisation, its boards and committees.

Gilmore tells us that the single IWF event that most affected her own career was in the late 1980s when she knew she would be taking on the regulatory role described before. The general economic trends stalking the UK mortgage market had already precipitated the well-known "savings and loan crisis" in the USA, which had cost the Federal government and its agencies many billions of dollars to repair.

Close friends in the IWF, particularly a former global president of the organization, were able to arrange direct interviews for Rosalind with key players in Washington, New York and other financial centres, allowing her to comprehend the structure of the crisis and its aftermath. It was, of course, on a far larger scale and with many more facets than what later happened in the UK. But understanding the American case made it easier to see how the UK situation might evolve in any similar asset price collapse, especially after a time of some deregulation.

The beginning of the new millennium saw the emergence of new governance structures in the growing International Women's Forum. A focus was placed on increasing European presence, as well as starting chapters in other continents.

"By then IWF had begun to be a very successful provider of global events. The conferences provided access to people that you wouldn't normally meet elsewhere," Gilmore remembers. "The British Forum had a rich programme of local activities as well. From private trips to museum exhibitions or theatres, to regular breakfasts where we could discuss diverse topics."

In Rosalind's words, "many IWF chapters were very successful, but members on both sides of the Atlantic began to feel something was missing. We were having a great time networking with one another, but was that enough?" And she goes on, "since it was an organization which had supported many high level women, the right project seemed one which would help bring on the next generation of women leaders. It was a way to give back to the future."

The Leadership Foundation was born in 1990 with a double purpose. On the one hand it meant to advance research on female leadership, and on the other, it wanted to provide a world-class female leadership course. A comprehensive training program was designed to help high-potential young women "get the toolkit they needed to cross the gulf of management into leadership," as Gilmore puts it.

The women carefully selected to become fellows of the program can't be members of the IWF, as the Foundation is an IWF charitable subsidiary. It must be at least two years after the programme, before they can seek to join one of the Chapters. Once they have left the demanding selection process behind them, however, they are shown glimpses of the powerful network of almost 5,000 female leaders that spans the globe today.

Gilmore was heavily involved in the construction of the Leadership Foundation from the beginning, serving on the board for a number of years, and then as President from 2005 to 2007. She describes how these young women spend three very intensive weeks of the year with peers who are at once so similar and so different.

Each year the Foundation aims to accept, through a stringent application process, a peer group of equal quality, but from different backgrounds, cultures and professions, and from as many parts of the world as the IWF can cover. Many are sponsored by their corporations, others by government or other public sector agencies; and the Foundation now also has some bursaries available from other charitable foundations. As funding has grown, so has the class size, but not beyond a good group dynamic.

Each Fellow must commit three weeks spread through the year to the program. One is spent at the IWF Autumn Conference, where the introduction and coaching is done by IWF staff and members:

As well as attending the Conference itself, the second week in the spring is spent at the Harvard Business School. The third week is spent at a European Business school in the summer, now INSEAD in France, but previously Cambridge in England. Problem solving, communication and politics, positioning, and a variety of other skills are taught intensively and in ways that mean a good deal of team work is needed.

Rosalind describes an exercise in which one of them tells another of a difficult problem she has had to solve. The recipient is then required to explain and discuss the case in order to get the group's feedback on it. This is not only a case study but helps people understand how important it is to listen, and how communication plays a part in leadership.

Additionally each Fellow is assigned a mentor from among the IWF members. "She can express a preference for someone in her line of work, or from a quite different sector, or from her own country or another," explains Gilmore. But the actual choice of the person is made by the Foundation. The mentor is there for the Fellow throughout the year, and sometimes long-lasting friendships are formed. "Mentors are from outside the Fellows' own organization which gives yet another dimension to the experience."

Most of all, the Fellows gain from each other. "Taking it all together, I think the most striking effect is that after the year of Fellowship each member of the group emerges with a much more firmly based sense of confidence about herself and her relationship with the world." And Gilmore continues, "this is of great benefit both personally and to their organizations, present or future. They develop an international peer group of friends for life. It must be enhancing for everyone."

On a warm May afternoon, from a cosy little house on a remote Greek island, Rosalind Gilmore still finds the time and energy to share her thoughts with us: "I have always been committed to the IWF and in particular to its Leadership Foundation. I hope that as time goes on we can continue to grow the programme, which all the participants love and which many describe as a life-changing experience. In that way every IWF member has available a legacy which they can make to future women's leadership."

CHAPTER 5

BARRIERS TO BEING
A BETTER YOU

Far away in the heavenly abode of the great god Indra, there is a wonderful net which has been hung by some cunning artificer in such a manner that it stretches out infinitely in all directions. In accordance with the extravagant tastes of deities, the artificer has hung a single glittering jewel in each 'eye' of the net, and since the net itself is infinite in dimension, the jewels are infinite in number.

There hang the jewels, glittering like stars in the first magnitude, a wonderful sight to behold. If we now arbitrarily select one of these jewels for inspection and look closely at it, we will discover that in its polished surface there are reflected all the other jewels in the net, infinite in number. Not only that, but each of the jewels reflected in this one jewel is also reflecting all the other jewels, so that there is an infinite reflecting process occurring.

Francis Harold Cook described the metaphor of Indra's net from the Huayan perspective in the book *Hua-Yen Buddhism: The Jewel Net of Indra.*[1]

5.1 KNOWING IS NOT ENOUGH

We all know that contacts are important. And we all pay attention to people who are "thought to have a lot of contacts", or we envy the ease with which the most successful managers are promoted, or are offered attractive jobs, invitations to parties and exclusive meetings thanks to "their contacts", but we can't work out the difference between "their contacts" and ours.

Have we ever wondered how much of their personal and professional success is due to their intelligence or their understanding of theory and how much to their network of contacts? What exactly is the relationship between what they have achieved in their professional careers and the people they know? Or, to put it another way, what is the connection between what they didn't achieve and the people "they weren't lucky enough" to know?

Although over the last 60 years a great deal has been written about networks of contacts and how they explain the world, we have yet to see a scientific study clearly showing beyond a shadow of doubt the exact relationship between professional success and a suitable network of contacts.

What is certain, however, is that it would be impossible to demonstrate scientifically and precisely why such a study would be needed. Modern science has developed on the premise of isolating a series of variables within a closed environment, and playing with them to see what happens in that environment. In its simplest form, we study what happens with a single variable to draw conclusions. Of course, the computer means that we can play with an ever-increasing number of variables at the same time, but that is already way beyond what our brains are capable of grasping.

Any sociological or statistical study which sought to explain the causes for a certain individual's success and the lack of success of others would have to identify and isolate so many variables that even if this were possible, it is more than likely that we would be unable to draw conclusions.

No irrefutable demonstration has proven that good contact management speeds the manager towards his goals and helps him to succeed better. What we can say, however, is that the vast majority of successful leaders and businessmen are excellent contact managers, in touch with a rich network of talent, power and potential. We are all aware of the popular saying – it exists in every language – "money attracts money."

We could waste hours debating this subject and we would never reach a convincing conclusion. But we should beware. Questions which have no answer are an excellent excuse to put off unsatisfactory efforts until tomorrow. The "I musts" turn into "I oughts" and then become watered down into rational discussions for and against which finally bore us and we fall silent, sidetracked towards some other more immediate problem.

Maybe that's why you're still reading this book, to find out whether by reading it you'll get a little closer to an "I ought," to see if this book reveals a magic secret from the Knowledge Guru to make you act at last.

But no kind of knowledge is going to move you to take action. Knowledge and secrets provide food for thought, but by themselves they aren't enough to shift us. Knowing that our contacts can help us to achieve our objectives is not enough. Imagining that some individual is more successful in his profession because he had the good luck to be born in a particular social circle, or secretly dreaming what fun it would be to earn a living doing what we like doing while we are counting the minutes to the end of a day doing some unsatisfactory job will never lead to a change.

We have all probably attended a seminar at some time in our lives which really scared us, when we discovered great truths about ourselves, even though in reality they told us nothing new. Yet the next day making a change in your daily routine seemed less difficult and more important. The same logical decision for or against which had been posited hundreds of times in the past about doing something differently now rested on a completely different emotional footing.

The arguments in favor of change were more credible, they were associated with more examples of success and were better related to the uncertain success than before, while the arguments against were reduced to weak, pointless criticisms and excuses which now carried no conviction.

The battle must be fought on the field of the emotions before it reaches the arena of logic. That's why many of you, well aware of the fact that you should pay more attention to your networks of contacts, have never done anything about it until now, because the battle has been fought before you realized. Meshes of inherited beliefs interact with lifelong emotional associations and with your attitudes to yourself and to your future, and imbue any conscious reasoning with emotions which shape the final response of the logical discussion because of the power of inertia they deploy.

In short, knowing it is not enough. You have to feel it as well. You have to question the absolute truths you never doubted, taunt yourself to try out new things, and they will produce new sensations within you.

We find a series of obstacles repeated between managers who neglect their networks. While you read over them, ask yourself how they affect you, how much you believe in them, or in whom and when you noticed them. You may be surprised by what you find out, and you will probably find yourself even more keen to read on.

5.2 WE ALREADY HAVE NETWORKS, BUT THEY'RE TOO COMFORTABLE

For those who work in the commercial world, networks of contacts are a clear priority in their lives, even a fascinating necessity which devours their time by the hour or by the day. The objective of selling demands that they should depend not only on their existing customers, but that they devote effort, imagination, and a great deal of energy talking with prospects and attempting to convert them into customers.

The rest of us live in a cloud of affectionate comfort which protects us from having to expose ourselves to strangers too often. It doesn't confront us with uncomfortable silences at parties or make us fearful of planning complex management moves involving alien interests.

Some of us can't even remember the last time we had to force ourselves to establish new relationships because we never went to live somewhere else, or because we all went to the same school and we keep on having dinner with the same friends we've had for 20 years, and because we are already so committed to our family and friends that we almost wish we could "un-introduce ourselves" to people. It doesn't occur to us to devote any time to a stranger.

There would be no problem with this as long as we "non commercials" had no goals or needs in our lives. But the reality is very different.

We should clarify a couple of things:

1.   We've all been managing contacts since we were children. The simple fact of making friends, exchanging the time of day with the baker or choosing our partners are everyday matters which we do intuitively because that's what everybody else does, and because we live in families, towns, cities, and countries surrounded by people, so that establishing relationships with others forms a part of our lives, whether we like it or not.

2.   The times when we have aspirations to something more than we are or we have are rare. We proceed from making efforts to approve of and fit in with our school friends to choosing a university career which will satisfy our parents and a partner our mothers can stand. Then come children, dogs, mortgages, and other complications, and before we have time to realize what is happening we have a heap of commitments which we would love to escape from every now and again, and there are many other factors which are beginning to appear much more interesting than before. We are creatures who desire. We desire something until we have it, and then we move on to desiring something new.

Most of us collected the most important contacts in our lives at no cost. They simply appeared: siblings, cousins, schoolmates, friends who are the children of our parents' friends in their turn. More people seem to have appeared in our lives by chance. They have remained because we are comfortable with them.

We may recall having made some efforts, more than likely in the field of romance. This is the best example of contact management in the teenage years. During adolescence you have to find a person of the opposite sex who seems to suit you.

Going out on dates, whispering in class, university drinks – these are the kind of scenarios in which we have done our best to please someone, have been rejected for saying the wrong thing, or even just for not being tall, or pretty, or funny enough. And we kept making the effort with this person or that (although some try much more than others), being happy and miserable, until at last we find someone with whom we don't need to make the effort.

Losing the habit of making efforts to build contacts with new people is one of the major restrictive obstacles facing today's managers. Look at the difference between friends who have never moved and maintain the same friendships along with everything else in their lives and compare them with friends who have lived abroad, or who went from school to school, following their parents around the world, or who have had frequent job changes. It is the latter who seem more open to strangers, having less difficulty talking with people they don't know and a variety of friends and aspects in their lives which we know nothing of.

Their contact management muscles are well exercised, and they make use of them frequently. People who have never had to leave their social circle, however, have lost that muscle and lack contact management reflexes, which is why moves to develop personal connections are much more like uphill work.

A slightly extreme example of this phenomenon, albeit one with which we are all too familiar, either through friends or our own personal experience, is what happens after a separation or a divorce. This is a classic moment in adult life when individuals are forced to once again try out emotional contact management, and it is precisely because they are looking for something so intimate and committed that the associated risks are greater and the disasters are particularly keen.

Some people decide to go back to their partners to avoid battling with the new loneliness and huge effort to meet new people, and others put up with it until it seems less painful to appear as a single at a party of strangers. They get used to striking up conversations and suggesting an outing to companions at the health club. And little by little, as they start to exercise their contact management muscle again, it becomes less uncomfortable and easier.

This obstacle is overcome with determination, a clear strategy like strong motivation, and patience. We can use the broken heart to illustrate with exaggerated clarity the difficulty which limits the majority of managers when it comes to changing or initiating their contact management activities. It is applicable, with less intensity, to any of the contact management applications noted in the introduction. Just like any muscle, when you start to use it, it starts to strengthen, and you start to wonder how you managed to get by so comfortably in your old world.

5.3 INVISIBLE OBSTACLES

When you have reached this page in the book, and have come to the conclusion that you're in worse shape than you thought, you have already overcome some very tough obstacles, but more are lying in wait. It's like starting a car. You're in first gear and you used quite a bit of fuel getting moving, but now you have to maintain the momentum, and even increase the speed a bit to climb a slope that looks steep.

This steep slope consists of a series of invisible obstacles when it comes to deciding whether to join a sports club to meet more people, or to ask a question out loud at a conference. From the moment the idea occurs to you of what you "ought" to do to bring your new contact management to life until you do it or leave it for another day, a whole range of reasoning processes and deductions will take place in your head about which you know nothing.

It's like the computer screen when you tell it to open a document and it shows you a collection of colored pictures before providing you with what you ordered. It is in these processes, which unfortunately are "user transparent," as IT buffs say, since nobody places little explanatory colored pictures before their eyes, that the serious obstacles make their appearance, obstacles which can drain your energy and slow you down to a stop, or even throw you into reverse.

We are talking here of deep-seated beliefs about the way life works, or who we are, what we can expect from the future, which restrict our actions.

We accepted them as ours at a time we can't recall, and we sustain them with a myriad of examples, comments from friends, proof seen with our own eyes and heard with our own ears. They have been, without doubt, fundamental to our crucial analyses and decisions all through the years, and they are partly responsible for what we have achieved.

There are also pre-programmed emotional reactions, associated with the data and with the interpretations we make. Just as that special song makes you sad every time you hear it, or a smell that sweeps you back to a certain moment in your childhood, you will find you also have various emotional reactions pre-set in your being from way back. And the awakened emotions in their turn call on other beliefs and thoughts which fit with them. In this way a chain of beliefs, emotions and deductions is repeated which ends up with the responses that leave you flabbergasted: "best leave it for tomorrow," or charge into action.

However, some of these beliefs and emotional responses may be restricting us imperceptibly, giving rise to those feelings of tiredness and lassitude when we intend to implement a change of habits which we had planned and decided upon.

The most disturbing thing about these beliefs is that you aren't even aware of them. This means that they can drift in and out of your decisions and actions with total freedom, never being questioned or detained for a moment by you.

A good example is the case of an expert in logistical operations and procedures with a long career in the luxury industry. After working abroad for two of the top European luxury brands he came to Spain to join a family group which wanted to improve their management efficiency to move into the front rank of the luxury business.

George had plunged into this exciting project three years before with all the delight of the young manager who has been given a chance to grow more quickly, and he thoroughly devoted himself to the project. But the tensions within the family owners, and the inertia of continuing to work in a fairly casual way, acted as a drag on important decisions of all kinds.

George started to become convinced that he had to seek other horizons, because he seemed to be giving his heart and soul to a project that he couldn't get moving, despite what he was sacrificing for it, and he felt he was likely to be bogged in the mire for another five years if he didn't move soon. That was the moment when George was clearly motivated to resuscitate his network contacts.

After a few initial weeks during which he carefully examined his network, he took a good hard look at himself. Having planned a strategy for finding a new job which would make the most of everything he had learned in the family group, he found himself in conversation with his coach, telling him of the progress he had made (and not made) during the month:

> The fact is, I didn't manage to call the five ex-colleagues you suggested. I've no idea how it happened, but the time just seems to have slipped through my fingers.
>
> And then the last time I had decided to make use of my coffee break to make the calls, I got nervous, and I ended up doing something else. It's not as though I was hysterical. There's no need to look at me like that! It's just that... as I was checking the time on my watch, it occurred to me that it was a damned cheek! I'd shown no signs of life for such a long time, then to suddenly call out of the blue... it wasn't natural, I would have had to force myself, and I was scared that someone would notice that I was uneasy.

When he was asked about the breakfast he had shared with his Italian ex-boss who had just come up to Madrid on a visit, he replied:

> It was all very pleasant, but I didn't mention what was on my mind. It didn't seem the right moment. We hadn't seen each other for quite some time, and he seemed more interested in talking about girls, you know.
>
> To tell the truth, he did ask me about the job, whether I liked it or not, but when I started to tell him that things weren't going so well, he started to look awkward and took out a cigarette as if he was getting bored or distracted and wanted to change the subject. I don't know... I would have told him all the neat stuff I'd done on the operational side, but all of a sudden I didn't want to talk about me. I felt as uncomfortable as hell and changed the subject to girls and how they drive you crazy.

George was losing speed in his development process. First he let himself be persuaded by the excuse of not having enough time, when really what was happening was that he was uneasy at calling someone that he hadn't spoken to for a while. It was fairly obvious that this nervousness would have to be investigated and its roots identified so that ways to overcome it could be found.

Then the meeting with his ex-boss threw light on another decision of the same type, since the discomfort and the cigarette which he described as indicators that he wanted to change the subject could mean a lot of different things, but the way George interpreted it left him feeling that he couldn't seize the moment to talk about himself, his successes and his new ambitions.

If we could have taken a look at George's brain during these events on an imaginary computer screen, we would have seen thousands of lines of coding which were jumping at the speed of light (well all right, very quickly, then). But there would have been one we would have seen repeated every now and again, a line that said something like "I don't believe anybody is interested in my work", and that line would call in subprograms of negative anecdotes or events in his life which emphasized the truth of this statement.

In other words the invisible obstacle preventing George from developing his networks was a loss of confidence in his own work, the result of working for so many years without seeing any results, because the family business couldn't produce them. Yet George has always been so ambitious and confident that he could not believe that this had happened to him.

The most common invisible obstacles managers run into when developing their contact networks are confidence in themselves (and in their work), confidence in the environment, ethical confusion, self-satisfied short-sightedness and lack of strategy, as we shall see in this chapter.

But if they were asked, nobody would ever give that as an answer. Indeed, if we asked them why they didn't manage their contacts more thoroughly and more satisfactorily, almost all would say that they didn't have time. This is a perfect, politically correct, response from today's manager, but it is a response which makes uncertainty responsible, and thus there is no solution.

And don't breathe a sigh of relief if you come up with the same answer. Just keep thinking, and ask yourself why you can't find the time. You may come up with another reason, one which is less visible but more manageable.

Glass ceilings

A glass ceiling is difficult to describe or define, but it separates networkers from everybody else. While for some people networking is a complete science, registered and announced as an essential skill in books, top management seminars and business schools, for others its message is politically incorrect.

The second group approaches networking with unease and suspicion, evoking the image of "social climbers" and "pushy" people in our environment whom we see as rather undesirable, unless they happen to be "commercial." They claim to have a good excuse to manage their contacts in working hours, as long as they leave us in peace outside the office.

Although we all talk about "having a contact" for this or that, and ideally we would talk about "contacts" in the plural that we might want to brag about to our friends, many of us would prefer to leave contacts to generate themselves, or to leave it to chance.

People who have "good" contacts have them because they were born in a privileged family, or because they are more attractive and they tell more jokes than we do so they get invited to more parties, or maybe because they're "close" to the CEO and thanks to that they've managed to build up a privileged network which we would like to have because it would solve a lot of problems for us, but it doesn't seem to be within our reach.

Most management books which talk about contact management are in English and come from the USA, which leads you to the conclusion that the American people, descendants of all the Europeans who set out for the New World because they were "out of luck" in Europe, don't see it quite the same way.

In the land of the "American Dream," the European newcomers wanted to create an environment which was radically different from what they had known in old, traditional Europe: there would be no closed shops or inaccessible social classes. Anybody would be able to be anything they liked in life, if they were willing to put in the work.

This fundamental belief is what makes networking something natural and essential in US business, while for classical Europeans it seems pretentious and opportunistic.

Adopting the conservative position as a response to the question of what we want of our professional careers condemns us to fabricate a whole mosaic of logical reasoning which is rooted in the conviction that we were born in the wrong place, so there is no sense in forcing ourselves too much to develop our own network.

It means we can take refuge in the superficial excuse of "not having the time." We can spend five, ten or 15 years in a professional limbo or confused suspended animation. We wonder why our lives haven't gone better. We look down our noses at those who always seem to be concerned with who's who, who by chance seem to live like film stars, because they fail to respect the passive and submissive rule of life as we do.

There is a principle of Zen philosophy: what happens to us in this life is a product of what lies within us. In other words, the managers themselves made the glass ceiling which prevents them from rising. The most representative minority of this phenomenon is that of female managers, which gives rise to studies and statistics where the results curiously end up reflecting the beliefs of the authors.

It's not that they laid one brick after another until they had closed the doors to future advances – rather it is their own inner fear of not being accepted because they are different which causes them to reject their difference, the very thing that makes them special, and because of that, they lose their essence, and what's even more important, they lose the will to fight to prove that anything is possible.

Anyone who dares to adopt the response given by an immigrant newly arrived from a war-torn or drought-stricken country, feeling he had left everything at home for what he might gain in a completely unknown country, has already gained a great deal; even though he might be scared to death.

Believing and feeling that you can achieve everything is the existential attitude which pushes networkers to devote time, effort and wisdom to the search for people with whom they can create new and lasting mutual aid connections. Their optimistic belief in their new possibilities becomes a kind of magnetism which attracts others to them, and powers the emotions of conquest, goal-orientation and satisfaction with their own efforts.

One very interesting study I have not been able to reference set out to elucidate what determined the potential for success in a sample of individuals from various different social classes. The study showed that the people whose parents were well off did in fact have more prosperous professional careers. But the determining factor was not the availability of resources, or access to privileged circles of influence, which, although clearly important, were not enough to explain the differences between the professional careers examined.

The determining factor in the potential for success of the individuals studied in the sample was much more subtle and powerful than the material circumstances in which they grew up. It was their belief in themselves: the children from wealthy families had listened to their parents when they were told that "they could be anything they wanted to be as long as they made sufficient effort."

The children from more modest families, however, had received a message which was completely the opposite throughout the whole of their childhood, which included remarks such as "life isn't fair," "money attracts money," "nobody will ever take you seriously," and a long litany of underdog conclusions, repeated ad nauseam by parents who had learned exactly the same thing from their parents; and who had therefore allowed themselves to be overwhelmed by the first signs their parents had warned them of for so many years.

This view of life as a series of options already selected according to where we were born is the first glass ceiling which condemns some to a life of mediocrity, while launching others to the stars. This ceiling is invisible because most of us are already sure we are on top of it, even though the results don't agree... and yet in some hidden part of our logic a bunch of remarks we have inherited from our friends or parents which justify our not being where we want to be are still working.

Internal vacuums

Another barrier it's almost so subtle, invisible, yet very common, is concerned with the culture of being at the service of others rather than at the service of yourself.

The barrier consists not so much of an approach whereby you put the needs of others ahead of yours, but rather that you never consider yours at all.

Women of previous generations, educated to care for their husbands, their children, their sick, and their parents, tended to have this self-denying attitude.

And while it is a fact that the social models which gave rise to this form of female service could not function without it, the current model of gender equality offers both sexes the same type of professional goals, but with a difference. While many men believe that it is right for them to pursue what they want, some men and any number of women don't feel at all comfortable with the idea of wanting something for themselves.

No careful studies have been carried out to discover why women more than men fall into this trap, and it is not our intention to contribute to the creation of generalized stereotypes, but here is an anecdote which illustrates a kind of story which has been relatively common for men and women in their forties and fifties, and for whom this expectation has been a real Achilles' heel.

Laura was the systems manager for an engineering company which had experienced a growth rate of over 20% per year for the preceding ten years. When she joined the firm it was just a cluster of engineers who were keen to work, and the company ended up with a payroll of hundreds involved in a whole range of projects.

Laura had given her life to this project, and at 50 she was like the mother of the company. She was the only woman on the management committee, responsible for more than 60% of the workforce, and with a long list of successes to her credit. She had redesigned the customer service procedures that generated so many problems before she arrived. She'd also been responsible for most of the increase in sales in the following years. She was the one who rescued them from a computerization disaster five years earlier. She still maintained strong relationships with the major customers of the organization.

But Laura didn't feel she was given the recognition she deserved, and her suspicions were confirmed when the managing director decided to take on a 35-year-old manager, forcing her out of the management committee.

Laura left the company out of the sheer incredulity and indignation caused by this change, but she felt deeply betrayed, both professionally and personally by the man who used to be her boss, and by the management committee as a whole, the majority of whom had joined at the same time as she.

How could it have happened? What did she do wrong? She had worked so hard for them – how could it be that not only had they failed to reward her sufficiently in the past, they had now tossed her aside completely?

The answer to these questions is that Laura's attitude to others drained all her energy, leaving not a trace for her personal needs and herself. Laura had been brought up to be caring, to make life easier for others, and to ask for nothing in return.

In Laura's opinion, people who wanted something in return for their work were too selfish and mean, and so she never complained that her reward for what she gave to the organization was never enough, and she never reacted when her own department shrank, nor when her colleagues on the committee were paid salaries which awarded bonuses for sales she herself was responsible for.

Laura devoted so much care and affection to ensuring that the job was done as well as possible that she never found time to make it known or tell anybody about it. And if anybody ever had a flattering comment to make about her contribution, she would feel uncomfortable and try to suggest that it was all the work of the others.

Laura's personal network was full of bloodsuckers. There was no single associate, friend or family member who would fail to call on her to solve an urgent problem.

Laura was wonderfully generous, so generous that not only had she no time to manage the contacts who contributed something to her, but when she met new people she usually only felt at ease with those who needed her for some reason and would not feel they owed her anything when she had supplied the help they wanted.

Laura would feel guilty if someone in her environment needed something and she failed to drop everything to run to their assistance. Anybody who didn't do the same she saw as selfish, which means that she rapidly fell out with ambitious managers.

This internal vacuum is to be found in the professional attitude of many men and women today, people who are surprised to find that as the years pass no one seems to remember what they contributed, nor is it seen as important that they do.

It is a breach of the principle of reciprocity self-imposed by the managers themselves, because of their feeling of discomfort with recognition and success. The result is that their contact management is always pure, altruistic generosity, and the bitter surprise comes when it is the selfish who are promoted.

You may feel that Laura's story is an exaggeration, but the case is real, and the likelihood is that her life is actually even more unequivocal and clear-cut. If you hesitate to present your work to others with pride, and if you usually leave the greater part of the negotiations to them because it isn't worth fighting for a better balance, this may well be the internal vacuum which is operating in your life and in your contact management processes.

Armour to conceal wounds

We all protect ourselves. We have masks for going out into the street, masks for coming home at night to have dinner with the family, masks for the health club, and masks to talk to the boss.

The mask and the armour are the protection we need to feel comfortable and stop the others from seeing what hurts us or what bothers us. A businessman preoccupied about the imminent collapse of his business wears the mask of success and confidence for the negotiations with his new buyers. Meeting people at clubs becomes increasingly a question of disguises and masks as the years pass, with the increasing load of personal secrets we feel we have to hide.

An armour is of the utmost importance in the achievement of goals of all kinds and to sidestep surprises and ambushes. But sometimes these very masks block connection with others.

For each complex or insecurity the manager accumulates, and for every painful wound from the past, there is a mask or piece of armour which protects that manager in the daily battle of the business world. The deeper and more sensitive the wound, the harder and tougher is the corresponding piece of armour, so that he ends up over-protecting each part of the body, the strength and solidity corresponding to the vulnerability of the region.

That armour establishes a distance between the wearer and whoever is in front. And while riot policemen will at last become used to all their layers and end up feeling as though they weren't coated with multidimensional disguises, the armour worn by the manager cannot be breached. No entry is possible if the manager doesn't lower his guard.

Trust and friendship are like gases which keep on flowing until a screen is placed in front of them, and if you're wearing armour, it could be that you are holding back the progress of those gases which might be so good for the soul and for your professional future.

Managers clad in independent and self-sufficient armour tend to get on only with other individuals who are also half robot and as unwilling as they are to reveal themselves as they really are. Or with bloodsuckers who take everything and ask for nothing, nor are they concerned to check whether anything is missing behind the mask of their unknown saviour.

Have a good look at your masks and armour before you set out to network. A sticking plaster may be helpful for a while, but it's designed to be taken off once the wound or the problem has gone. The masks we develop to protect ourselves should never turn into eternal burdens – ideally, they should have a use-by date.

If you recognize masks and armour as part of the way you connect with others, think about them. Which ones are new, and which have been there for a while? And, most important, which are the ones which keep you isolated from everybody? Your partner is usually the person best qualified to identify and point out your masks, so maybe that person is actually in the right in some of your arguments.

But if you identify a mask you decide you want to be rid of, make sure first that you can handle the weakness or the wound that lies beneath.

Ethical confusion

The term ethics implies a concept full of deep-rooted emotions, inducing in many people a feeling of suspicion when contact management is under discussion.

I don't think there has ever been a seminar or course at which no one has raised a hand to ask about the ethic which supports the principles and techniques of contact management. This is a very important subject, and can be either a huge source of energy or a massive obstacle causing everything to grind to a halt.

In actual fact, ethics is a concern to be found in all areas of management. I like to ask my students if they can tell me what the difference is between a good leader and an excellent manipulator. We need to be able to unfailingly recognize the features or characteristics which distinguish them so as to be able to avoid any manipulators we may encounter.

After some discussion about the behavior patterns which are typical of a manipulator, there is usually someone who comes up with an answer which is very intuitive, but definitely on target: a leader is someone who tries to achieve the best for all, while the manipulator is the one seeking his own benefit, even at the cost of the well-being of everybody else involved.

Both make use of the same techniques and both manage their own and others' emotions, to the point of blurring the line which separates the ethical from the unethical, even for themselves. It is very difficult to judge from the outside whether a person's behaviour is ethical or not, because only the individual in question knows what they are feeling and thinking, running the risk of being wrong and bearing the blame for ever.

Laws and customs collected in the popular wisdom of each country define a few minimal limits, but the truth is that even when a huge effort has been made to tell good from evil, millions of cases set up a grey area or a loophole in the law which puts both sides in the right and converts the ethical debate into an un-winnable battle because of the certainty with which each side defends its motives.

Contact management certainly evokes the same doubt, but it is also certain that it is each party's job to establish the philosophy and principles which guide their efforts. Contact management is a tool of equal usefulness to anyone applying immaculate ethics and to the unscrupulous robber of souls. It is a set of techniques in the service of all kinds of motivations, and later on we shall tackle the new contacts filter as a key technique for avoiding entrapment in inappropriate networks.

All readers will have to formulate their ethical principles or moral values, so that the way they manage their networks, their personal practices and their method of perfecting the techniques I shall describe further on will stand as an eloquent product of the crucial choice concerned. They will also have to study the practices and behavior patterns of the others in order to choose the ethical and moral values before incorporating them in their network.

A common mistake is to confuse ethics with coldness in a strategic plan. Strategic network planning certainly involves initiating a search for personal objectives as a primary objective, but the need to think about yourself is directly related to the shortage of resources.

In the process of developing management skills there is a time to be strategic and another to be authentic. Shortage of time, of money to give gifts or to introduce yourself into various social circles which appear crucial oblige you to prioritize and choose how and where to use the resources you have. Setting aside time to analyze what you are doing helps you optimize this process.

Then comes the time to be authentic, you must enter life's stage and forge friendships, sow trust and make allies. At this moment premeditated calculation and lack of warmth is detectable. It is almost impossible to dissimulate, and although you may be able to pull it off for a few minutes or even days, the fact that you live in a social community swapping information about you means that sooner or later unethical behavior, insincere motivation and a feigned personality will be discovered.

Most American literature about contact management is not exportable to Europe because the cultural protocols which inspire trust in others are very different from country to country.

This is so much so that in the Latin cultures, for example, we tend to be very demonstrative, generous in our gestures of affection, indeed, we even speak more loudly and from closer up to others. We are much more disposed to see human relations as a center of priorities than other cultures, and it is because of this that we tend not to question the range of personal closeness reactions we indulge in.

Some people are worried that contact management must be some kind of "bad" thing because it seems more premeditated, and because it questions the very reactions of the people around us. It introduces an additional layer of thought into the way we connect with people which tends to make us mistrust the very people whose personal interaction we seem to enjoy most.

This is another invisible obstacle which supports the mistaken belief that you stop being spontaneous because you've started to think before you invite people for coffee, chat or express affection or trust. Once again, this question is hard to answer and very personal.

From the point of view we shall be defending throughout this book, contact management helps the manager to select those with whom he can be spontaneous without finding himself at risk of harm or having his confidence betrayed, and those with whom he cannot. He never stops being spontaneous, but he does choose with whom, and this allows him on the one hand to protect himself from deception and on the other to direct his spontaneity at those who will appreciate it and respond to it with the same level of trustworthiness and honesty.

At the end of this chapter you will find another exercise you can use to analyze your personal positioning regarding the warmth or coldness of your gestures of affection, and how you can develop this perspective so that it will support your contact management.

Wandering aimlessly

The weakest point which I have been able to find in the literature available on contact management or networking is that this ability is treated as though it were a solution in itself, when in reality it is no more than a tool in a manager's service.

More than one management committee has asked me to give them some training in strategic contact management, and when I have asked what for, they have been unable to come up with an answer.

Clearly defining the basic objective and strategy of our efforts in the field of relationships is vital for us to be able to distribute our resources effectively, particularly the time and energy we have available, which are inevitably bound to be limited.

But this is also a way of placing theory and tactics in a relevant context with real individuals and problems. I remember one client who wanted to train his young high-potential staff in networking techniques, but who at the very same time found himself replaced as CEO by somebody else, because the company was in the middle of a serious financial crisis.

The greatest barrier to the development of the participants' networks was not lack of technique or a weakly developed conversation muscle. They had not had the time to reach this point because 90% of the managers I had in front of me couldn't decide if they wanted to stay with the company and help to build it up, thus gaining extraordinary opportunities for personal leadership, or if they wanted to cut their losses because they didn't believe in the new CEO and wanted to abandon a sinking ship.

When you are not sure about this it means the messages you send out are ineffective, because they are vague and their emphasis shifts from one interaction to the next, the allies you choose are not consistent and that there are no alternatives, since neither are clear in your mind, and that the efforts you devote to policy management are a waste of time.

It may be that at a given moment your "because" may be specifically to gather information to take a complex decision, but that is a rare situation in a professional career, and that's why I recommend that you make your decision before setting out to confuse your people with unclear conversations and uncertain requests.

As we are about to see in detail, contact management is work which pays off in the medium term, so setting immediate goals is pointless. A lot of people start to manage their contacts when they want to change their job, for example. They start calling all the people they knew on the MBA course or former work colleagues whom they haven't spoken to for several months, or maybe they directly send a mass email to everybody they know seeking information about possible vacancies.

This is not contact management. And the "because" in this case is so immediate and obvious that you could almost call it a commercial transaction, quite apart from the fact that it usually doesn't work. The response level that managers like this receive to the petition published on their network is proportional to the effort and dedication they have applied to their network in the past.

5.4 ANALYZE YOUR INVISIBLE OBSTACLES

Divide a sheet of paper in two with a vertical line, write on the left all the reasons why you haven't achieved more success in your personal and professional life, and on the right, put down all the reasons why you have achieved the things that you do have and value.

Don't just set aside five minutes to jot down three or four trivial items on one side and then go on to the next page. A question such as this should wake up all kind of thoughts and memories in our brains, in such a way that two or three days later even more ideas or examples should be appearing to be added to one side or the other.

Nor should you hide anything from yourself. Write down everything that occurs to you, however unlikely it seems. This is a private exercise which only you will see, and the greater the number of answers you put in each column, the more you will get out of it.

Once you are satisfied with your responses in both columns, go through the list, and, using colors or some other symbols, classify each sentence in one of three categories:

(1) Underline or highlight the idea that what I seek is out of my reach.
(2) Underline or highlight the idea that I am able to achieve anything which is proposed to me.
(3) Underline or highlight anything which has nothing to do with this discussion or where I can find no relationship with either of the two preceding ideas.

If you find yourself with a lot of material in category 3, I suggest that you reformulate the response or increase the level of detail somewhat so that you coincide with ideas which fall into the opposite categories (1) or (2).

Don't let yourself be over-influenced by the column in which each response is to be found. Both categories can appear in both columns. Once again, try to be objective with this classification, as though you were dealing with somebody else, or if you're willing you could even hand over the job of categorization to another person, without providing the details about what these responses mean or why you want to perform this analysis.

If at the end of the exercise you conclude that there is a large majority of responses in category (1), it is possible that you are starting to unmask the more or less obvious presence of this invisible obstacle in your psyche.

This is neither good nor bad in itself. What is interesting is now you can see it more clearly, out in the open, and that means you can do something about it.

And from now on you can begin to make a mental note – or even jot down in a notebook – the number of times that this thought comes into your head. This is the first step towards being able to confront the obstacle, since as long as it is invisible it can operate at its ease, but once its subconscious disguise has been torn away, you will find yourself in a position to question it.

5.5 KEITH ANDERSON, CEO OF SCOTTISHPOWER RENEWABLES

Keith Anderson was born and raised in Scotland. Leader of a young adventurous company and full of ambition, he uses his networking skills to improve his performance and that of the organization he leads. As business becomes ever more international, he shares his adventures and learning of cultural differences at work.

ScottishPower Renewables is part of Iberdrola Renovables, the world's largest developer of renewable energy. With over 30 windfarms in the UK, the Scottish business unit is the UK's leading developer of onshore wind.

Keith Anderson, CEO of ScottishPower Renewables, is also responsible for Iberdrola Renovables' international offshore business, developing projects all over the world from his Glasgow headquarters. Such ambitious goals are possible because Keith "has become a lot more proactive about networking than ever before," as he puts it.

It all started at the end of 2006, when Iberdrola, the Spanish energy group, acquired ScottishPower Renewables: "When you work in a company that's been taken over, it's easy for people to think they're getting things forced upon them. They tend to think their own way of doing things is better than what they're asked to do by their new colleagues. Networking helps you realize it's not better, it's not worse. It's just different."

Anderson says, "networking is a critical skill to help you understand why things are done the way they're done and why the systems are built the way they're made. It really helps you get beneath and beyond the obvious."

Of course in a merger between a Spanish company and a UK-based country the culture clash was intense. "One of the difficulties when we first became a part of the group was you would try to do business by email and you'd get a response that seemed pretty abrupt and directive. We almost took offense until we realized it was a cultural thing," remembers the Scottish-born executive.

"It quickly became apparent I should get on a plane to Madrid in order to get a bit more context to our email exchanges", explains Keith. "It's partly to do with Spanish culture, where personal relationships are far more important, and people put far more emphasis on face to face interactions than we do in the UK," a preference that many Latin and Arab countries share.

Anderson confesses that in the UK people have become too dependent on email. "If you need something from a colleague down the corridor you'll email them and expect a response within the day. Even if cold, it's quite fast and effective at one level. Emails are an efficient way of exchanging information, but they're not enough when you do business internationally."

Another curious example of the cultural differences that make Latin email management so different from Anglo-Saxon approaches is how and why people reply to emails. "If you ask a question or announce your plans to someone on email in the UK, you assume you will get a response. But in Spain you wouldn't use email to ask a question, you would call the person on the phone. So unless you specifically send a clear signal that you need a response, you're very likely not to get one," something the executive learned by flying to Madrid and spending time with the executives who should have been so similar, yet were so different to himself.

Anderson had worked in The Royal Bank of Scotland and Ernst & Young in the past, with a lot of exposure to international initiatives, where "email didn't get relationships built or develop trust," he reflects. "You really need to spend more face to face time explaining who you are, what your background is, what you've done for the company. You get much more colour, flavour, and warmth to the relationship by meeting the person, seeing the person, interacting with the person," Keith elaborates.

A big cultural difference encountered is family. "If you walked into a meeting for the first time with someone in the UK and started talking about your family they would look at you as if you had two heads!" he compares. "In Spain it's quite natural to discuss family details. A meeting will typically start with five to ten minutes of personal questions to get to know how the other person is doing. The whole personal side of networking is certainly much more important in the Iberdrola group than in any other company I've worked for."

But building personal relationships is increasingly necessary in multinational companies, as Anderson explains. "Geographical distance and differing company cultures often break processes into silos. An email or a paper can easily get stuck as it moves between departments because the people there don't know how important it is to you and to the company."

"You really need to go out of your way to get to know people. How can you ask someone from the other side of the world to support your ideas or approve a huge investment paper you've written if you are nothing more to them than a name they can't even pronounce?" exclaims the international executive.

Most life-altering career opportunities are heavily influenced by the trust the organization places on an executive, as Anderson often tells his teams: "You need to be known by everybody who is anybody in the organization. If the group needed to fill in a new post, why should your name be on the list of candidates?"

In Anderson's opinion the biggest mistake executives make in terms of connections is "relying too much on email. Unless people understand who you are, what you stand for and where your loyalties lie, you will find your job to be a lot more frustrating," and he continues, "when you actually go and see people you need to approve your projects, you are socializing the papers you will write. A paper that isn't socialized can easily get stuck in somebody's inbox."

The CEO of ScottishPower Renewables also relies on networking to get his job done: "I need to play the political game in Edinburgh and also in Westminster in London. Some projects require a lot of lobbying to be done in decision spaces I have no access to, such as the Scottish parliament or Westminster. People will only fight for my priorities if they know me, trust me, and believe in the projects I am pushing forward."

A lot of the networking I do is critical to achieve the public engagement and perception renewable energy needs. Getting all the necessary players around an ambitious educational center three years ago is a good example. We built a visitor and educational center just outside Glasgow, on the biggest onshore windfarm in Europe, which has a capacity of 322 MW. It's an opportunity for people to relate to what we are trying to achieve. Children engage so much more easily to renewable energy than adults do!

Networking really does make the world go round. As Keith puts it, "if you don't have strong relationships with people and you don't know who's who and what's what, life is a lot more difficult!" Slowly but surely, windmills populate the lands and the seas of the world we know today, preaching cleaner energy and driving worldwide networks of people towards a more respectful use of the planet's natural resources.

CHAPTER 6

YOUR FUTURE: START WITH YOUR PERSONAL SWOT ANALYSIS

A client I worked for some time ago was experiencing double digit growth in new markets such as Russia, Brazil and China. The company was very fast at opening new operations, while they knew that their logistics and process efficiency were far from perfect.

Because they were very aware of these Strengths and Weaknesses, they knew it made no sense to try to compete in mature retail markets like Germany, UK or Holland. In these markets the Opportunities for entry were small, and the great Threat of a price war with competitors was not one my client could ever win. Their strategy was soundly based on Porter's SWOT analysis tool. When I applied the same tool to my own position versus the company's dynamics, I realized my services would no longer be required. It was time to make an elegant exit!

Michael Porter is still the major reference on strategy at world level. His model of the five forces is taught in all business schools and you have no doubt been familiar with it for years.

Most managers who decide to embellish their professional careers with expensive courses or MBAs devote hours out of each day to understanding and in some cases shaping their business strategies. Most of them, however, have never sat down to create a strategic plan for themselves.

In other words, if we were to select all the managers with over five years' experience who have just spent tens of thousands of euros on upgrading their intellectual capital, and if we subjected them to an online survey, asking them whether they have set down their personal strategic plan in writing, the vast majority would say that they had not.

Have you? You've already laid out the money to buy this book, and no doubt several others, to help you to improve your professional situation. Don't you have a formalized business plan which explains how these costs are actually investments?

6.1 STRATEGY BEGINS WITH YOU

Do you agree? Read that sentence one more time. If any manager with reasonable experience of the business world would be shocked to discover that the company for which he was working did not have a strategic five-year plan, why wouldn't that manager be concerned to realize that his own strategic career plan consisted of nothing more than a collection of castles in the air and scattered ideas which had never been formalized into a plan?

If you're smiling as you read these lines because you already have a special notebook for the purpose, or a folder full of ideas and a collection of reports or essays where you put down in writing what you want to do with your life, give yourself a pat on the back. You are an exception. And what's more, the examples of professional success with which you are familiar have also had it set down clearly for some time.

Companies which have no clear strategic plan, which are not well adapted to their market, end up going out of business. Not without having lost a good deal of money on the way, spending on senseless projects with badly managed costs. In the medium term the forces of competition in their reference markets will punish them financially until they cease to be profitable. Managers lacking a strategic plan fail to pick up clear signals from their environment because they are not independent business units. Instead, they end up with a more or less fixed salary plus the odd telling-off or a labour dispute which they can interpret as their superior's fault. But bosses who have no plan wind up working for those who do.

This means that if you really want to win in business, the first thing you have to do is define your mission in life. Who wants to be more than they are now? Where do you want to be in five or ten years?

Answering these questions as part of a formalized and exhaustive exercise is no guarantee that you are bound to succeed, but it does qualify you to compete with the other captains who are navigating their vessels in the sea of executive talent with you.

This chapter will take your hand and lead you through a series of questions and important analyses which you will need to complete your personal strategic plan. Once you have completed it, keep in a special place with the date on which you finalized it. You will have to revise it again in time... and again, and again, and even yet again.

Because, just like the sailor on the high seas, once you have studied your navigation chart, analyzed the weather conditions and estimated your sailing time, every day will be full of unforeseen breezes, changes of course due to losing the way or the problems of the sea. And if you don't regularly check your chart, you are in serious danger of becoming lost or turning up at the wrong place.

6.2 YOUR MISSION

The management committees of the great companies of Europe have sunk considerable sums of money in the matter of defining their missions. Some of them have managed to get by for years operating without a written mission, but some consultant will have convinced them that today a company without a mission statement should blush with shame.

Fashions and opinions apart, the mission is, or ought to be, a simple way of explaining who a company is and what makes it different from the others. The mission expresses the company's *raison d'être*.

It is a difficult exercise in summarizing, often requiring a number of people to reach agreement. A fine mission statement applies an existential consistency to all existing analyses of the markets in which the business is competing, the type of people it hires and chosen business model: the processes, people and information systems that determine who does what.

Whether it's yourself you're selling in the labour market, or whether you're promoting a certain product or service, a company or an artist friend, if you don't have a pithy, concise sentence which explains why what you do is special, it is highly unlikely that you will have set out a coherent strategy with no loose ends. It's like a subtitle which underpins the name of a product every time it's introduced.

The personal mission is also a good starting point for you yourself. Think about consultants. One of the most important apprenticeships in the consultancy world is that each consultant learns to operate like a one-man business, offering his services to a market consisting of project managers and partners from his own company who are recruiting the most interesting consultants for their client-based projects.

In this way, when a manager sells a project to a client, he goes back to the office and checks a list of the available consultants who might make up his project team. Naturally, the manager wants the most highly qualified and hardest working team possible, and to find them he will go through lists of dozens of consultants with various levels of experience to choose the most suitable. He becomes a demanding customer, in search of the most appropriate companies to provide him with the mix of know-how and talent he requires to complete his project and leave his own customer satisfied.

Since the list all too often contains names that mean nothing to him, he may well stick his head out of the door and ask a colleague "who is this Margaret Smith?" The answer he gets from his colleague will be an approximation of Margaret's mission, which will be all the more accurate if Margaret has done her networking duties well.

In other words, the consultants who have clearly defined what they want to learn and to bring to the company, and who network conscientiously, will win positions and projects which are well suited to their professional expectations, and hence which fulfill their strategic plan. The rest will have to make do with what they get, even though it may be of little interest to them, because being idle is not an option.

The maximum professional yield is derived from people who love what they're doing and do what they love doing very well. They also have to be earning sufficient money so as not to be squeezed financially. Building and shaping their personal mission statement requires that three basic questions be answered:

(1) What do you find exciting? Make a list of all the things you get huge amounts of pleasure from and which have always captivated you. These will be the activities inviting you to strive harder and practice more, so much so that you often lose track of time when you are involved. Write down everything you can think of on a sheet of paper.

(2) What do you do much better than everybody else? On another sheet of paper write down, or stick some photographs, of all those activities and areas where you do especially well; the fuller the list, the better. The aim is to identify the most simple and apparently unrelated things, like cooking chocolate cakes, pacifying your sister's children, or winning short-story writing competitions.

(3) What brings money into your home (or could bring you earnings)? On a third sheet of paper, write down what you would be willing to sell in return for financial income. It may be that you actually frequent markets or websites and are involved in selling directly, or

rather you're selling your time to a company which pays you your salary. If you're a manager, your sole source of income is probably your current salary. Investigate whether there are other enterprises, compatible with your work and expertise that could earn you extra money.

Once you have filled in the three separate pages, look for the subject areas which recur on each of the three sheets. Begin a list of possible activities and professional careers which could satisfactorily answer the three central questions.

This list is not going to jump up fully formed like an alphabet soup on the newspaper puzzles page. It will require a great deal of thought and the weighing of alternatives, which right now might seem completely ridiculous or imaginary. But it will do no harm to jot them down on a fourth page and scan the list each day, or maybe go over it with friends and close colleagues.

If you manage to come up with a simple sentence which meets your passion, your talent, and your financial requirements, you will have found a mission which can carry you to success. It is a first step – and a very courageous one.

Suppose that Margaret Smith, having worked for a large international auditor, collecting analysis projects for acquisitions in the energy sector, suddenly realizes that even though her salary is good, she doesn't actually like what she is doing and she decides to carry out this exercise.

What happens if Margaret defines a mission which has nothing to do with what she's doing at present? What if it turns out that her true passion is scuba diving, and dolphins in particular, yet she has been outstanding as a consultant for her team work and her skills in training her most inexpert workmates. She cannot imagine any professional career which brings together dolphins and her expertise as a trainer without starving to death.

The first thing to happen to Margaret will be frustration, and a decision that the exercise is futile. But if she is bold enough to explore it, and deploys effective contact management, she might take a trip through the professions which would bring her to a more satisfactory version of herself.

When they reach their thirties and forties, quite a large number of managers decide to break with their past careers and make a 180° turn in their professions. It usually takes between three and five years, and those who succeed in managing to find a new employment identity, which is profitable, exciting, and successful, display two basic abilities: they have been able to manage their contacts to consolidate and develop their employment dream in the direction of something doable via transitional scenarios, and they have been daring enough to take the risk. This phenomenon is particularly well illustrated in the book *Unconventional Strategies for Reinventing Your Career* by Dr. Herminia Ibarra, lecturer in organizational behaviour at INSEAD.[1]

6.3   YOUR COMPETITIVE CONTEXT

To do your personal SWOT analysis, you must begin with your competition context. The context to be defined will differ according to the objective you are pursuing with the networking tools.

In the case of a company, your context is your market. For a telephone company your context is the totality of the homes and offices which contract your telephone services. For an airline catering company your market is all the airlines which use such catering services in their airplanes. But in your case, defining the market will be a touch more complex.

The model of social capital can be of use to us here. This model distinguishes a person's human capital from their social capital as follows. Your human capital is the totality of all the knowledge, abilities and experience you possess at any given moment. This includes the languages you speak, the ability to type, and your friendly nature, which provides you with a lot of business opportunities.

Your social capital, on the other hand, is all the people who might seek your help, thus providing you with the opportunity to demonstrate and gain by your human capital. This includes all those contacts who know you, trust you, and are prepared to exchange favors or information with you, thus helping you to achieve your objectives: friends, family, workmates, school friends, and a sizeable group of acquaintances without whom the years you have devoted to investment in human capital would be lost.

Your reference context is all of the people who might be likely to enrich your social capital. Just as the market of customers might require the services of a specific company, you have around you hundreds or even thousands of people who could be the "purchasers" of your human capital, or at least, who could recommend it.

And in just the same way that a company can compete in several markets at the same time, you are sure to have a presence in a number of strategic contexts. So you can then do your SWOT analysis for each of the specific contexts or markets.

Clearly defining the reference context is one of the most difficult, but most critical, steps in the design of your personal strategy. Let's look at a few examples to get an idea.

Take Margaret Smith, again. One of her contexts, the one which is of immediate relevance for her, consists of employees at all levels of the consultancy where she works. She is asked to work on a project for which the other consultants or managers recommended her.

However, as we know that Margaret is not satisfied with her current work, she must not only handle day-to-day matters, but she must also concern herself with analyzing her career plan in the medium term. Her work as a consultant requires her to manage marathon days which are impossible to reconcile with the management of her personal course, which is why she has decided that her first step will be to move to a client company with more predictable work schedules.

In other words, Margaret is also going to analyze her SWOT with respect to all the companies which recruit consultants in-house, prepared to pay a salary which is compatible with her current income, and which is located in Madrid, since she doesn't want to have to move house. Once she has selected the companies which meet these requirements, the relevant individuals in Margaret's context are the managers and heads of these companies who are required to recruit consultants. Given the people with whom these managers deal, from whom they seek recommendations and the type of associations and events which they frequent, Margaret can define a second analysis context: heads of IT, strategy and organization sections in companies with a payroll of over 1,000, based in Madrid, which are planning to make some acquisitions in the market (don't forget that this is what Margaret is able to do, and for that reason only those companies which have a problem of this type on the table are the ones who will need her).

Another example is the case of Roger Robertson-Robertson, or "R3" to his friends. R3 is the new chief of the Barcelona office of an important pharmaceutical laboratory. R3 has come from an American multinational where he has been working for the past ten years, and he has taken over a crucial goal from the venture capital company which bought the laboratory a year before and is intending to re-launch it commercially.

Roger has to analyze two crucial contexts in order to succeed: on the one hand is the organization of the 500 staff he must manage in the

Barcelona office. These 500 employees, with an average seniority of 15 years and strongly opposed to the new capitalist owners, may be the wheels of Roger's car... or the brakes. In other words, if they decide to trust Roger, to listen to him, become his allies, they can help him undertake the actions needed to re-launch the business in the region. But if they fail to become part of his social capital, they can make his life impossible.

The relevant context for Roger is the collection of managers of equal to or higher rank than he in the company, together with the board members and representatives of the venture capital company who are involved in the management of the laboratory. If these people form a good opinion of him in the upcoming months, they will be more likely to let him in on the in-house policy secrets, and give him a break if he puts his foot in it. Generating credibility and trust among the upper management echelons of the laboratory located in Madrid, Paris and London is crucial if R3 is to be able to defend the interests of his 500 subordinates and to influence the strategic decision of the group.

Once the context is defined, we can go on to list the opportunities and threats which it proffers. Once again, correctly identifying these opportunities and threats is vital if the resulting strategy is to be successful. When we say that the business vision is important, this means that you have to be sure about your reading of the competitive context in which you are acting, and before others catch on.

Three important considerations must be taken into account when making a SWOT analysis. The first two levels are like the two halves of the human capital, and the third level of analysis is the social capital itself:

(1) The technical level – concrete, intellectual, objective. This means the product, the intellectual capacity or knowledge, which we usually refer to as 'non-subjective'.
(2) The emotional level – subjective, managerial skills, values, sensations. This means the emotions evoked by a perfume, or the work values displayed by a manager, or the characteristics which people associate with his or her personality.
(3) The social level – this means the structure and operating modes of the social networks.

You should try to place each personal strength and weakness, plus every opportunity and threat from its context, in one of the three levels described above. You should end up with a table with six boxes for the context and six boxes for you or your product. Or if you wish to make use of the classical strategic representation, which places the whole SWOT in four boxes, set up a SWOT graph for each analysis level or dimension.

The purpose of differentiating between these levels is to achieve a better degree of detail, but it is mainly interesting because the development tactics of each dimension have different achievement periods and affect different levels of your persona.

If a technical opportunity in the IT subcontracting market comes from there being a shortage of expert knowledge in an area of technology which is much in demand, you can take advantage of this opportunity from the day on which you have taken on the necessary knowledge. The tactics will include books, courses and exposure to actual problems.

If, on the other hand, it turns out that your company prefers highly extrovert and competitive profiles, while you tend to be quiet and withdrawn, the development plan for this gap is more complex and may not be viable.

And lastly, the social level is like the packaging, including the pricy model who recommends the product advertising. In the case of many perfumes and creams the container may end up costing more than the content, and depending on the prestige of the model or actress displayed, the cost of the image and the communications for the product may be even higher.

Your social network, analyzed from the range of aspects shown in Chapter 2, is in itself a source of advantages or weaknesses which position you in your context with several starting points. The typical method of exchanging information or favors used by the players in their context, their minimum requirements for establishing trust and their preparedness for change are the limitations of the game which determine the level of difficulty at which you are currently located.

Your SWOT analysis should factor in the three variables, both separately and jointly, because the objectives you decide to pursue and the strategic pathway you select to achieve them should allocate a relative weighting to each of these types of capital or added value.

6.4 THE OPPORTUNITIES AND THREATS OF THE CONTEXT

If we were selling a product in the market, we would have to ask ourselves about all those factors which affect a given customer's decision to buy. If we are seeking funding for, say, an NGO, we will find out what kind of investors or foundations are looking for projects like ours. Translating this into the problem scenario of marketing our human capital, we will also be interested to know what will be the effect of the decision of a possible candidate to become part of our social capital.

Because the fact is that, although we may be keen to increase our social capital, and having read this book and many others we may have set down on paper an infallible plan, reality offers us a result which also depends on the wishes and interests of those we would like to conquer. Always remember that when it comes to contact management, as with practically all other managerial skills, there is a time to be strategic, like the time you've set aside to read this chapter, and a time to be genuine and to accept the reactions your persona gives rise to in others.

Below is a list of questions which you may find useful in defining the opportunities and threats of your context. It is not intended to be an exhaustive or exclusive list, but it has been thought out so that each individual can choose and answer the questions they feel are useful, or their own versions inspired by the question in this list. You are recommended to give detailed answers and to allow yourself the opportunity to come back to the questions so that you can add or delete material if you see fit. The point of the exercise is not the speed with which you answer, but the accuracy of your responses.

Who needs your services, knowledge and the other components of your human capital? Make a list of their typical profiles. You may even include actual names of real individuals if you wish.

Which of your characteristics or skills is valued to the point that you will be selected in preference to somebody else? Factor in technical features and technical expertise, but also bear in mind preferred stereotypes of success, particularly valued managerial skills, and the need to be associated with someone or a member of some special circle to be considered.

What are the features displayed by the "clients" who prefer your style of work or your product more than those offered by other competitors?

Who by their actions or opinions influences the others in regard to you (or other candidates)? If the company is submitting a project for the construction of a windfarm, is there someone with a high level of technical knowledge working for the politician responsible for the decision? What matters is not so much who makes the decision but who has the power to veto it if they think that it is technically unsuitable.

What kind of middle-men or product consultants are operative in your context? Doctors recommend certain drugs to their patients, head-hunters choose managers for their clients, and senior managers or HR ask for suggestion from their superiors when they have to select high-potential profiles.

How long is the buying cycle or the decision to change a supplier? In the case of the labour market you should consider the average length of stay in the position in which you are interested, and the average period of time which lapses between a resignation and the fresh start in this position.

What level of visibility do you have in the various groups of clients or those who seek your skills? Do you know if they exist at all? Can you quote their names and put a face to them? Are their opinions sound?

What percentage of the relevant players are up to speed with what you are offering at this moment? What percentage of them have heard anything about the successes or failures in your past?

What economic, social and cultural circumstances influence the level of demand for your specific product or service? To the ice-cream vendor obviously the weather is important, but for the ambitious manager working for a foreign multinational it is important to check how many national managers are promoted in this multinational, and what accreditations or lapel pins are required to be considered as candidates.

What access do you have to the communication channels which inform the players who are the objective of your context? If it is easy to publish an article in the relevant review which is read by all the players in the market in which you operate, this is an opportunity. If, on the other hand, there is a lot of competition to appear in this medium, or if attending the events or meetings where your targets are to be found is impossible, then your capacity to communicate with them or influence them is limited.

However, an economic crisis context like that which has been hammering at the doors of the Spanish market for some time now affects not only business sales, but also their investment projects, their rate of outsourcing services, the output standard and the level of their requirements regarding certain functions, such as budgetary control.

You should be careful when defining and formulating these factors as personal weaknesses or as threats of the context. The threats of the context are not a consequence of who you are; rather they were there before you located yourself in respect of the context, and will be there afterwards. Representing an investment fund with more restrictive criteria may be interpreted as a weakness in your product, but given that this is not easily changed, it is more useful to interpret what is a threat of the context: lack of investment opportunities.

Toward the end of the chapter you will find an additional "table" which may help you to analyze the social context of your environment (see page 149).

6.5   YOUR STRENGTHS AND WEAKNESSES

The second part of your SWOT analysis concerns yourself, once again on three levels: technical, emotional and social. Your study of the context and the definition of the opportunities and threats will definitely already have pointed out the corresponding strengths and weaknesses in each area.

But what you might do is have your friends and companions give you some feedback about you, asking them to describe what they most value or appreciate about you, and what they think you could improve. The wider the range of the sample, the richer and more varied will be the information. Choose both friends and people who have nothing to do with your work, as well as family members with whom you live and office colleagues who wouldn't recognize you if you weren't wearing a suit. And prepare yourself to blush at the compliments as well as face the embarrassment or frustration at the difficult truths that perhaps no one ever told you because you never asked.

The emotional skills framework described in Chapter 5 may also be useful to you if you give yourself a score between one and ten for each ability, as shown in the exercise at the end of this chapter.

And in conclusion, the analysis performed in Chapter 2 of your existing network will help you to complete the social dimension of your SWOT analysis.

6.6   YOUR STRATEGY AND OBJECTIVES

Now you are ready to take the important step which separates the dreamers from the high-performance doers: you will now prepare your one-, two- or five-year strategic plan, the period depending on your actual situation.

Formulating your mission or the *raison d'être* of your current activity was the first step which defined an actual procedure, whether it was work-related, commercial, financial or of some other kind. But once this procedure is defined, it is essential to plan its concrete terms for the near future.

This is why you undertook a three-dimensional SWOT analysis, which will have shown you the gaps between what you contribute to your context and what your context needs and values, for which it is prepared to pay a cost in more or less tangible terms.

Leadership is a word repeated thousands upon thousands of times every day, referring to actual people in the business, social or political world, as well as to companies themselves, scientists, and indeed every phenomenon which represents faster progress than the others.

Definitions of leadership are therefore two a penny, they are repeated and renewed. But there is something which inevitably distinguishes leaders, and that is their speed of adaptation, as well as an ability to anticipate the opportunities and threats of their context. Whoever sees what is coming first and is ready to take advantage of it first is the leader. And the others are not.

This is why the SWOT analysis is the tool par excellence to support the creation of a strategic plan, since it reveals all the gaps or failures to adapt, allowing the company or the manager to choose the pathway which minimizes these shortcomings in the shortest time possible. Or in some cases it may recommend a change of direction to a less difficult context.

One of the most useful lessons from the treatise on war strategy developed by Sun Tzu thousands of years ago, equally appreciated by strategists from all fields, is the recommendation to choose your battles.

Choosing a battle which is too difficult to win is possibly the most common error committed by managers and companies when they define their strategies, and the most unwitting of all, since once the battle has been joined it is very difficult to stop to assess the situation, and all the more difficult to abandon everything which has been invested and wasted in the battle itself.

This was the case of Monica, who, after completing a two-year MBA which had her marriage on the rocks, and five years of breaking her back to make up for her past as an economist in a team of lawyers among whom advocacy was the only way to promotion, she sat down in desperation in the office of the company founder and asked him what, precisely, she was doing wrong. The devastating answer was to the point: "You aren't doing anything wrong... it's just that you're in the wrong place."

It wasn't that Monica hadn't thought about changing jobs any number of times over the past seven years, and it wasn't that she didn't know that being an economist counted against her. But she was unwilling to give up everything she had already invested in this battle. She had underestimated the downside, in both intensity and the length of time required, arising from not being a lawyer. The only thing she did wrong was to invest seven years of her life in a battle she couldn't win, and finding this out late is a really hard blow.

Nor is it enough to turn these questions over in your mind in a chaotic way in the hurly-burly of the trip to work and in relaxing conversations with understanding friends. You must set aside quality time to the job, write down formal observations and descriptions to complete the necessary from start to finish. And even then it is only the few who become leaders of the rest.

Here you will find questions which help you to define your strategy at two levels: the overall and integral objective designed to be achieved in the estimated period, and the sub-objectives which are derived from it in each of its three development dimensions: technical, emotional and social.

What do you want to have achieved within X months (minimum 12 months)? If you could visualize yourself at this moment, how would you describe yourself? Include every detail which occurs to you, from your work rate to the content of the things you do, the place where you work, the type of people to whom you relate, and the kind of future goals which excite you.

What knowledge and experience, both technical and emotional, do you think you ought to have accumulated by then?

What will your contact network look like? For greater rigor you can make use of the POTENCIA model. What is the profile of the people in your future network?

What level of visibility will you have in your company, in your market, and in the social environments relevant to you?

What will you be known for?

What kinds of stories or anecdotes will be included about you in local gossip?

How will you feel and what will your personal life be like?

And the most important question of all:

On what day and at what time will you come back to revise this formulation of your strategic objectives?

When you have honestly and carefully answered all these questions, with repetitions where required, write down your objective and the secondary objectives which are derived from it, and then put them to the "SMART" objectives test.

S   Significant
M   Measurable
A   Attainable
R   Relevant
T   Time-bound

If they fail to meet any of these conditions, they must be reformulated.

Add the date and everything else which completes your strategic commitment to yourself. Place the text in a special place, somewhere as special and important as it is to you to be professionally successful in your life. If, when you have read all this, you haven't put it down in writing or immortalized it in some way, we shall have to conclude that professional success is not one of your priorities.

6.7   BUDGETING

Your strategy will not be complete if it is not accompanied by a budget. You have already decided what it is you wish to achieve, and by when... but you have not yet made it clear what you are prepared to spend to get it.

And yet the available budget will be crucial when it comes to defining the tactics and actual steps of your action plan. This section may be very simple or very complicated, but if there are no clear answers to these questions, your contact management processes will remain unchanged.

By this point in the book two factors concerned with the art and science of networking, or managing contacts, should be very clear:

(1) Place upstream bets on trust and invest with acts of generosity to generate value around you, following a combination of selection criteria and fortuitous chance events.
(2) Always maintain a minimal rhythm or frequency. OVERDOING IT IS A WASTE OF TIME.

In other words, you have to budget your plan to win a marathon, not a string of isolated hundred yard sprints. Your budget should estimate the theoretical consumption quantity for each period (weeks, months, years) for your plan to produce results in the medium term.

The theoretical quantity will already be in itself an indicator of the output which will allow you to check whether your actual performance matches the plan or not, before you waste a great deal. It will be enough for you to check for each period the level of outlay you have made in each resource category.

This check can be as thorough or as "quick and dirty" as you like, but you can be sure that if you have set a theoretical level, very soon you will feel and will know automatically when you are drifting away from your plan, just as you intuit when your outlay is being wasted on idleness or when you can afford to indulge yourself because you made some savings in the previous month.

You don't have to put a rope around your neck or beat yourself up in front of the mirror every morning; it's just a matter of ensuring that the budget is being followed up. If you find out that you are drifting noticeably away from the theoretical level repeatedly and continuously, then you will know that (1) you have set a rather unrealistic theoretical level or that (2) some other barrier or restraint exists which must be resolved before you can devote yourself to developing your networks.

Time

Your resource par excellence is your time. Nothing is more limited than the hours and minutes of the day, especially for anyone in enthusiastic pursuit of a goal. And here is the first key question:

What percentage of your time must you dedicate in each period to managing your contacts?

The time period depends on what suits you. A week is the most common period, but depending on your situation it may be a fortnight or a month. If you find yourself tempted to use the day as the time standard, it may be that you are setting objectives so urgent that they cannot be achieved via networking.

This percentage will consist of a definite number of hours. It's up to you whether these hours form a part of your working day or of your free time, but in the interests of reconciling this with your personal life, and of restoring your creative and magnetic energy, it is recommended that network management activities with professional objectives be kept to work time. Someone with red eyes, a crumpled tie and limp gestures is not an encouragement to the development of a relationship and communicates nothing attractive, neither tranquillity, nor harmony, nor trust, nor efficiency.

Once this key question has been answered with a realistic theoretical level, one in keeping with your strategic plan, you can then answer the following detailed four-part question to keep the risk of a failure to accomplish it to a minimum:

- What days of the week and what times will you actually set aside?
- Of the total number of hours you will set aside in one month, how many hours will be for evaluating and adapting your networking efforts? At what time during the month will you do this job?
- What percentage or number of hours will you devote per week to generating new contacts?
- What percentage or number of hours weekly should you devote to each category of contact? (Read Chapter 8 to see the categories of contacts.)

Diary analysis exercise

This exercise will help you to work out how you should now divide your time in respect of contact management, and will help you to arrive at reasonable answers to the questions asked before.

Choose a recent week in your diary which looks representative, that is, not atypical, but which reflects what happens in the majority of your weeks. Transcribe to this framework your main meetings and the managerial tasks you undertook during the week. You might also prefer to perform the analysis on last week, which will still be fresh in your memory.

Try to fill in each available half-hour with what you did, especially with the objective of what you were doing. If you made any calls, were they about managerial administration or were they calls to contacts for the purpose of developing the relationship or communications?

Although there will be many tasks which will be difficult to categorize in one way or another, don't devote too much time to thinking about them. Give each an objective and press on, so that the exercise doesn't go on forever.

If it then turns out that the exercise doesn't produce reliable results for you, wait until next week and then do it again.

	MONDAY	TUESDAY	WEDNESDAY	THURSDAY	FRIDAY	SATURDAY	SUNDAY
9h00							
9h30							
10h00							
10h30							
11h00							
11h30							
12h00							
12h30							
13h00							
13h30							
14h00							
14h30							
15h00							
15h30							
16h00							
16h30							
17h00							
17h30							
18h00							
18h30							
19h00							
19h30							
20h00							
20h30							
21h00							
21h30							

GRAPH 6.1

(A) When you have completed the activities of the week, with a pencil or black marker, blot out the spaces occupied by tasks which cannot be associated with networking or contacting management.

Write down how many hours of the week were spent working, how many were devoted to contacting management, and how many to your private life (including eating, sleeping, sports, etc.).

(B) Now classify your contacts in three levels, as a function of how important they are for you and your current objectives. You can call them "class A" contacts if they are the most crucial, "class B" if they are the next, and "class C" if they are the least relevant.

With three pencils or markers of different colors, go over the calendar marking the spaces which correspond to actions with contacts of each class.

Now, write down how many hours of the week were devoted to class A actions, how many to class B actions and how many to class C actions.

146

(C) Using a fourth color highlight the hours you devoted to getting to know new contacts, either by paying a deliberate visit or going to conferences and events which would make it easier for you to get to know new people.

Write down the total number of hours you devoted to collecting new contacts.

(D) And finally choose a new color to fill in the spaces you devoted to analyzing your network, planning new networking activities and analyzing your contacts.

	No. hours	%
Personal		
Work		
Networking		
TOTAL		**100**

	No. hours	%
Class A		
Class B		
Class C		
Recruitment		
Analysis		
TOTAL		**100**

GRAPH 6.2

Write down the total number of hours invested in this activity and transcribe the results of points A, B, C, and D to these tables.

Note that the number of networking hours on the upper table should be the same as the sum totalled on the lower table.

Calculate the percentages resulting from this analysis and assess how near or how far this is away from what is thought to be best in theory.

In order for a certain likelihood of achievement of contact management plan to exist, you should ensure that the objective percentages which you set for each section should be achievable without excessive effort. In other words, they should not be dramatically different from what you are currently doing.

Other resources

Time, however, is not your only resource. The next resource to be budgeted is money you are going to invest in subscriptions to associations, gifts, trips, meals, and coffees, and everything else you find yourself involved in when adding value to your contact management.

This parameter can also be calibrated or defined according to theoretical standards via the detailed questions set down before.

And lastly, it is worth considering what other resources you have available to invest in the trust associated with new and not-so-new connections. There are many ways of upgrading the value of another person without spending money, and by deploying a reduced quantity of time.

The best contact managers are efficient because they get the most from the resources they invest, and since time is the scarcest resource, the following exercise could make important time savings for you in the future.

You need to make an inventory of available resources, a list of everything in your reach and which you can make available to contacts to assist them with their targets.

Below you will find a table which classifies the types of resources you may have available, so fill in the column with the actual resources, specify whether they are direct access resources or whether you must go through a third party to acquire them, and grade the difficulty of access and preparation of each resource.

With this table you can be kept constantly aware of the cost of offering each favor or actual item of help, such that then you can more speedily associate one of the resources with the priority and particular interest which each social encounter presents.

It is recommended that you mention in this inventory such resources as you have in abundance. It is assumed that, when you are on the lookout (and spending) you will be in a position to acquire any resource proposed, but it those which can be offered without too much effort which it will be of interest to note.

Graph 6.3 describes a suggested list of types of resource, but you are free to add or remove those categories you feel are relevant in your case.

1. Privileged information
   - press articles and reports which you may collect
   - politically delicate or confidential gossip which may be difficult to obtain through other means
   - specific information about a sector, a product, a technology
   - examples: solving your friends' computer problems, helping them with income statements, supplying the names of websites of good ceramics suppliers

Type of resource	Resources available	Access (direct or via a third party)	Difficulty of access: (H) High, (M) Medium, (L) Low
Privileged information			
Contact with third parties			
Privileged access			
Promoting their interests			
Gifts			
Support and exchanges in sports and hobbies			
Home hospitality			
Emotional support and help with private problems of certain kinds			

GRAPH 6.3 Available resources for value generation with my contacts

2. Contact with third parties
   - Providing contact data for a friend or work colleague
   - Forwarding a sales document or CV to a third party
   - Organizing a lunch or a dinner to introduce a third party
3. Privileged access
   - Managing directors or exclusive personalities who happen to be your friends or family members
   - Invitations to exclusive events like the corporate box for Real Madrid or membership of an association which is very selective as to members
4. Promoting interests
   - Making recommendations to your contacts about the person or his or her services
   - Making your offices or events available for promotions or presentations
5. Gifts
   - Books you find interesting
   - Objects of various values which you can give as gifts without them seeming too personal, but which say something about who you are (corporate gifts don't count unless they are difficult to get hold of or are particularly valuable)
   - Handwritten greetings cards on special paper
   - Personal calls to special events
   - Concrete favors
   - Invitations to events which are appreciated by or are the special favorites of the person in question: the opera, guided visits to museums, invitations to fashionable spas, etc.

6.8 FRANCISCO BELIL, CEO OF SIEMENS SPAIN AND THE SOUTH-WEST EUROPEAN CLUSTER

Born and educated in Barcelona, Francisco Belil has lived and worked in the U.S.A., Germany, Mexico and Spain. The interview we did in 2008 for the Spanish edition shows his seasoned and worldly vision of business, innovation and networks. Full of energy and drive, Belil tells us how organized interpersonal networks at Siemens cross borders to create innovative solutions for the future.

A prudent, yet provocative conversationalist, Francisco Belil is head of Siemens Spain and the South-West European cluster, which includes

14 countries. It's the last step on a formidable ladder of international success amidst German work environments and multinational corporations. Barcelona, Pittsburgh and Fontainebleau saw him study as a youthful engineer. Several cities in Germany, the Unites States, Mexico and Spain have witnessed his unending striving to increase performance while pushing innovative paths in everything he does.

Without a shadow of doubt, having fun and networking have been a constant throughout his life: "I can only produce good results if I enjoy my work. That's probably why I'm always on the lookout for people with big smiles!", he begins.

Belil remembers he found himself in huge and complex organizational environments very early on in his career. Valuable and diverse talent spread out among countries, departments and hierarchical levels. So much so that finding what was needed for each business challenge was no easy task. Using personal relationships to navigate the corporate world proved essential from the very beginning.

On the other hand, "you also had to try to align your personal goals with the organisation's needs. Frequent interactions and exchanges of valuable information with players from different corners of the company were the only way to build my personal vision."

Belil claims that, even today, "networks are an essential part of my work. I spend more than 50% of my time listening to colleagues and hearing others' opinions before making my own decisions," a leadership style that fits like a glove in the Siemens model of excellence and innovation.

The executive describes his company as "a knowledge network spanning 191 countries. Such a global reach brings a privileged diversity to our analyses, in-house projects and innovative efforts." But the Siemens networks don't stop there, since, in Belil's opinion, "they also include customers, universities, and research organisations. We seek talent wherever it might be, and if we can't find it in-house, we go shop for the best in every field."

Belil illustrates this with an example: "We have the best gas turbine in the world. To achieve this we had to work with specialists in high performance materials and coatings. We had recourse to highly sophisticated equations and mathematical models which analyse fluid dynamics. In some cases these calculations required extremely powerful computers...very hard to find!" he exclaims.

The Cluster leader thinks that Siemens "encourages networking because it's the only way to find the excellence we require. It all starts with the questions we choose to challenge our people with."

Siemens believes that technological innovation begins by carefully selecting the very questions to be researched and invested in: "We look out into global trends to learn where things are going. How much of what happens isn't just another passing fad? Which novelties will have a significant effect on society and its future needs?" he clarifies.

"The population of the world will grow from 6,300 million to 8,000 million in the next 20 years," reflects our friend. "2007 was the first year in human history to have more people living in large cities than in the country."

"The percentage of people over 65 years of age, nearing 8% worldwide at the moment, is set to double in the upcoming generation," Belil argues. "Millions of people will be commuting into and out of growing mega-cities on a daily basis. What are the implications of all this for urban infrastructures, clean water supply and electricity consumption? How will we provide for this?," he asks.

"This is exactly what the founder of Siemens was doing 163 years ago. He asked himself the big questions about society's life quality," Belil reflects. "Why isn't there a quicker way to send a message to America, for instance? Can't I receive my reply in less than two months?," he quotes, alluding to the unease which led Siemens to invent the first pointer telegraph.

Nowadays Siemens is especially focused on finding answers for energy, health and industry challenges. Belil specifies that "we are working very seriously on domains as extensive and diverse as the automation of industrial processes, mobility, water supply, early diagnosis of sickness and energy efficiency. Environmental protection is our topmost priority."

"Think of how we build relationships over internet, with cell phones and social networks, for example," he argues. "It's creating new needs to guarantee individual's personal security." Life in small towns used to groom high levels of trust between neighboring families, so that there was no need to lock doors when people went out to work. Some families took care of other neighbors' houses because they had trusted each other for generations.

"This is no longer the case in the huge cities we live in today," Francisco tells us. "I was lucky to live in Mexico City for six years. The truth was that the number of people I knew was minute compared to the millions of citizens who surrounded me," recalls the executive. "In large cities security becomes a strong priority."

At Siemens the observation and strategic selection of trends and priorities gives rise to a number of research paths supported by geographically widespread teams. Team members are permanently connected to each other by email, telephone, physical meetings, videoconferences, and other new formats made possible by current communications technology.

"But it's the people behind technology that make things work. Finding a subject matter expert among 400,000 employees around the world is never obvious. Our executives are encouraged to cultivate these crucial personal relationships over time," Francisco explains.

"It's like an orchestra, if you think about it," continues our friend. "The head of research is the conductor. He guides his orchestra through the music, while he searches for the missing parts. If he can't find the exact violinist needed in-house, he goes outside. The MIT, the Max Planck Institute, or some other specialized organisation may have it."

Belil stresses that "innovation is part of our DNA," even though it is done differently today. "In the nineteenth century an innovator was some wise man with a brilliant idea, who more than likely put his idea into practice in his own workshop. Nowadays our greatest achievements are made possible by interpersonal networks, ever more sophisticated as technology advances."

Siemens is, in fact, a worldwide web of networks. It integrates smaller sub-networks of all kinds and varieties to produce the results Siemens strives for with such determination. "Research teams are in constant contact with our client base. Commercial teams talk to end users while our technology experts talk to clients' technologists to ensure that what we are doing matches what they are looking for."

Belil describes the reciprocity of these exchanges. "We push to keep information flowing, thus benefiting all members in the network." And he goes on, "I believe a dialogue between individuals with a minimum of interest and knowledge is always enriching for its participants. There's always a chance to learn new things. Right now I'm learning a great deal from this conversation!" he exclaims, with a broad, friendly smile.

"Naturally, everything depends on the people. Every organisation is the sum of the people who make it up. This is why positive attitudes are so crucial among our employees. They have to enjoy what they are doing, and make their colleagues feel good about it as well," he explains. When the time comes to take on new people, he adds, "we know that transferring technical knowledge is much easier than spreading good attitudes."

Francisco Belil concludes our interview with a colorful comment about human relationships he learned while living in Mexico. "You need to share a kilo of salt with another person to get to know him or her. That's a lot of salt!" Still laughing, he walks us back to the lift before making his way to yet another meeting of innovative Siemens networks.

CHAPTER 7

NEW CONTACTS

No action plan to improve your networks would be complete without a section on building new connections. The burden of the activities involved with analyzing, planning and carrying out tasks involved with tracking down and taking on new contacts will depend on your strategic plan. And, in theory, it will be established by the responses you give to the section on budgeting in the previous chapter.

At the same time, this is probably one of the tasks most ignored by managers and most frustrating to record, since you have the feeling that you are wasting time. This is the job offering the fewest apparent results for each minute invested, but it is actually the foundation of everything. Without new connections, there is no rotation in your network, and hence no possibility of the appearance of candidates as customers, investors, bosses or any other positions in your life.

Defining the number of hours to devote to creating new relationships is crucial, because even though every hour you spend on it has a goal, you still come home empty-handed from time to time. Or another possibility is that you reach home with great expectations about a new acquaintance who is revealed at the next meeting not to be promising at all, or to have absolutely no interest in you.

This is the first purge of your social environment, and this means that a large proportion of what you select now will be wasted further down the track. But you must try to bear in mind that a minute invested in a six-month-old contact which turns into an amazingly advantageous result is no more and no less than the sum of all the minutes you devoted to assessing and researching who you should talk to, how to capture their interest and how much time to continue to invest in cementing a connection which may provide you both with good times and nice surprises in the future.

Imagine yourself as one of the judges of one of those television programs which train young unknowns to be stars in a house with no privacy. Those judges didn't start work on the first day of the program in the midst of the glory of introducing the guest to the magic house – they would have had to see thousands and thousands of candidates of all kinds, endlessly sifting the best to end up with a list of no more than twenty interesting candidates.

This chapter is devoted to the first calling or casting process inviting candidates to take part in your life, to researching where best to track them down, to preparing for those meetings and to spending plenty of uncomfortable moments in very boring monosyllabic conversations as the price of a handful of interesting and exciting meetings laden with potential for the future.

And never forget that, unlike the judges on the TV program, you're both judge and candidate, subject to the decisions and preferences of your new encounters. You must prepare yourself for disappointments as a candidate and satisfaction as a judge.

7.1 WHERE TO LOOK FOR NEW CONTACTS

There are many ways to go about meeting new people:

- Get to know the friends of your current contacts, a one-on-one meeting, and this will depend on, and sometimes be limited by, the nature of your current network.
- At dinners, parties and leisure events with your friends, family and workmates. Under these circumstances you get to meet a range of different people at the same occasion, but often it will turn out that it is the same guests whom you will meet again and again.
- The everyday life of a neighborhood, going to collect the children from school, church or mosque on holy days, sport or exercise at the local health club. Each activity increases the potentially profitable use of your time because this is time you would have to spend anyway and because you can involve yourself in launching a variety of relationships at the same time without too much effort. Even so, the majority of these relationships will have little or nothing to do with your professional concerns.
- The everyday work situation, particularly if your job exposes you to customers, suppliers and other people external to the company.

This introduction mode guarantees a shared interest in the work because you share a relationship to the same company or activity sector, although many limitations will arise due to the fact that your interests will clash both inside and outside the company, which may, on occasions, sabotage any possibility of a real relationship.

- Participation in professional associations, events and conferences, or attending fairs in your sector. This is a most efficient means of meeting contacts who are already self-selected, since they are interested in the same area as yourself, and they are also interested in establishing contacts.

This is why I have prepared a section of the book devoted to selecting, assessing and preparing your participation in associations, events and fairs, because there are many ways of going about this, and although many managers do it because they intuitively feel that it is a good idea or because everybody else does it, many do it really badly.

Indeed, once you have acquired a critical eye for evaluating the totality of the events, conferences and meetings on offer every month, you will be amazed at the huge number of them which are poorly designed to facilitate contact with new friends. Absorbed in the confusion of finding speakers, solving logistical problems and seeking sponsorship funding, they abandon visitors to their own resources the moment they arrive.

It's actually quite surprising how often you leave these events with exactly the same number of contacts you had on arrival. And then there's the fact that starting a conversation with a stranger requires a courageous effort to overcome the personal spaces around the coffee table to grab a few fleeting moments between speakers, and indomitable tenacity to keep on trying to start conversations with other managers who are just as uncomfortable and unmotivated as you are.

Plan your strategy for making an approach

First things first. If you've already set your objective in terms of time and the other resources to be devoted to making new contacts, you must now shape and adapt your strategic plan to suit existing offers of events, associations, leisure organizations and virtual networks.

One way to do this is to draw up a list of requisites or a checklist which will clarify the more general of the principles in your plan, so than afterwards you will be able to put the opportunities which present themselves to the test.

These requisites must answer the following questions:

- Is the *raison d'être* or mission of the association or event compatible and compliant with yours?
- Does the typical profile of the member or participant correspond with the type of contacts you would like to make? What proportion of members or participants are actually your competitors?
- How often are the meetings or events held, and how easy is it to establish new contacts or cultivate existing contacts under these circumstances?
- How important are new ideas, and how assiduously are they followed up, and how much effort is dedicated to choosing and involving dynamic and interesting members and participants?
- How flexible is the balance of power in the association or at the event? You can tell this by how hard or easy it is to organize future events, to take part in its publications, or be involved in decision-making bodies or working parties, for example.

But there is also one critical principle which you must keep in the fore-front of your mind when deciding upon the exact mix of associations and events in which to invest your resources: they must all satisfactorily meet two fundamental criteria:

(1) They must offer the necessary potential to provide results for your strategic plan.
(2) They must be comfortable, pleasant and interesting, because they are a framework for you – for the things that interest you and your personal characteristics.

You must be sure that even though you don't know one interesting person, you're going to have a good time and will be unstressed. Learn things which interest you, do things you like doing, but at the same time feel at home with the people around you.

If the association or event meets the first criterion but not the second you will take on the air of a shark in pursuit of a weak contact, and you will have drifted away from the principles of trust and reciprocity which should form the basis of all contact management.

And if it meets the second but not the first, that's okay, but you must accept that this is just a whim, a gift you give to yourself, and don't expect to get any further with your personal objectives. In this case you're putting money on a personal fancy which has nothing to with your life objectives, or you've decided to give away your time and talent because one of your life objectives is service to others. In that case you actually are complying with the first principle, because your personal strategy is basically orientated towards selflessly giving to others.

The association or club of your life

In many cases you can't find an association or club which best represents your identity and personal interests and which is frequented by the kind of people you want to relate to. In that case you can decide to try to establish that very association or club yourself.

The association-founding movement in Spain is less active than in other countries and there are many opportunities to set up work, analysis and enjoyable groups which offer opportunities to practice contact management skills, not to mention those associated with political management and leadership.

The first requirement for your association is to be different from those which already exist and to contribute something new and important to your sector, your business or people like you. If you feel tempted to set up an association because they won't let you be the boss in the one you're already a member of, don't do it, it isn't a good reason.

You must define this objective as clearly as possible, and make an investment in your image, which might involve spending a few hours creating some attractive documents, even a website and logo if you can afford it.

The second important thing to realize is that getting people to join an association is very difficult. Everybody is interested and likes to be asked, but very few people will really make a commitment. A good idea is to involve some important individuals in the association at the earliest opportunity. Personalities, people with influence, those with connections and those who are interested in the project and will contribute by their very visibility.

Number three is to set up a leadership structure as soon as possible. There must be no doubt about who makes the decisions, and leadership must be based on availability to contribute to the association, but the individual in question must also possess the necessary leadership skills to attract other members.

Setting up an association is a very enriching learning curve, since you have no authority to motivate or influence others, and because feelings can become heated in an environment where people have often come to seek the recognition they are denied in their own company or other forums.

The most important law governing the functioning of an association is that of reciprocity. People must be rewarded, tangibly or otherwise, for their contributions, and you must steer clear of those who come to the association to take what they can and give nothing.

Keys to the efficacy of events: the 6 Hs

The first thing you must learn is to select the events you attend with the greatest of care. This method will help you to decide whether to go to an event or a fair, or to stay at home; and if you decide to go, with what degree of involvement (and investment).

The 6 Hs method should help you to analyze each opportunity. wHat, wHo, How, How much do I gain, How much do I spend and How much does it cost.

1. wHat
   - What do you want to achieve? Find commercial prospects, meet pretty girls, be seen, build the visibility of your brand or business, gain credibility among your competitors, raise finance for your NGO...?
2. wHo
   - Who is the target public of the event?
   - Who is being targeted in advertisements, websites and other marketing materials?
   - How much does it cost to take part, and how many participants are expected?
   - What types of participation exist (sponsors, exhibitors, visitors, speakers, etc.), what are the profiles of the participants in each type, and what advantages are to be gained at each level of participation?
   - What is the strategic reasoning which persuades the participants to be involved? What do they hope to gain?

160

3. How
   - What potential for interaction does the event offer?
   - How are the dinners or drinks organized – standing? Sitting? and are the seating positions named?
   - What other options exist to facilitate contacts, are there round tables or discussions broken up into subgroups, is there room to set up ad hoc private meetings?
   - How much help is offered to participants for them to distinguish between the participants: are there name cards with names and positions of responsibility to participants; are there member lists with names and positions; are there hostesses or members of the organization whose job it is to make introductions between people who don't know each other; are initial introduction rounds organized to break the ice in discussions or to make round tables more manageable?
   - How many of the participants did you already know from before, and how many new ones will there be?
   - What is the background of the event? How many times has it been held before, according to the organizers and according to the participants? What do your friends and contacts say about the organization and the practical usefulness of the previous invitation?
4. How much do I gain?
   - What clear opportunities for value generation can you see before you go (or pay)?
   - Who are the speakers and contributors, how long do they stay at the event (do they arrive, speak and leave, or at least stay for a coffee?), what opportunities do you have to ask them questions during their presentation, and what chances are there to talk to them in private or in small groups before or after their talk?
   - How many of the organizers, sponsors, and exhibitors are possible targets for you, and what is their quality, with one quality factor being their ability within their organizations to make decisions to deal with you?
5. How much do I spend?
   - How much does this cost as an opportunity? How much work must I leave undone and what other valuable opportunities must I leave to one side?
   - How much work time do I lose?
   - How much travelling is required?

- What are the average costs of the move as a whole without including subscription costs?
6. How much does it cost?
   - What is the cost of participating in the event?
   - Registration costs, including or not including meals, the cost of putting up a display stand or sponsoring the event in any form.

If you find an event or fair which answers all these questions positively – please, tell the rest of us! They are rare. But at least, if you have asked yourself these questions, you will know exactly what you can expect in return for your investment, and you won't come away too disappointed.

In the end it will be for you to decide how many of these events to attend and what level of involvement to seek depending on the potential benefits in terms of visibility, reputation and gaining high-potential contacts.

And if by chance you are an organizer of events and meetings, please apply the above to yourself. You will upgrade the success and interest of your fair, and you will really boost business in your sector instead of having it boil down to four photographs and a note in the local press.

7.2 YOUR NETWORK OF NETWORKS: THE MAP OF CIRCLES

Another interesting analysis is to make a more exhaustive inventory of your network. The greatest gain from this study is while not knowing the exact number of contacts in your network, or the names and surnames of all your acquaintances, to understand the structure and interconnections between the worlds or social circles you move in.

To do this, I recommend the circles exercise. You will need a fairly large sheet of paper, A3 or the like, and you should attach it to a wall or whiteboard so you can look at it a few times before you decide it's finished and earmarked until the next panoramic study.

First draw your personal circle in the middle of the paper, then carry on to draw around it all the other circles in your life: the school circle, the circle of the sports you play, of your weekend pastimes, your family, work, previous jobs, neighbors, the parents of your children's friends, religious or spiritual communities, the circle of friends abroad, and any others you can think of.

Try to keep to the following visual criteria when you draw your circle of circles:

- Draw the size of the circle to suit the number of people in it.
- Locate the circles at distances proportional to the impact they now have on your life, and the impact they have on each other, as if they were planets and stars between which there are gravitational attractions or repulsions.
- If there are circles with divisions, you can draw them in as satellites.
- Try to write in each circle the number of contacts there are in it, and if you are eager to go deeper, draw up a list on another document in an Excel file of all the names which are associated with each circle.

Here's an example of the circle of circles.

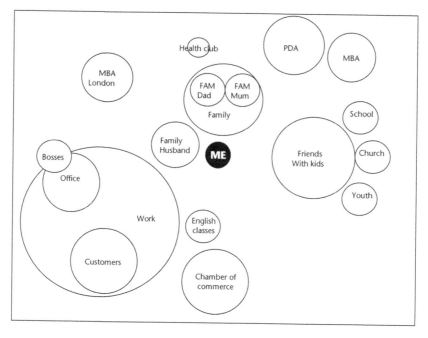

GRAPH 7.1

Once you are satisfied with this diagram, try to set down on paper how this map of circles explains who you are and who you want to be.

There will be some circles from the past, and others more associated with your present and your future. This panoramic view will help you to understand how you should devote your resources to cultivating some circles rather than others, and may give you ideas about other circles which are not in your diagram but perhaps ought to be.

What this means is that you can create the circles you need to make contact with certain types of people, people who are less accessible and require a better use of your time, so that it is difficult to follow the more laid-back steps of more natural initial encounters and their developments. These are contacts which must be made with a valuable proposal from the word go.

At the end of Chapter 6, you were asked to think about what your medium-term objectives were, but also what would be their immediate effect on your network, on the type of people you need to know and the circles you were keen to penetrate. Which circles are the ones to boost to achieve your goals?

When you look at your diagram of circles, don't forget that social circles can be boosted to give you access to distant personalities or to make contacts of a specific type, establishing priorities among circles.

High priority presupposes your spending most of your free evenings making your way to the chosen circle or circles. It will also mean visibility, adding value to the network, and becoming involved in the relevant projects.

For precisely this reason you must take another look at your circle diagram in six months or a year. The effect of your actions on each prioritized circle can only be seen in the mid or long term. But at the same time, your life is evolving, and with it the opportunities you seek, which is why the way you prioritize your circles must be subject to constant adaptation.

Let's take the case of a manager who wished to change the sector in which he operated after doing an MBA. He's the manager of a purchasing department of a construction company, and he wants to make a move to the energy sector. He draws up his circles diagram and decides to start up a club of ex-students from his business school with a focus on the energy debate in Spain.

He devotes himself body and soul for the next six months to consolidating the club, increasing the number of members and upgrading its visibility, but despite his efforts, the political tensions within the club frustrate his work, and he finds himself six months later exhausted and with the same number of contacts in the energy sector as before he began. This will be a sign that the system is not working.

However, at the same time, he started going to Arabic classes, and this has put him in contact with some businessmen who are working on various large-scale projects in a several Arab countries. A few months later he gets a chance to attend an international conference of Arab countries interested in setting up renewable energy stations.

If this manager had failed to retain the panoramic view of why he had started the energy club, he might have been so exhausted by his efforts with the club, and so short of money, that he couldn't have been bothered to attend the congress in Abu Dhabi, and would have put it on the back burner as a nice idea for the following year. But the fact is that he is keeping an eye on his circles and watching how they affect the creation of opportunities in the energy world, and he clearly sees how he must reduce his dedication to the club, and ask for some money to make the trip to the energy congress.

Which circles does he need in his diagram to help him to achieve his ends?

There can be two types of circle: circles which already exist and which you know, but which you cannot access, and non-existent circles. These non-existent circles can be allowed to exist if you can create a method of approach or a reason for their existence.

In other words, to achieve your medium-term goals, it may be that a number of associations, friendship or interest groups or project teams already exist which will help to reveal short cuts to your expectations. But maybe they don't.

In this case, you can try to create a circle from scratch. If its a professional association, take a look at pages 157–9. But there may be other ways of getting to know specific people.

A party, for example; if you can set up a party sufficiently interesting and lively to attract this type of person, you're not calling on them empty-handed – you already have something that will create value. At Harvard we learned about the business-related case of a popular investor from Silicon Valley who was famous for the parties she threw at her home, to which she invited guests from the very top level. Her parties became a meeting machine for specific people, which contributed value for everyone involved.

Of course, you have to throw a large number of parties and work very, very hard to become a hostess famed through the whole of the

Valley of the Microchips. Structures like this are not thrown together in a moment.

Another method could be a professional association, or a club of friends with a shared interest. Clubs or associations exist which have succeeded in generating an unusual notion of power and status, thus always attracting people of greater influence. Setting up a medium like this is hard, tiring and competitive work, and there are many which go nowhere.

Other value drivers you might consider range from establishing a taskforce or project team within your company to solve a problem of interest to the company, to setting up an NGO with a purpose and an image which is clearly distinguishable from others.

Another case of an excellent contact manager who triumphed precisely because of the value drivers he built is that of Lyndon Johnson, who became the thirty-sixth President of the United States of America following Kennedy's assassination.

Indeed, Johnson had revealed an exceptional skill in handling networks since he was very young, and he devoted his energy to a value driver known as the "Little Congress". This was a group of Congress staff, mostly new university graduates, from the Congressmen's secretaries and assistants to lift attendants, which met in discussion forums to practice their skills as speakers and learn how the House of Representatives worked.

In his famous work on Johnson,[1] Robert Caro described congress as a "moribund organisation," founded in 1919, which had degenerated to the level of a social club with occasional meetings. Lyndon Johnson managed to become president of the club, revitalized it, calling a meeting every week, and inviting important personalities to give talks.

This was how he created a valuable system which permitted him not only to establish relationships with more or less unapproachable leaders, but also to get notices and increase his visibility in the media, until the members of Congress themselves began to ask for their bills to be discussed in the Little Congress to give them some publicity before the actual vote was cast. In this way Lyndon Johnson managed in a spectacular fashion to become better known than all the other staff in under a year.

This means that every panoramic review of your network should include a POTENCIA analysis of your nucleus network and a map of your current circles. Both views will help you to select one or two social circles to build from scratch by means of a value driver, or to re-build and re-orientate, or simply to develop an existing circle which you haven't paid enough attention to.

Each panoramic review will be a good chance to see whether your efforts still match your personal medium-term objectives, or if they are becoming swamped in the details and difficulties of a particular circle which has as yet contributed little to the plan, or which prevents you from achieving anything because it's too complicated.

It's better to look ahead than to realize after devoting everything to a pathway that you later do not find quite so attractive, or which stopped making any sense some time ago.

7.3 OPENING CONVERSATIONS

The beginning of each human relationship is an exchange which is often uncomfortable, and agony for many, particularly if a long time has passed since they left their comfort zone.

Let's talk about before, during, and after.

Before

Many things will have to be done to improve the likelihood of success of your first encounter. In this context, success means a comfortable or even pleasant conversation, leaving the door open for other opportunities. AND THAT'S ALL.

If you're very lucky and a single meeting is enough to solve all your problems, you are one of the fortunate few, but that isn't a success for your contact management skills, that's just winning the lottery, and it shouldn't be your aim. Managers who would like to scoop the pot with a single meeting usually turn out to be overbearing, interfering and unpleasant. What happens much more frequently is that you lose the lottery and also lose the chance to get to know the contact in question.

(I) The raw material

The raw material is you, and unlike most of the literature available on the internet and in management manuals, this book will not recommend that you dress in red, or have yourself spray-tanned brown and spend the day practicing smiles and pre-programmed greetings.

Managing contacts is said to be an art because there is no single way of achieving success via your personal network. If that were the case, it would mean that all the great leaders of the world would be nothing but clones, and it would not be so easy for impersonators, mimics and other critical comedians to mock and caricature them.

Mastery of an art demands knowledge of the techniques and tools available, but this is just the start. If you wish to distinguish yourself, you must adapt these tools to your personality, blunt their edges making cuts which stand out from those of the others, and little by little you will gather your favorite and very personal techniques which go everywhere with you. This is a little like becoming a good chef with his kitchen knives which he takes everywhere in a case, or like top hairdressers.

Are you acquainted with your raw material as far as the opening conversations are concerned?

Think about three first meetings you had which in your opinion went very – and I mean very – well, and three that didn't. Now answer these questions about each of them:

- Why did they turn out the way they did? What were the positive factors?
- If you could repeat them, what would you do differently?
- How did you feel during each meeting? Try to describe the different intervals: slightly nervous during the first ten minutes, then more interested in the next period, etc. As always, the quantity of adjectives and useful qualifiers will require you to think for a while.
- Where were you coming from before the meeting, and what had happened during that day? What level of energy and receptivity did you feel as far as others were concerned at the time when you met that person?
- What did you talk about during the conversation?
- What gestures and non-verbal body language drew your attention regarding the person you were talking to, in the way of smiles, tones of voice, expressions, etc.?
- And as for yourself, what gestures or postures did you adopt?
- What did you have in common with the people in the cases where the conversation went well? And what did you share with the others?

When you have analyzed these examples of success and failure, try to highlight a few ideas you can use to create your own "X-ray of success."

Jot down in a table like this the two or three pieces of advice you would give to yourself and the two or three pieces of bad advice, or errors you would recommend avoiding.

ADVICE	ANTI ADVICE
1.	1.
2.	2.
3.	3.

GRAPH 7.2

(II) The appearance of the raw material

Whether we like it or not, appearance plays a crucial part in first encounters. The appearance and adornments of the first *Homo Sapiens* showed the tribe he was from and told the others whether to stay and chat (or get drunk) or run for it. Today we still use what we see as a basis for deciding whether to approach a stranger or not.

Remember that perceiving is not just seeing, but also hearing, smelling and intuiting. Here the guideline is you yourself: be the best possible version of yourself.

If necessary, invest a little money in a personal shopper or image advisor, but in most cases you'll achieve major improvements just paying a little attention to your appearance and seeking the advice of friends and colleagues.

Here's a list of points typically forgotten by many managers when it comes to making first impressions. With the excuse of being in a hurry, or not interested, or having too much work, it is amazing how many executives ignore the details shown in Graph 7.3.

You can use this checklist as a verification tool to make sure that you haven't forgotten something important when you set out to impress the world, or even for self-diagnosis in your regular control and follow-up sessions, as detailed in the next chapter.

This table is divided into four sections, starting with the most obvious, and moving on to the most ignored. Even so, there are many business people and executives who are unaware of crucial points of personal hygiene like dirty spectacles or who drench themselves in cologne. Defining a personal style which is expressed in the way you dress, your accessories and body language not only gives a clear impression to those around you, it also helps you to build confidence in yourself and what you are like.

An attitude of confidence, ease and fun is critical if you want to attract others. The best contact managers get huge pleasure from meeting other people, and you can tell from their smiles and gestures, which broadcast the fact that they are comfortable to all around.

The recent mania for checking your mobile all the time is particularly unpleasant, since it gives the impression that you aren't available to get to know or talk with those present, or worse, that you don't find them interesting in comparison with the unknown callers on the phone.

And finally, your promotional instruments are so, SO, important. Read on to discover the risks of not being prepared in this department.

	IMPORTANT ITEMS FOR FIRST ENCOUNTERS	Yes?
Hygiene	Nice breath	
	Presentable hair	
	Clean spectacles!!	
	Clothes clean, ironed, well cared for	
	Pleasant aromas	
Style	Colours and cuts which suit you and are up to date	
	Accessories to create an impression (business card case, watch, briefcase, etc.)	
	Define your style: find out what suits you best on first impressions and reinforce it with expressions, posture and gestures	
Attitude	Relaxation in advance: tension dissolving exercises	
	Mobile off or on silent. Make the most of "the power of now"	
	Crib: typical questions or lists of current subjects to get started with and chat about fluently	
Promotional instruments	ALWAYS CARRY business cards	
	SHORT promotional materials about your objectives	
	Multi-channel consistency as regards your image: website, documentation describing your business, services or project, sending and receiving, follow the same line and help to reinforce the impression you want to give	

GRAPH 7.3

During

The "during" part is the most important part of the whole contact management procedure. This is the part where authenticity matters, more than before, and regardless of how much we may have planned or prepared.

"During" is when the unforeseen may occur, the surprise, which on the one hand may disappoint us because sometimes we fail to make the desired impression on the other person, but at the same time we may be delighted by unexpected and chance occurrences the implications of which we usually don't understand until much later.

We can offer a few action guidelines, too, always keeping in mind that being yourself is crucial. Once again, each reader is free to seek tricks and recipes on the internet or from other books, if you really feel you need to.

The approach.   At events, two approach strategies can be observed.

- Some people feel they have to talk to as many people as possible. Because of this concern they tend to force the opening of the conversations, and what is more serious, cut them short because they feel they have to keep moving.
- Others, however, leave it to chance or coincidence, and allow themselves to be pushed by each instant of the event without trying to get a special output from every minute. Although it may seem unlikely, this strategy provides the best results in the long run, because it doesn't upset anyone, and it is also likely to leave more room for the random chance factor which often causes the unforeseen to turn out useful and different.

At the kind of events where no thought has been given to helping people to mingle, instead of staying in a corner trying to look involved with someone on your mobile phone, you could:

- Move to the drinks table, where it is easier to start a conversation with another guest who is drinking;
- Head in the direction of others who seem to have come by themselves and undoubtedly will be feeling as uncomfortable as you are;
- Go to the event with a friend or colleague, since this eases a lot of situations and gives you the opportunity of making introductions, and you can pass this back and forth;
- Bearing in mind that body language speaks before verbal language, avoid defensive postures like folding your arms or looking at the floor before you send your receptivity message, and just smile, say "Hi" or "How's it going" when you make eye contact with someone.

And in the approach one very important factor should be borne in mind, which is the accepted and shared protocol for approaches in the venue in which you find yourself. The only way you can pick this up is by paying attention and watching how people greet each other.

There are some situations when a direct approach can be interpreted as too invasive; there may be well-rehearsed modes of greeting, and even facial expressions may be interpreted in a different way from what you are used to.

This is the main mistake made by managers who travel to other countries and assume that they will establish contacts in the same way that they do at home. Each country and each culture has its own formula for behaving at the first meeting which is designed to communicate trust, and then how to proceed with the relationship. It is very important that you seek information in this respect if you want to fit in successfully.

Conversations. The art of conversation is another critical element in the first meeting. While still making sure that you are natural and honest, a few basic principles are worth remembering.

Conversation is a procedure. The more formal it is, the more it adheres to the rules of the procedure, but sometimes we forget that strangers may not trust us as much as we think they do, and we tend to skip the basic steps.

The conversation procedure begins with the introduction and then moves on to what we might call small talk, casual conversation. We then proceed to the subject of the conversation, and finally take our leave.

The introduction and the leave-taking are almost more important than the actual conversation, since the first sets the tone of the conversation and breaks the ice, while the leave-taking gives you the opportunity to refer to the next meeting, to smooth out any tension which may have appeared in the foregoing minutes with a more trivial subject, and above all to leave a final comfortable and positive impression.

The duration of each step in the procedure is up to the speakers, and must be adapted to the nature of the meeting, but as a general rule the speaker who is on the lookout for negative signals and adapts himself to them is the one who does it best.

Some books about networking talk about conversational transitions, referring to the moment when one person stops making conversation for its own sake and launches the message or request, drawing attention to the problem or challenge in which he or she is interested.

But here again common sense must rule and your eye should be on the middle distance or the long term. Common sense would dictate that trying to jump to a subject of your own interest on a first meeting could seem very abrupt, and, in general, ill-advised.

Later conversations are the time for testing the possibilities of touching on specific targets or subject areas, and here we have two strategies:

- The transparent tactic of announcing what you want to talk about. Here it is advisable to leave the door open for a negative reaction so that your interlocutor is not cornered. Approaches such as, "I would like to talk about this sometime when we both have a moment," for example, raise the question without any obligation that it has to be dealt with immediately.

Our contact will either respond with "whenever you like" or "sure, me too," which gives you carte blanche to make the transition, or if there is no such response then the conversation continues as before. This is a clear signal in itself – he hasn't taken the bait either because he doesn't think it's important or he would really like to avoid the subject.

On occasions the opposite outcome may need a little more small talk to reach the level of trust which means you can go straight to the request. In this case it's advisable to change the subject of the conversation to something fairly entertaining, and wait for a more favorable opportunity in the future.

- The tactic of beating about the bush and hoping it isn't noticed is a great favorite in Latin cultures and is the most common where the subject matter is uncomfortable. In this case the speaker attempts to raise subjects which are close to the one he is concerned about, to see if the interlocutor will be the first to tackle it.

This is a tactic which requires practice and it may be fairly obvious to the other party, particularly if both parties know that there is something serious to be discussed. Even so, it's a fact that geniuses exist in the art of conversation who can ease the subject out with skill and even humor.

On the matter of conversations, two other guidelines should be highlighted: the importance of stories, anecdotes and colorful expression on the one hand, and the clarity of the message on the other.

The checklist in the previous section on how to prepare for your meetings recommended the clear formulation of your promotional messages about yourself and your goal. You would be surprised how important this is and how often it is forgotten by many managers.

Jotting down the two or three outstanding characteristics or qualities about yourself and your objective will force you to think before you speak, and the more thought you give to it, the clearer and more understandable you will be to you listeners.

If you have to invent your description of yourself every time you open your mouth, the most likely upshot is that your messages will vary from one conversation to the next, robbing them of consistency and credibility. And you will also forget to say the most important thing because you are nervous, or because of the distractions of the moment, or your explanations will start to wander, confusing the stranger in question, and ultimately boring him.

The use of stories, anecdotes and memorable expressions is crucial if you want to maintain your audience's interest. If you remember what was said in Chapter 3 about the rumor mill, you will see that everything which gives the impression that something special is taking place will be better remembered and is more likely to be passed on. Stories and anecdotes add feeling and imbue the facts with immediacy, they mark a personality and a style, not to mention making things easier to understand.

The worst thing about talking to people you don't know is that they will not have gained enough confidence yet to tell you that they haven't understood what you said. Make it easier for them with examples, metaphors, anything that fits.

Body language. Remember that what you say is the smallest part of what people understand about you. The impression that stays with others is much more affected by your appearance, your gestures, what your eyes say, the tone of your voice and whether they get a handshake or a peck on both cheeks.

Cultivation of a relaxed approach and self-confidence is the best way to ensure that the totality of what is communicated by these rebellious and involuntary messages is consistent and successful.

Again, you will be able to find all kinds of superficial advice in books or from snake-oil sellers about how to shake hands and how to hold yourself.

Start by observing yourself in the conversations you have in your day-to-day life and note your tendency to interrupt or not to speak, where your back is and what your eyes are doing. Listen to the tone of your own voice.

Write it down, think about it, see what others think. Work out what sensation and beliefs cause you to behave in a specific way, and you will come to see how you can free yourself of it. You will start to develop a body language which matches what you want to say, so that your hands and your eyes will emphasize and underline your message instead of distracting the attention of your audience.

There are no tricks, and if you have to concentrate on controlling your sweaty palms or smiling when you don't feel like it, you are certainly paying no attention to what is being said to you, and certainly not thinking how it might be useful.

The business card. Your business card is fundamental to the networking procedure. It is the most convenient way of collecting the contact data of a new acquaintance, and a vital tool for everybody with a tendency to forget names or who are being drowned in the flood of information they receive throughout the day.

It could be said that the main reason for carrying business cards is to make it easier for your new contacts to track you down. But if in addition you have an unusual – or a very common – name, or a combination of hard-to-remember details, or you're abroad where the way you spell you name is hard to understand, the business card is a great aid for your new acquaintances.

It is therefore advisable to make a real investment in this aspect of your image. If your card shows the logo of a well-known company, you will benefit directly from the effort invested by your company in marketing, but if it is a personal card or is attracting attention to contexts in which your employer is neither relevant nor pertinent, you should seek some opinions and even consider hiring an image consultant.

Ignore all the superficial advice which also clutters the world of information about networking, seeking your attention, telling you to design a card which is very different, outstanding. Remember that the most important thing about your card is that it should say something about who you are, via its colors, the type of card used, the way the information is presented. And for practical purposes an unusual size may be a mistake because it won't fit in a card case, and so will be easy to lose.

But it is still a fact that the card is associated with professionalism, with the expression of commercial intentions and opportunism, which means that special attention should be paid to knowing when to offer it and how.

The principle "when in Rome do as the Romans do" is the basic standard. You can actually attend a breakfast where nobody makes any attempt to offer or ask for a business card because it will be seen as vulgar, but on the other hand you could be taking an aperitif where everybody has their name in huge capitals on a card hanging round their necks and cards are flowing faster than the drinks.

Aside from these contextual factors, individual cases must be governed by the preferences expressed by the others and by sensitivity. If someone asks for your card, obviously you give it, but if they don't it's not so clear whether you should or not.

As a general rule it's more advisable to ask the other person for their card. That means you have the ideal excuse to offer yours, although it should be noted that the more important or desirable (in the professional sense, of course) your interlocutor is, the less likely it is that they will want to exchange data with you.

Perhaps one of the most difficult principles for many contact managers to accept, although it is very obvious to those who are successful, is that everybody decides whom they find interesting and whom they don't, and the larger the number of interesting acquaintances building up in a manager's diary, the more miserly he will be with his time and attention.

It tends to be the case with speakers at big events, politicians or famous personalities that they can't avoid feeling like a honey-pot in the bears' den. There are many more people trying to attract their attention or ask them for something than is comfortable, and you can even observe this in the forced dynamics which take the form of waves around the epicenter of the mouth-watering honey.

If you really want to form a relationship with some high-level personality, you will have to choose an occasion when you can shine and be remembered. Chasing the speaker or politician at their public events and taking umbrage when they don't give signs of recognition is frankly amateurish and not very practical.

Forming a relationship with someone like Bill Gates or Nadal is difficult. Full stop. If it is really essential for your future, you will have to devote a great deal of time and effort to buttressing your presence among the connections of your objective contacts or creating a service or unique business which attracts their attention on its own account.

Setting up magic expectations is fun, but not very practical. Be realistic and make the very best of the advantages that you do have.

To help you to analyze and memorize this list of points or ideas – which many would say are just common sense, and others rocket science – I recommend the following table as a model. The idea is for you to be able to score your own output level from time to time, and complete this numerical assessment with relevant comments and notes.

	LEVEL	AREAS FOR IMPROVEMENT
Approach		Number of people approached per event and quality of the meetings
		Occasions used to tackle possible contacts
		Body language before and during the meeting (look, posture, gestures, etc.)
		Knowledge of, and adaptation to, local and cultural networking protocols
Conversation		Gestures and expressions which communicate my style and personality
		Description of my conversation procedure. Duration of pauses, feelings following each step, etc.
		Transitions. Style (transparent or not), fluency, reactions observed, results achieved
Presentation of self		Effectiveness of messages about me and my projects (clarity, consistency of messages, feedback received, doubts generated)
		Use of stories, anecdotes, metaphors (how many, effect produced, difficulties encountered, favourable surprises)
		Gestures which betray your emotional state. Level of confidence or nervousness, nervous gestures to be avoided, exercises which have succeeded in raising your confidence, etc.
Conclusions and results		Business cards: impression caused, doubts sensed, moment of exchange, acceptance of card with surprise or displeasure, practices to improve on receipt of a card, etc.
		Feelings generated in the other person and outcome of the conversation

GRAPH 7.4

Afterwards

This stage of the meeting is the one which requires most discipline and organization, and it may be here that you will observe faster improvements in a short time.

Afterwards is when you process all the information you have received, prioritize the possibilities arising, together with the cost of the opportunity this implies, and set effective action in motion. It may be that the greatest errors arise from prioritizing the opportunities, since managers tend to forget that their resources are limited, or to avoid de-prioritizing anyone, just in case.

The first typical problem experienced by many managers is to return home with a stack of business cards and be unable to associate a face with each one. And if you leave the job of organizing them until much later, the association task will be even harder.

What is advisable here is to store the information and impressions received as soon as possible. Some people actually write on the card they have just received, while others scan the card and put a paragraph into the database. Any technique will do as long as it is practical and helps you to record the data you need to make your decisions regarding priority and subsequent action.

A classification system for your contacts will be a great help in time-saving and deciding when necessary which new contacts to follow up and which to set aside.

One thing you can do is take advantage of this opportunity to design an initial classification system, with the idea that it can be adapted on the occasion of your next strategic review of your networking according to how well it has appeared to fit in with day-to-day operations.

The important things which will ensure that your new contact classification works are simplicity, attention to the emotional nature of the chemistry and personal trust, and the application of strategic criteria.

With this in mind it is advisable to deploy no more than three possible grades or scores for each category. Let's look at an example.

George is a commercial representative who works for a large pharmaceutical laboratory. When he goes to a fair he uses the following system to classify his new contacts.

The first criterion is professional. Since George is on the commercial side, his objective is to find new customers for the laboratory, and with this in mind he tries to allocate each business card to one of the categories used by the laboratory.

The laboratory has classified its customer database as prospects, product consultants, first-time customers, regular customers and VIP customers. So George goes through the cards, slotting each into one of these categories.

George then makes a second pass through the cards, but this time he adds a score for the chemistry and personal affinity he felt for each individual. He gives a 1 for those who seemed really interesting and fun, to 3 for those who made him feel really uncomfortable.

Spending five minutes going through his cards like this, George is making the best possible use of his personal energy and his resources.

The cards which fell into categories which are especially critical for the laboratory right now, and which also have a top affinity score, are the obvious candidates for most investment on George's part. But there are others which aren't.

For example, there are contacts which are very important for the laboratory, and hence for George's professional strategy, but with whom he didn't feel comfortable or at ease. In this case George can choose to do nothing, or just add the contact to the laboratory database, or make efforts to cultivate the relationship for the benefit of his profession. It's his decision, and we must all set our own personal criteria in this regard.

The same thing happens with the contacts which seem to be very good company, but haven't really got much to do with his work as a commercial representative. There's nothing stopping George from cultivating the relationship with them for pure pleasure or his personal development. Each stage in George's life will impose the criterion to be adopted, so that when George was single and without commitments he would have been more likely to explore opportunities for friendship, yet when he's exhausted by family duties and work needs, obviously he wouldn't.

The important thing is to think about this instead of doing it without thinking. If George had made his classification, and during his latest review of the network had realized that he should have more contacts outside of the pharmaceutical world, then his impulse to keep in touch with his new contacts would have a certain intuitive or impulsive component, but also a certain strategy.

Consolidation is the most obvious step in cultivating relationships, and yet it has a fundamental impact on the ability of the new acquaintance to retain you in his memory.

Consolidation consists basically of sending an email, making a telephone call or paying a visit immediately after the first meeting, to strengthen this beginning and to show the other party that you're interested and keen to continue to cultivate the connection.

When the first contact has been exciting this usually takes place as a matter of course. But in all less striking contacts managers tend to forget this step and leave fate or chance to decide whether this connection will turn into something or will remain just a chance encounter.

Depending on how important this new contact is to you, whether for strategic or friendship reasons, your reinforcement of the root will merit a proportional effort and investment.

The minimum expression is a brief email of thanks, or expressing how interesting the chat was, with some formula about the future.

The maximum expression is a gift. Flowers, a book, a symbolic expression like a tin of asparagus or an electronic photograph of something which came up in the conversation.

It's up to you to decide which is the most appropriate measure for each contact, always within the allocated classification.

After consolidation it may be that nothing happens for months or even years; or a professional relationship nurtured by a mutual interest project may begin, or a genuine bond of friendship may grow out of weekly table-tennis sessions or other shared pastimes. After consolidation you move onto development of the connection.

7.4 INGRID WÜNNING TSCHOL, HEAD OF HEALTH AND SCIENCE, ROBERT BOSCH STIFTUNG

Women are significantly underrepresented in leadership positions in the academic world. In 2010 only 12% of the highest-paying positions at German research institutes were held by women, as is the case with important boards and commissions that decide on prizes, appointments, and grants. AcademiaNet is the simple instrument conceived by Ingrid Wünning Tschol to change this. And it's working!

AcademiaNet is a singular initiative to bring excellent female scientists and scholars to the attention of those who sit on academic boards, hold executive positions or report on research. Anyone who is responsible for conference planning, or requires an expert's opinion when making decisions, will find the women who used not to show up easily before.

Ingrid Wünning Tschol conceived the website, gained support from major research and scientific institutions in Germany, and even convinced Angela Merkel to participate in the site's public presentation. In her own words, "I thought it was going to be more difficult, but instead, it was incredibly easy!"

The idea came up when she co-chaired the Euroscience Open Forum in Barcelona in 2008. More than 4,500 attendees joined journalists from all over the world to participate in over 70 scientific sessions and inter-disciplinary meetings of scientists, young researchers, politicians, pol-icy-makers, innovators, business people, media and communicators.

"It was a huge success, except for one thing," explains Ingrid, "we failed to have enough women among the plenary and keynote speak-ers." When she checked her meeting minutes to find out why they hadn't included more women, she discovered that "sure enough, we had invited women. But when they said they didn't have the time to come, we just went on to the next best person in their specialty."

This got the science policy-maker thinking: "There must be a very simple instrument to collect all the best women in science so that conference organizers and high-level committees can find them," she remembers. "Women don't come up at the top of your head because men do much better networking," she reflects, alluding to a well-observed trend across industries. While many evolutionary thinkers claim women are very good at navigating social structures to find a husband, a nanny or a house cleaner, women don't seem to apply equal effort to publicizing their own achievements in the workplace.

A little online research showed that there were quite a number of plat-forms around, but any woman could submit her own profile. "It seemed to me to be like searching on Google. We needed a more credible filter if women were to be taken seriously in the higher levels of the Science world," she thought. "And I knew that in Germany there are many research organizations with very high reputations that use well tested fil-ters of excellence, such as the Leopoldina National Academy of Sciences, the German Science Foundation, the Max Planck Society or Acatech."

Wünning Tschol came up with "a rather simple idea, not a genius idea" to collect all the women who were already retained as excellent by such organizations in one database to make them visible to every-one. She immediately went to visit the presidents of all these major scientific institutions to tell them about her idea, and "I was surprised to find they were very easy to convince!"

Ingrid had hit upon something that these men would have liked to do, but didn't have the means to do in a professional way from their own organizations. Their response was unanimous, "Yes, I would be willing to sit on a steering committee to define the criteria of excel-lence and then I will nominate only women who comply with such requisites." After the first few meetings at the beginning of 2010, the German scientific journal *Spektrum der Wissenshaft* became engaged as primary media partner. All Ingrid needed now was money.

She went straight to the board of trustees to ask for €500,000. "It was the first time in the 11 years I'd worked at the Robert Bosch Foundation that I thought I was going to fail entirely because most of them were men. But again, it was a big surprise. Not only were they all for it, but they commented rather loudly that they thought it was an excellent idea," smiles the Head of Science as she looks back on that meeting.

Six months later the AcademiaNet portal was created with 558 women who had been nominated by prestigious German science institutions like the German National Academy of Sciences Leopoldina, the German Research Foundation (DFG), the Max Planck Society and Leibniz Association. The Alexander von Humboldt Foundation, the Helmholtz Association and Fraunhofer Society, and also the European Molecular Biology Laboratory (EMBO), or the German Council of Science and Humanities also participated, as did Acatech – German Academy of Science and Engineering – the Association of German Engineers (VDI), the German Chemical Industry Association (VCI) and the German Rectors' Conference (HRK). It was time for a party to celebrate the launch of the portal.

Once more, Ingrid pointed as high up as she could get, and she called German Chancellor Angela Merkel's office. When she explained the project and asked whether it would be possible to engage Merkel in the launch, they answered, "this sounds like something Angela Merkel would certainly like to do. We receive many, many requests like this, and she only has one day a week to participate in such activities, but we will ask her and let you know."

Three weeks later a positive reply came back. Everything was set for a spectacular presentation of the website, until the Chancellor received a letter-bomb on the same morning of the event. When Ingrid heard the news she thought, "Oh well! There goes Angela Merkel! But once more I was surprised. She not only showed up, but she even left her protocol speech to one side and shared personal anecdotes in a friendly and smiling manner. Her presence helped us enormously, with lots of media hits to officially inaugurate AcademiaNet in November of 2010."

Since then traffic statistics show high visit rates with people drilling down to level eight of the website information. "I know the President of the Deutsche Forschungsgemeinschaft, the biggest research granting agency in Germany, asks his staff to use it when they compose a list of referees to assign a grant," states Wünning Tschol as an example.

"The purpose of AcademiaNet is to make committees that decide over a lot of money or make policy a lot more feminine. It's not a career development tool, even if this may be a byproduct for some of the women listed," clarifies the science policy-maker.

AcademiaNet's next goal is to become European, both by translating everything into English, and by including other highly qualified organizations with strong quality filters such as the European Research Council. "While we raise the money to develop the English version, we are going in concentric circles around Germany, speaking first with German-speaking institutions in Austria and Switzerland. Hopefully we will soon involve the Royal Society of Scientists in London or NWO in the Netherlands, for example."

When asked about including an online social network in the project, Ingrid admits it is not her first priority. "I guess we are traditional in this sense, but it is also the way of the scientific community. It is more important that these women meet each other in a high level committee in real life."

The yearly conference organized in Berlin to discuss science policy issues, which are then sent to the government, is the preferred networking channel to help these high-profile women scientists network. "And of course we mix them with very powerful men such as the President of the Deutsche Forschungsgemeinschaft or the chair of the European Research Area Board. We mix all these people making sure that we have sixty to seventy percent of women in there."

Ingrid thinks it is really crucial for women to jump on the professional networking wagon if they want to get to the top of their organizations, as much in the science industry as in any other. "Real jobs are being given away at the bars. Men naturally assemble together to catch up on things at every conference I attend. Women need to start doing it too!" she recommends. She insists that women should apply as much effort to participating in coffee break networking as they put into preparing their speech.

An especially funny example of this gender-biased approach to networking was a special evening talk organized with another program of the foundation, where a famous professor travels to Germany to share experiences with participants. After the talk all the women said they were tired and going to sleep, thinking they wanted to be bright and attentive during the talks of the next day.

But the famous professor knocked on the table and said: "You're not going to bed! I am a lot more jetlagged and tired than you are, but I am willing to go out and have a drink with you. This is what we guys do. We discuss all the gossip and unofficial details of business over beer and wine."

"I also believe women need to become a lot more realistic about power and competition once you hit 45," Ingrid tells us. While a lot of women in their early thirties feel that they will be naturally promoted all through the next ten years of their career, "this stops when you reach the level under the CEO. All the kind mentoring and helping suddenly comes to an end. You become a competitor, and it no longer matters whether you are a man or a woman. You are an obstacle to be overcome by those who want the same jobs you do."

Ingrid is one of those women who have often been the first to do this and be elected for that. She still finds herself to be the only woman on many committees and powerful forums, but she has learned to be a very proactive networker, even when she is tired after a long day of meetings. She hasn't only conquered new territories for future women scientists. She's also leading the way with her example, and actively supporting the best in Europe with the AcademiaNet project.

Now it's up to you to do the rest! Please do network your way to success.

CHAPTER 8

BETTER CONTACTS

Once I attended a conference on life balance where an expert said that "the problem with quality time is that you have to watch Toy Story thirty-six times with your son before it hits you. He turns around half way through the thirty-seventh replay and says 'Daddy, I love you!' You can't plan for that to happen during any given quality time-slot."

The key to taking relationships to the next level is to spend time and effort on them. Let's just hope your contacts don't require 36 movies to get down to business!

The previous chapter dealt with an early stage in the contact management process, covering its effect on generating openness and the

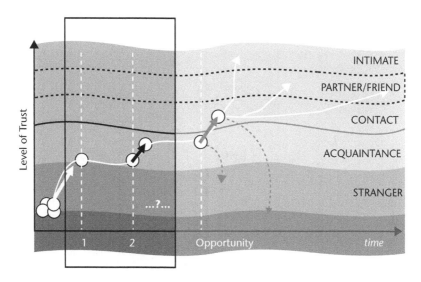

GRAPH 8.1

185

renewal of ideas and opportunities in the personal network, as well as everything else which is at issue in a first encounter.

Although the first conversation with a new acquaintance will take place at a party or a conference, and though consolidation has proceeded correctly, this is just the hesitant beginning of a relationship, the fate of which can be neither predicted nor forced.

The above diagram shows that after the first meeting (1) and the consolidation (2), there follows an interval of time during which no new interaction will take place unless there is an opportunity of interest to both parties. Once this opportunity has arisen, and the subsequent interaction is established, the result may be an improvement in the quality of the connection, or an immediate rupture.

Every interaction you are involved in with your near and distant contacts tests the bond between you. None of us is immune from losing a close friend through a misunderstanding or a trusted associate because of an unexpected problem or a failed transaction.

This first contact is a wager, on which, as discussed in Chapter 4, a level of trust and the resulting expectations have been staked, which time will clarify and appropriately position. This means that the development of the current connection is in itself a source of work and will take up hours on end.

Consider the following variation on the diagram above. Instead of tracking the development of a specific contact over time, we are now looking at the appearance of the network at a given moment. This

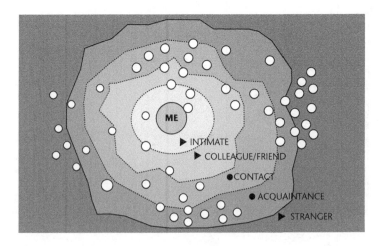

GRAPH 8.2

snapshot will show the status at a given moment of all the contacts present in a manager's network.

This cross-sectional diagram offers an intuitive picture of what is meant by the development of the connections; the job is to move all these contacts towards the interior of the diagram.

Developing contacts means undertaking actions, being involved in interactions, paying visits and making telephone calls which help every established contact to become more trusting of the manager; and to demonstrate that trust with deeds and examples in return so that the mutual bond which unites them steadily grows in strength.

Given that many variables lie beyond the manager's control, particularly as regards personal preferences and the individual trust filters of contact, developing connections in real terms means planning actions which make the best use of the manager's resources, and rapid adaptation to the outcomes of each interaction.

8.1 THE DIFFERENCE BETWEEN CULTIVATION AND PERSECUTION

The most popular networking manuals, and some of the speakers who are well known in the field, recommend a regular rate of contact. In other words, if two months is the period decided on, then absolutely every one of the contacts in the manager's network must receive some kind of contact from him at least once every eight weeks.

An American manager who moved to Madrid some years ago had obviously read the books, and she showed herself to be a very serious student. Blonde, with beautiful blue eyes and a spectacular figure, she had no difficulty recruiting new contacts at parties and drinks, following which she would sit down to feed her Outlook software with contacts with a great deal of assiduity.

This particular woman put a great deal of time into filling in the "quality" fields regarding her contacts, setting down all the personal details she had gleaned on the first conversation, and charting the people she knew who were the friends and contacts of each new acquaintance.

According to the rule books, this manager was outstanding. But according to the criteria and philosophy upon which this book is based, she committed some fundamental errors. The evidence is that this particular manager left Madrid some months ago, after discovering that her devoted efforts at pursuit had not borne the expected fruit.

She had indeed set a deadline within which she had to renew contacts with each name in her database according to its classification. When she made the acquaintance of each new friend she classified them as VIP, quality and quantity. The VIPs had highest priority, which meant she had to contact them once a month. Those of quality had to be contacted every two months, and quantity received her attention once a quarter.

The first mistake in her classification system is that she failed to factor in what these contacts thought of her, or their own policies for "cultivating" connections. Of course, she neither noticed this nor guessed, particularly because Latin people find it very difficult to suggest to someone that they are irritating or annoying. The best way to say no is to say yes, delighted, of course, and then to casually make yourself scarce.

Perhaps this is something of an exaggeration, but a story with a little garnish added to it will help communicate a powerful idea and from time to time raise a pleasant smile. What happened was that our dogged student diligently applied all her contact standards and for the first months her contacts felt effectively obligated to respond to her approaches in some way or other.

However, apart from not noticing the feeling generated upon each contact, she was also uninterested in the concerns and preoccupations of the contacts themselves, and so much contact with so little content began to tire the recipients.

The standard of connecting with a contact merely to cultivate a relationship has the problem that it fails to meet the principle of mutual benefit, which is crucial for networking. Calls and emails which add no value do not count, and in the long run they feel like persecution.

There is a huge difference between chasing somebody to make them your friend, and cultivating a friendship between you. The first case is what the protagonist of our case history did, and she ended up being boring and even sinister. She thought that starting her sentences with "I'd love to see you to..." or "you're the only one who can help me with this..." were effective devices to stroke the egos of her contacts and get them to trust her more. It is possible that it might just have worked in some cases, too.

But appeals like these, flattering though they may have been, really contributed nothing useful, and could never be seen as genuine. The only really genuine thing is what you are actually feeling and thinking, and the only thing that will really create trust, interest and curiosity is real added value.

In other words, cultivate a connection if it requires a certain regularity of interaction, but the gold standard is the contribution of obvious value. If you have nothing to contribute, it isn't worth making the call.

A "hi" from time to time may be acceptable if you have already established some kind of relationship, and both parties know that a certain amount of time has slipped by between meetings. But this is not a resource which can be abused.

Another problem of regular pursuit is that it can be technologically programmed. And because it can be technologically programmed, anybody can copy it and apply it. This is like the birthday greeting which has turned into a marketing tool, or the little phone calls in series which lots of people like to make on New Year's Eve.

This adds no value. It pursues your connection, but doesn't cultivate him, and on occasions it may cause the opposite effect to what you're hoping for: you become tiresome. If in addition you commit the error of striving to achieve immediate objectives using connections which have not been allowed time to mature, pursuit turns into manipulation, one-upmanship and other contorted versions of networking such as have been responsible for so much hesitancy and scepticism among executives world-wide.

8.2 CLASSIFYING YOUR CONTACTS

In Chapter 7 we spoke of the importance of designing a classification system which would allow you to decide how to focus the relationship with each new contact you make, using as a basis the impressions you received during a short meeting, and in most cases also making use of the comment available from current friends and colleagues about the reputation of the contact in question.

But there is one critical indicator you can only test by interaction with the individual in question over more than one occasion, and which is yet crucial for being able to satisfactorily assess the use of the resources available to you: the transaction level returned by the connection, or in other words, their reciprocity index.

When we measured the POTENCIA of your personal network a few chapters ago, we were focusing on the quantity and quality of the exchanges you share with the members of your network. The T in Transaction allowed you to see the contribution made by each connection to the whole, and the C in Credit helped you to examine the level of reciprocity existing in each relationship.

One of the most extensive barriers to increasing the manager's output in his quality as a networker occurs at exactly this point, at the complex and taboo ethic whereby it can be seen that a member of the manager's network is not productive, and in some cases is actually a large-scale consumer.

While for a banker an account with red numbers on it is clearly a business problem, and for a call center a lonely old lady who calls up to talk about the weather is bad for business, it is very difficult in many cases to recognize that there are people in a network who are not only contributing nothing, but who are actually profiting by it, whether or not they are aware of the fact.

This is another area rich in material for ethical debates and existential doubts which obstructs action and prolongs unbalanced situations for years. And this is where you should think carefully and adopt a clear position, one which helps you to take complex decisions in this regard, and one which matches your personality, your values and your strategic objectives.

When relationships begin, the classification which allows you to distinguish between them is based on two variables: the emotional affinity you experience; and objective or strategic compatibility. However, as time passes and interactions take place it becomes less important to make a distinction between the two dimensions. We can assume that the relationships as they develop within the spectrum in question have exceeded the minimum levels of affinity and strategic compatibility.

In other words, the classification proposed for new contacts is rather large and complex for measuring what is happening as bridges and interchange situations are being set up between the parties, and is somewhat lacking when it comes to measuring the real level of reciprocity in the relationship.

Let's take an example from an area quite unconnected with business strategy, but painfully common and well known to all of us. Cast your mind back to that magic princess or white knight that you once knew, who seemed a real soul-mate because of all you had in common, and how wonderfully attractive they were because of it.

That platonic infatuation, which at the time seemed mutual and almost written in the stars, would have received top honors in the classification system of any contact manager; exponential affinity and strategic compatibility to the end of the world.

But as the meetings and interactions continued, they brought in more information. Some no doubt very positive and heart-warming, even exciting and heralding a future romantic involvement. But other less obvious hints pointed at a fatal ending that nobody wanted to see.

And so it turned out that one fine day, having ridden the roller-coaster of emotions in conflict, it became clear that the soul-mate wasn't as interested as you thought. Calls were not returned as quickly as you would have liked, nor with such interest. There were still smiles at compliments and jokes, but none in return, and those crucial moments in any relationship when you have to stand your ground and reveal your commitment vanished or were marginalized.

There may be no greater disappointment in life than this. For many of us this story is a part of our collection of adolescent anecdotes, and for others it is the standard fare of the single life. But it is also the example par excellence of zero reciprocity. The story warns the intelligent and demanding traveller not to stop here, never mind how attractive the prospect seemed from a distance.

It doesn't just happen in romance – it can happen in any relationship. It's a fact of life, and it's something you should measure with every contact you meet.

What you do after checking your measurements depends very much on your personal strategy. There are friends or professional mentors who can contribute so much at times of difficulty that no amount of favors returned afterward can balance the account. So let it be.

There are the personal commitments we make to a sibling who "never had any luck," or to a friend who's "always putting his foot in it," and whom we respect more than anybody else. Despite the fact that it won't help our personal strategy. So let it be.

But if glaring cases exist of workmates, colleagues, friends and acquaintances for whom you are a constant source of added value and whose return isn't remotely comparable, you are investing your resources in an asset that will never be profitable for you.

The opportunity cost which you accept is everything which a more just and reciprocal version of your contact would bring to you and to the others. It's your decision, and nobody is going to disagree with you about it. But you must take it in the knowledge of what you are giving up.

This may seem a touch boring and uncomfortable, but from here on you are advised to classify your existing contacts according to two criteria: the level of trust (both cognitive and emotional) which you have accumulated with each individual, and the level of reciprocity which you identify in the other person – the win–win quality which exists between you.

When you have established the habit of paying attention to this variable, you will have a much, much clearer perception of what is happening when your personal frustration with the poor fruit you have harvested is directed at your company or the anonymous group of decision-makers who don't recognize you, or identifiable individuals who let you lavish your attention on them and give nothing in return.

It's important to know. Deciding what to do on this matter is one of the big decisions which make or break people. Alas, this book cannot help you with it.

And, of course, if it turns out that the non-reciprocator is you, beginning to measure the reciprocity of your relationships will bring home to you the guilt or correction required if you want to preserve this connection. The only relationships which never stop giving are the ones between your parents and you, and even in these cases there are limits which can be exceeded if they aren't respected.

8.3 THE LAWS OF SUSTAINABLE DEVELOPMENT

Once we are clear that the purpose of development is to improve and strengthen the connections in your personal network, that this is achieved by contributing value and not simply because the contact exists, and that the black holes which consume everything they suck in are hazardous to any personal network, we still have to discuss some principles or laws which are essential for the socially responsible contact manager.

Ongoing addition of value

Not making contact if you don't have anything to say seems obvious when you read it, but it turns out to be tricky when you try to put it into practice. How is it going to occur to anybody that they may have something for them, if they don't speak first?

With difficulty, with imagination and a lot of creativity – this is how we play the game we played at the start. There is a need for information so that we can understand what is bothering our contact, before we can contribute something from our repertory which he might find useful.

Sometimes just our own personal time is a help in itself. In the cases where the foundation exists upon which we might build a friendship or have interests in common, just swinging by for a coffee is appreciated, and it also might supply some information so that we can think about future contributions.

In other cases it's a question of putting in some time and paying attention, and trying to imagine the situation of the contact you have in mind and the associated difficulties. Sometimes you just have to take a chance on sending something that you don't know will be accepted, or whether it will be seen as some kind of interference.

And sometimes you just have to wait until fortune supplies an occasion which is welcome to you both. It can be frustrating if you have great expectations or hopes of a certain connection, but productivity is the cure for frustration. Continuing with new contacts and nurturing them can eat up a lot of your waiting time, but it may have some nice surprises for you, too.

Facilitating the negative

This is a golden rule, to be followed at all times. When asking a favor, making an invitation or proposing a project, you must frame your proposal in such a way that it is easy and comfortable to say no. If you don't your opposite number feels cornered, and this could mean the end of the relationship in the worst case, since your contact begins to associate this feeling of discomfort with you and your personality, and will avoid you until eventually you are no longer to be seen.

Suppose you need to ask for some money to make a mortgage payment, and you make a list of family members and close friends whom you intend to call. Anyone who receives that call is going to feel they are in an awkward position, to say the least.

Many people's tendency when asking such a delicate favor is not only not to facilitate a graceful negative response, but to blackmail the recipient of the request with the moral dilemma which arises if they don't help, with detailed descriptions of all the negative consequences arising from a failure to receive the necessary loan.

This is exactly what you must not do if you want to preserve the relationship. When you make the request you must make it very clear that (1) you understand that this is a tough ask, and you're only doing it because of the important relationship of trust which exists between you, and (2) that your contact absolutely must say no if they have any difficulties of their own, based on that same trust.

In less compromising examples, it is enough to include informal phrases and expressions to close your request or to remove the sting from a possible refusal in advance. "I'd love to see you Saturday if you've nothing else to do," "This could be an important get-together for you, but, obviously, you decide," "Do you think you could spare me an hour – there's something rather urgent I'd like to discuss with you. Not if you can't make it, of course." And so on...

Accepting rejection

Rejection is unpleasant, but also essential for you to adapt your efforts and upgrade the output from your contact management procedures.

Rejection often takes the form of silence rather than a direct negative, and you have to be able to understand it and accept it. Great emphasis has already been placed on the matter, but I'm repeating it here because it is one of the areas handled worst by beginner contact managers.

There are two ways of taking rejection. You can blame the agent of the rejection and the context, or you can blame yourself. The advantage of blaming everybody else is that you retain the comfort of being the victim, and hence are exempt from any self-assessment, analysis or correction.

But if you blame the others and bad luck, you don't learn much. Questioning your own motivation is tough, but it is much more productive. Analyzing the reason for the rejection, and seeking possible grounds for it in the product, the offer, the style employed, the way a service was requested and all the other variables which affected the outcome highlights new factors which will help to improve your own contact management skills.

Perhaps the difficulty of accepting rejection in personal relationships is the fact that this rejection is just that: personal. However much you try to justify the rejection on business-related grounds, any manager who has placed himself at risk and devoted time and care to cultivating a connection which, in the final analysis, changed into a locked door is bound to feel that it is his personality which is at fault.

Sometimes there are objective and strategic arguments justifying the rejection, but at other times it's just because you didn't go down well with your opposite number. That's the nature of the situation and there's nothing to be done about it. It's in the rules of the game, and anybody who thinks they get on well with everybody is lining up for a lot of pressure and a lot of time pretending to be or think differently, which dramatically reduces chances of success.

Accepting a "no" or a negative response with grace and elegance is typical of the experienced contact manager. Experience shows that it's better to receive a clear signal in time than to keep on banking on something which doesn't work, and that, as we say in the world of romance, "there are plenty more fish in the sea." There are many more contacts waiting to be known and who will have a lot more in common with you.

The quality of personal details

Personal details are definitely important. They are the most genuine and hard-to-fake content of all relationships. Nurture them, spoil them, pay them all the attention they call for.

This is the case in your personal interaction style, with handwritten cards, personalized gifts or a few sensitive words that require quite a bit of thought as to what would work well in an email, or in the way you listen to, and learn from, others. Learn what they like, how they take their coffee, what they like to say about their lives. People talk about what matters to them.

In every conversation and every interaction your interlocutor is revealing his personality, his desires and his goals. Pay attention with all your senses and remember the details of the meetings and the anecdotes told.

This is the aspect of personal relationships which it is impossible to imitate or automate. However much software programs try to include empty fields for you to include these kinds of details, the fact is that they are hard to get down in writing, and require updating at a great rate.

What is also important is that as you listen to all these details, you will be processing them, and in doing so intuiting small important facts about your contact which he would never tell you explicitly. The personal details he communicates are the trees at the edge of the wood, but being able to see the wood in its entirety, to respect it and accept it with suitable comments and appreciation is what cements the personal aspect of all relationships.

This is what the Dunbar number, mentioned in Chapter 3, refers to. We are unable to store intangible impressions loaded with emotional labels about more than around 150 people. Our brain can't handle any more. And any effort to double that by skimping on personal details won't work. It just won't seem real.

Consistency over time

In the interviews with great contact managers consistency of response and style over time is quoted as being of great importance.

You must comply with some self-imposed minimum standards of quality and reactivity if you wish to generate a consistent reputation. Handling people in one way one month and differently the next doesn't work.

Our minds are programmed to look for patterns in everything we perceive. This is a very important process as we learn about our world, and is what helps us to learn even when information is wanting, since we fill it in so as to comply with the law of consistency as we perceive it.

The same thing happens when we learn about an individual's trustworthiness. If we are to retain a lasting impression, we must see a consistent form of response over time. People who appear and disappear for no apparent reason tend to arouse suspicions and hesitation. People like that are... strange.

Maintaining consistent standards over time as regards friendliness, reactions to requests, attendance at events and functions and in other areas is difficult, and all the more so the more extensive the personal network of contacts, and the more important or needed you are.

Some successful people end up depending on one, two or a whole team of secretaries to keep pace with the calls for attention or the expectations of friendliness on the part of the outside world.

Although this may not necessarily be your case, nevertheless it is advisable to acquire support tools which will help you upgrade the productivity of your networking time, and handle the expectation you give rise to around you. Don't bite off more than you can chew, or become involved in long-term commitments.

Enjoyment

Enjoyment is the definitive rule of networking. You must never feel obliged to get to know people and to establish relationships. You won't be able to keep it up unless it brings laughs, fun and pleasure.

The best contact managers are able to find something unique and different in everybody they meet, and they are sufficiently curious to stop and chat with people they meet on their way until they identify something in these people which distinguishes them from everybody else they know.

You have to be a bit of a child to be a good networker. The ability not to be corralled by the prejudices and beliefs of the others, while still being fired by curiosity and spontaneity, lies at the heart of the great contact manager, and we all have it within us to some extent.

Seek out that aspect of yourself and spoil it with the time and the circumstances it needs to lure it out of hiding. You will notice how dramatically your relationships improve, and how your stress level sinks.

8.4 THE AGE OF MULTIMEDIA NETWORKS

Modern technology opens doors to ways of saving time and effort in the cultivation of our social connections, but it also imposes other challenges which many managers sidestep or forget.

The concept of the multi-channel connection implies that you interact with your contact via a combination of communication channels. You share meals, send emails, meet at association functions, leave voicemails on the fixed line and with the secretary and you call the mobile. Heaven knows what will happen when all computers are equipped with electronic noses and we can scent videos of each other!

However, what it's important to remember that the combination of communication channels must be adapted to match your contact's preferences as closely as possible. The greater his relative power or the less his accessibility, the more critical becomes your making the most of the attention you require, and knowing how to tell him something to make sure he gets it.

There are some people who use email only for emergencies, and others who only read it when on long-haul flights, and if you want to say something in a hurry to them, you have to leave a message on their mobile. Some managers never use a computer, reading only what their secretary prioritizes and prints out for them. Developing a connection with someone means knowing how they like to receive information. To find that out you have to either ask a direct question, or carry on probing and make a note of their reaction to each different test.

And though the huge explosion of matchmaking websites and virtual professional communities, sites for friends, elitists, populists and all and sundry might give you the idea that now we can manage all our contacts via the internet, this is far from certain.

Just think back to everything which has been said about trust and how it is generated and you will realize that there is a dimension to creating trust which cannot be done through virtual channels. To build genuine relationships there must be at least some face-to-face contact.

Face-to-face contact offsets communications in writing, delayed replies, tones of voice on the telephone and silences which you have no idea how to interpret in the opposite situation. Even when you have a good personal relationship which you have cultivated over a number of months sharing the same office, you can end up causing misunderstandings if communication is reduced to emails and the telephone.

In other words, after a certain number of emails you start to read conflicting emotions and rudeness between the lines. Spending time together should by no means be hard work, with coffee breaks, chats about the football match and the like, because it is important that there should be an opportunity to clear up the misunderstandings which arise from other, more arid, communication channels.

An interesting example of this arose from a survey of 50 women aged between 35 and 50 who used virtual meeting services such as Match.com or Meetic.com. The results of this survey showed that most of them had virtual contacts with three or four men at the same time, but they found it difficult to remember what they said to each one, or what had been said to them, until they organized a real meeting, face to face. Once genuine contact had been made, in later telephone calls the person acquired a much more clearly identified presence which was not confused with others.

In conclusion, here are a few basic tips for the use of the telephone and the email. Read them and only bother to remember those you feel are useful. What some people might think is very clever, others will see as obvious.

1. Making phone calls
   - PREPARE IN ADVANCE
     - What you want
     - A script for the course of the conversation
     - Practice it out loud
   - DURING THE CONVERSATION
     - Smile while you talk
     - Be personal and friendly
   - AFTERWARDS
     - Write down the things you have to do
     - Prioritize them and allocate a date and time
2. Receiving phone calls
   - Don't pick up on the first ring
   - Smile when you answer
   - Write down the caller's name straightaway
   - Take notes of the conversation
   - Always use the caller's name
   - Avoid distractions
   - Thank the caller for the call
   - Set a deadline for returning calls
3. Writing emails
   - Make sure your email service shows the recipient your name but not your email address
   - Use the subject line as though it were a newspaper headline
   - CC: only to be used when all recipients know each other and you're sure that they don't mind their personal email being known
   - CCO: Use this for sending to a large number of people, with your name in the recipient field
   - Use bullet points
   - Be sparing in the use of the high importance sign!
   - Always include the company in your emails and the company contact data

8.5   COLLECTING "RARE GEMS" IN YOUR NETWORK

A small number of people ("rare gems") possess outstanding and unusual characteristics, whose potential regarding the movement of contacts around them merits a section especially dedicated to them.

Connectors

This term was coined by Malcolm Gladwell in his acclaimed work *The Tipping Point* to designate those parties responsible for converting local diseases or rumors into epidemic phenomena of great proportions. While there certainly existed innovative agents who spotted what was new before everybody else, and regardless of the opinion of the others, for Gladwell it was the connectors who converted these innovations into genuine revolutions.

Connectors are people who have many more contacts than everybody else. They are the ones we used to call hubs, and their greater connectivity turns them into privileged bridges so that they can access may people at the same time.

David Rockefeller is thought by many to be a connector, thanks to his database with 50,000 names and addresses, and oracle Kevin Bacon wanted to position him as the Hollywood connector, although, as we have already mentioned, the real connector is Rod Steiger.

Sonia Fernández identified Juan Díaz Andreu as a connector in her 2004 book *Networking: Two Degrees*, and it is likely that many of the actual cases included in this book also meet the conditions for being connectors.

If those who take a lot and give nothing in return can be seen as black holes, this astronomical feature which tacitly warns you not to approach if you wish to stay this side of the universe, connectors can be compared with light bulbs or sources of light.

Connectors are defined by the following characteristics:

- They know and are known by the vast majority of the people with whom you have contacts;
- They are invited to all the parties and events, and these functions are seen as a success if they attend;
- They don't have to be famous, since few of them are interested in stardom, but they are motivated by the value which can be generated by networking;

■ When they are consulted about anything they are usually only too ready to help, and they can usually give you a name or recommend one or more articles.

Gatekeepers

This old term is used to refer to those who guard the entrance and exit gates. It is they who decide who passes and who does not, which means that they have a great deal of power among the members of the community seeking access to whatever it is they protect.

One example might be the person who is in charge of bookings in a top luxury restaurant in busy Manhattan, who, as we have seen in many films, can make or ruin any millionaire's evening with a snap of the fingers.

The classic example is the personal assistant or secretary of some great person, or in other cases the office head. These individuals are responsible for jealously protecting the diary and the availability of their boss, which makes them a special figure in the word of contacts.

No small number of them find themselves the recipients of expensive gifts, fancy compliments and the politest of attention from all the visitors keen to be included in the appointments list of the boss in question.

A great media star's agent is also a gatekeeper, since everybody who wants to offer a deal to the star has to get past the agent, has to be liked by the agent, and has to convince the agent.

Good contact managers know how to take special care of the gate-keepers of the world, since most of these special carers know that they can snap their fingers if anyone fails to treat them with the right amount of consideration.

VIPs

The term "Very Important Person" has become very common and shows up as a category in the databases of many companies. Every lounge worth its salt has a VIP zone for its important people, and the truth is that all of us get a frisson of pleasure when we are treated as VIPs. It is an ever-increasingly exploited honor in present-day marketing policies.

However, we intend to use the term VIP here to designate a specific kind of networker who is distinctive for his skills as an excellent and generous mediator. These are the contacts who are outstanding not because of their ability to influence or because of their political power, but because they are liked by everybody and their sociability is a byword.

VIPs attract other customers to fashionable shops, seasonable locations, restaurants in search of a certain ambience, etc. They are neither buyers nor investors, nor are they supporting you or your product, but they can certainly put you in contact with many who might be.

The VIP personality is sometimes initially discounted because he shows no special interest or gets deeply involved in planning strategies, but it's good to know him, appreciate him and keep on his right side, because in his usually great generosity and his love of bringing his friends together, he offers great disinterested help to those who treat him well.

The VIP agent par excellence of Spanish society in the not-too-distant past was the great woman behind the successful man. Without a clue about what their husbands did at their offices, some "little women" operated as brilliant hosts, influencing the results of their husband's work by their social management, raffles for good causes, and taking tea with their friends and the wives of important managers.

This female figure seems to have passed into memory, but if you look carefully you may yet be able to find a rare and exotic specimen still surviving in our most modern of societies.

Mentors

Mentors also deserve some respect because they are a type of contact of enormous value for anyone lucky enough to be able to rely on one.

Traditionally, the mentor is seen as a kind of experienced sage who devotes himself to teaching a pupil. And the title Mentor is still applied to anyone who hands on knowledge derived from accumulated experience to a pupil with whom they feel a special affinity.

But a mentor also performs a very important function, deserving of notice, which is that he has privileged access rights denied to the pupil. The mentor has already consolidated networks with other individuals of his age, experience level and power of influence, which would be unlikely to include the pupil because there are too many levels of difference preventing a spontaneous and easy friendship.

But the pupil in the care of a mentor begins to hear about such and such a person or about a world somewhat distant from him, and his name begins to be heard among the members of the select higher management level. He is seen in the corridor when he comes to visit his mentor, and when he achieves a goal or some special recognition his mentor tends to talk about him with the same pride with which he would speak of a son. After all, it is thanks to his investment that the pupil has achieved his objective.

The mentoring strategy has proved itself to be excellent for members of minorities who wish to become involved in organizations which are unaccustomed to diversity in any of its forms. Indeed, a mentoring program has been set up in London for women who are professionally qualified to sit on the Boards of Administration of companies quoted on the FTSE 100.

Given that the main obstacle encountered by these women is that they have no real contacts among the current members of Boards, the program aims to accelerate their inclusion in a community of Board Members to occupy the seats available which appear on the Boards.

This strategy is also portrayed in those stories and films about an outsider who arrives at a small town which is unused to outsiders. Attempting to start a friendship with the residents one by one can be very time-consuming and fruitless, since the outsider must overcome the trust filters operated by the various individuals.

But if the outsider should make friends with one of the town connectors, it will be he who persuades the others to accept him, by inviting him to functions and events which would otherwise have been closed to him.

The mentoring relationship is not just one-way, since the mentor can also gain significant benefits by virtue of the fact that his pupil is involved in areas and with groups in the organization to which he could not have anonymous access. There are cases of CEOs who end up gaining all their information from their direct subordinates, the members of the management committee, and who could benefit by receiving information directly from below.

There are some CEOs who make their way straight to the offices and ask questions, but nobody forgets who is asking, and that affects the replies he receives. The possibility of a mentoring relationship with young pupils will supply him genuine, unfiltered information.

An attempt to include one or more of these outstanding personalities among the ranks of your network could be very advantageous and profitable for you and all the members of your network.

8.6 MANAGING CONFLICTS BETWEEN CONTACTS

It is in all honesty difficult to avoid conflicts when managing contacts, indeed it is all but impossible. Friends and associates disagree with each other, and this affects their relationship with you.

In the kind of conferences and seminars you might have attended up to now, the question almost always arises as to what to do if a conflict arises in the contact management situation, so I have devoted this section to providing an analysis guide to help you to place the problem in context appropriately and to assess the different options.

The first obvious thing is that once the conflict has become apparent, it's almost too late. There is no easy solution. Practically all solutions come at a cost, and your job is to choose the solution with the lowest cost and fewest negative outcomes in the medium term for both yourself and the rest of the network.

Here are a few common examples of conflicts:

- One of the parties involved in the decision to purchase does not have real decision-making powers and becomes annoyed when the salesman attempts to make direct contact with the manager who actually does have the power to make the decision.
- A friend or colleague who bypasses your interlocutor to access one of his contacts, either by offering the name of the interlocutor as bait, or by offering privileges to the target contact which were not offered to the interlocutor.
- A complicated disagreement or falling-out between two close friends, between a married couple who are close friends or associates in the company which is so unpleasant for both of them that they both seek unconditional support from you.
- A misunderstanding which occurred after you connected two friends or acquaintances who, in their frustration, blame you for what has happened.
- A bitter, public struggle between two leaders fighting for power where all the members of the team or organization are required to side with one or the other.

In all these cases an emotional snowball forms which is often bigger and more complex than the situation calls for, and which becomes harder to manage the greater the emotional escalation arising.

And the fact is that it is very difficult to prevent a situation which affects personal networks from turning into an emotional snowball. The protagonists tend to anticipate exaggerated effects and to set up remedial tactics which sometimes do more harm than good.

Moreover, if the situation is being observed from the outside, this can seriously aggravate this kind of conflict, since both protagonists are aware of the "whatever will they say" factor within their networks, resulting in both of them striving to show themselves as blameless victims of the situation. When the conflict takes place within a network of contacts this network becomes, without wishing to, a public judge of the events, forced to dance to the tune of the conflicting parties to convince them that they are understood, backed and supported.

The costs and negative effects on the parties involved in network conflicts include:

- The effect on your own personal ego and feeling of worth and your ethics. This includes disappointment on observing that the other party has betrayed the trust which has been placed in them, and they have actually made the worst possible interpretation of the situation, casting into doubt all the trust which we presumed they placed in us.
- A direct effect on the connections shared by the protagonists; reduced communication, the deterioration and sometimes disappearance of prior valuable transactions, an exaggeration of alarmist interpretations, impulsive reactions, insults and in extreme cases, escalation to violent revenge.
- The effect on the credibility and reputation of both parties in the eyes of their shared friends and contacts. Falls from grace are often due to the appearance of negative rumors which injure the good name of the people involved, and as the rumor becomes more deeply embedded doubts appear as to the objectivity, professionalism and seriousness of both parties, solely because of their having become involved in the events.
- A direct impact on the relationships or connections shared by each of the players in the conflict with other neighboring nodes in their networks. Since in many cases the trust established between the players feeds on the trust which each party places in the third parties shared by both, the breaking of the bond between them also affects the other connections which braced it or supported it, leading to a very wide range of outcomes.

The best way to manage these conflicts is to anticipate them and head them off, since their extent will depend on many factors which you don't control, like the emotional momentum of the parties involved, for example, which can obviously cause them to react in more or less exaggerated ways.

The method described below makes it possible to perform a predictive analysis of possible conflicts and will help you to decide the most appropriate focus of your approach, or it can also be used to analyze an existing conflict and work out the best damage control method.

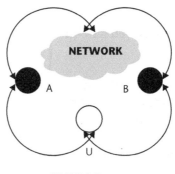

GRAPH 8.3

The network conflict situation is represented with four figures: (A), (B), you and the rest of the network. Each figure you should fill in the table below with the possible scenarios.

One of the scenarios should always be not doing anything, so that the situation remains the same. It may sound stupid, but a large proportion of conflict resolution mistakes arise because the analyst never considered the option of not acting at all, and yet a large number of quarrels and misunderstanding disappear over time if not too much is made of them.

OPTION	A	B	U	NETWORK
OPTION OF NOT DOING ANYTHING	+	+	+	+
OPTION 1	+	+	+	+
...	−	−	−	−

GRAPH 8.4

For each scenario you should assess the answers to two questions in each column:

- What can this player gain in this scenario? (+)
- What can this player lose in this scenario? (–)

Keep in mind the fact that these questions concern what MIGHT happen. It might take some little time for the effects on the network to reveal themselves, which is why it is important to assess all future possibilities.

What each player may gain or lose is a list of effects at all the dimensions quoted above: the effect on his own self-esteem, effects on his relationships with others, effects on his relationships with you and with the members of the network, and effects on his reputation.

8.7 RECOMMENDATIONS

The recommendations situation refers to a specific conflict case which gives rise to many misunderstanding and conflicts because the person making the recommendation, in his interest to help someone or other, leaves loose ends which end up tripping someone up.

Let's apply the table above to a typical example: you recommend your brother Andrew for a job where his boss will be your friend Brian. They meet, they get on well, and Brian hires Andrew. But after a few months a serious disagreement blows up between Andrew and Brian.

You are then directly affected by the conflict, you receive the angry emails and calls from both of them, and you aren't really sure which of the two is at fault. The only thing you do know is that you love your brother although you have never worked with him, and that your friend Brian is very demanding and ambitious.

Graph 8.5 provides an analysis table like the one above so that you can see what the situation looks like.

This reflects the main consequences and possible outcomes deriving from the available information, contingent on the "do nothing" scenario, which means staying on the sidelines and keeping quiet, or dealing with the misunderstanding. At issue here are gains and losses of trust and arguments, gains and losses in personal reputation, organizational costs and sometimes also financial costs.

The possible gains and losses produced by each situation are (1) uncertain, and (2) very intangible, but should they occur, the upshot

OPTION	A	B	U	NETWORK
Stay on the sidelines	+	+	+	+
	>lose job	>lose staff members	>low trust in A, B	>pressured to take sides
	>low trust in B, U	>pay for A's mistakes	>seen as poor recommendation	>goodbye to socialising between all 3
		>low trust in A, U		
Mediate	+	+	+	+
......	>blame U and fall out with him	>blame U and fall out with him	>take responsibility for whole problem	
	–	–	–	–
			>lose A and B entirely	
			>lose reputation	

GRAPH 8.5

208

in your life will be very noticeable, so you should give them serious thought, even though at the outset it may seem a little extreme.

A fight may be very important to one party and trivial to the other, since the interpretation of these effects depends entirely on who is analyzing the picture. If the battle arises between two members of the management committee of a powerful empire, it may mean that one will have to go, in which case the potential costs will be very high, and may even be seen as too high to accept.

Blaming yourself for the misunderstanding is a win for both parties because they have found a football they can both kick around. The intermediary becomes the messenger, and simply because of that he becomes the target for all the negative emotions floating in the air, even though he is not responsible for them. However, if, in addition, you made the recommendation, assuming part of the blame will allow the others to feel less at fault.

This is the difficult part of making recommendations: if it turns out badly, the likelihood is that the parties involved will blame you, because the collaboration was embarked upon only because they trusted you, not because they trusted each other. So if it turns out badly, what is destroyed is the trust they both had in you.

And we all find relief in locating a cause or object external to us onto which we can load at least a portion of our guilt. Otherwise we would all be obliged to question ourselves – uncomfortable, to say the least, and in some cases, devastating.

8.8   RISK MANAGEMENT

This is where we suddenly see clearly the risk lurking in the business of contact management. Depending on how you interpret this table, and on how you decide to act, you will be running one kind of risk or another.

If you aren't willing to run risks, you will never be a good contact manager. You can never please everybody, and anybody who adopts the strategy of getting on well with all and sundry will end up as the weakest link in the chain, since no one knows what you really think and stand for. That makes you an unreliable ally.

When it comes to managing risks, two important variables must be born in mind:

(1) how you perceive the risks: how likely are they to eventuate, and how serious are the worst possible consequences if they come to pass;

(2) how you see you own ability to emerge from the worst possible consequences still smelling of roses.

In other words, the above table may imply very different things depending on who is interpreting it.

If you know that your brother is a bit slapdash as regards work, and under no circumstance are you prepared to lose Brian's trust, or have your reputation tarnished, it may be worth attempting to mediate between them. You could mediate to solve the dispute and keep them working together, or you could apologize to Brian for having made a rather questionable recommendation, suggest that they stop working together as of now, because it isn't going to work, and help your brother Andrew to find a job better suited to his nature.

But if you don't want to risk fights, recriminations and unpleasant situations involving both of them, and you don't want to see your reputation even more damaged, and you prefer to discard the relationship you previously shared with Andrew and Brian, obviously your choice is to do nothing.

In both cases a choice of scenario must be made which does not eliminate the dangers of the alternative scenario, and in fact supports your perception of the dangers in question: obviously you will see the risks involved in the opposite scenario as less probable or less damaging.

The same intellectual mechanism swings into action when instead of risks, what are at stake are big opportunities, only in this case making the choice will be more fun and motivating.

So what do you do? First, you have to be very, very sure about recommendations. If you decide to recommend a third party, make sure you are 100% clear on what you know about them and the trust you have in each individual aspect of their character. In this case, if you had told Brian that you loved your brother but that he could be a bit slapdash, Brian would be aware that your recommendation went no farther than your affection.

Secondly, when you're intending to make a recommendation, to support one side over the other, to referee some dispute or become involved in any action which intuitively makes you nervous, both because of the pluses as well as the minuses which might arise, give yourself 24 hours to think about it and try to fill out this table.

Consider the most important wins/opportunities for you, see what others think before you make a decision, then put your money down. This is the difference between acting like a fool and taking calculated risks.

And thirdly, assume that the worst case scenario has occurred, and prepare a plan B for yourself. It will help you to sleep at night. One slightly kamikaze executive used to say that if his business plan failed, he would go and live in New York. He clearly assumed that he could recover in another city, and that this particular city might be an interesting and fun place to live.

Managing contacts means managing risks, and sometimes you lose. But if it is a calculated risk, taking it shouldn't leave you painted into a corner. Paying the bill and moving on to plan B will make you stronger, better prepared and more skilled at calculating risks in the future.

8.9 BREACHING THE LAW OF RECIPROCITY

Another dimension exists in the reading of the table which has crucial implications for you. There are two different ways to read it:

(1) Which option is best for all concerned?
(2) Which option is best for you?

Where the situation is such that you can choose to do the others a favor at your own cost, or to do yourself a favor at everybody else's cost, which sadly is quite common, then you must try to compare the respective losses, since life goes on, and we have to live with the choices we make.

In other words, if you have decided that at this particular time you have to watch out for your own interests and do what is best for you, even though this results in some degree of loss for the others, you must accept the fact that on the balance sheet of life between you and the others, you are now in debt. This means, according to the principle of reciprocity, that you will feel obliged to make it up at some time in the future. The opportunity may arise, but it may not.

If, however, you decide that it is vital that you protect the interests of the group, even though this may cost you dear, then do it. But remember that a group of people does not usually feel the need to return the value received, because inevitably responsibilities are diluted. Many problem solvers, trying to save the group, offer themselves as a voluntary sacrifice and then are surprised to receive no recognition for it, and indeed sometimes they are sacrificed precisely because of it.

Reciprocity works between two individuals. It is less effective between an individual and a group. In the group, the sense of indebtedness is diluted because the group is not always as united as it might be. A typical example would be the promises a boss makes to motivate his staff, but which he then fails to keep because the organization won't permit it, or because he is promoted to another position and his successor refuses to fulfill the obligation.

This question lies at the heart of the ethical and moral debate which permeates contact management. As you have seen, it is you who must give the correct answers to the question, and it is you who must bear the burden of what you decide to do.

On this matter, the only thing this book can do is present you with the available options. It is your free and personal choice, which defines your own identity, your values and the way you want to live your life. Your contact management procedure is merely the consequence of this choice.

8.10 HEIDI SINCLAIR, FORMER CHIEF OF COMMUNICATIONS OFFICER FOR THE BILL & MELINDA GATES FOUNDATION, AND NOW PRESIDENT OF THE GLOBAL TECHNOLOGY PRACTICE AT WEBER SHANDWICK

Heidi smiles often. Her creative approach to technology communication has fed 30 years of strategic insight and operational strength. In the interview we conducted for the Spanish edition of the book in 2008, she shared her views on networking, moving a family across the globe and stepping into the position she'd just begun at the Bill & Melinda Gates Foundation.

I really loved my job as CEO for Burson-Marsteller Europe. But I received a note from Bill Gates offering me a chance I couldn't resist. I had known Bill for some time, through technology conferences we had both attended over the years. He said there was a job opening at the foundation that could be perfect for me, and the mission was so compelling, I just had to do it!

This became the detonator of a new chapter in the life of Heidi Sinclair, a tall American woman who had just left Spain to follow Bill Gates on his mission to help make the world a better place for everyone. Heidi is a good example of what some like to call a "modern gipsy" and others refer to as "executive nomads": the most recent lifestyle evolution that is bringing modern executives back to the very roots of human living and bonding patterns.

Heidi Sinclair grew up in Seattle and went to university at Stanford, in California. She later got swept into a very successful career in which she created her first business venture at 23. A four-time Young Entrepreneur award winner, she soon became managing director of International Creative Management's New Media and Corporate Division. Senior executive positions for Borland and Lotus Development Corporation paved the path for the global positions she now holds.

Before being appointed director of communications for the Bill & Melinda Gates foundation, Heidi was president and CEO for Burson-Marsteller Europe, with responsibility over 18 company-owned operations and 34 affiliate operations across Central and Eastern Europe, Africa and Russia. She and her family of three children moved to Madrid in 2005, the new base from which she would captain teams in over 50 countries.

One of the most interesting things she's learned about landing in a new cosmopolitan city like Madrid and later, Seattle, is how important it is to "figure out the right networking organizations and events to go to in order to meet the right people."

When she arrived in Madrid she was immediately invited to join the Madrid chapter of the International Women's Forum (IWF). A global organization of pre-eminent women dedicated to advancing women's leadership across careers, cultures and continents, IWF provided an international platform of 5,000 members, of which 80 members are based in Spain.

The monthly lunches organized by the Madrid chapter helped her fast-track the learning process of every new city: different business routines and schedules, new schools, unknown brands and strange foods. The relationships she developed in the group compensated the setbacks of having to spend long hours travelling around the region for work purposes.

Two of the friends she made at IWF introduced her to the Young Presidents Organization (YPO). Looking back, YPO became a sort of spinal cord that connected her back to her father, supported her years in Madrid and smoothed her way back to the Seattle community. The intimacy provided by such networks allowed for networking to happen in a very deep and personal way, even though the Heidi that came back to Seattle in 2008 was a very different person from the Heidi who'd once lived there as a girl.

The YPO is also an international organization made up of more than 20,000 peers and their families across 100 countries in the globe. The role of this invitation-only group is to allow CEOs and top leaders, as well as their families, to exchange ideas and develop meaningful relationships with each other.

Sinclair remembers that the YPO "became an important touchdown, because my father had been in YPO forever. I loved that it embraced family and children. YPO connected me back to my father while it also enabled very meaningful relationships for my whole family while abroad."

Back in Seattle, Heidi also leveraged the support and personal relationships provided to her by the Young President's Organization and the International Women's Forum, not only to once again fit in to a new society and city with her family, but also to identify and develop opportunities for the Bill & Melinda Gates Foundation.

A good example was an invitation through the IWF network to a luncheon hosted by Jean Enerson. A well-known anchor, Enerson and Sinclair "just clicked." More lunches and meetings driven by good chemistry, shared laughs and engaging conversation followed. And as so often happens, work-related opportunities found their way to the table, such as the chance to do a story in the media about the foundation's new CEO.

Sinclair hadn't really networked intentionally before. "I never did it in a concerted, thoughtful, conscious way. It was more that I liked working with people. I would find myself really enjoying collaborations with colleagues who became friendly in a spontaneous way. It was just networking around the work instead of networking as part of the job."

Heidi describes the role of networking in her career as "serendipitous" until now, but she sees that going forward this is going to change. "I am now focussed on connections that have both a personal and work substance, which help me make a difference to the community I live in. Rooting back into my home town, these relationships also allowed me to bring value to the Foundation. One of the opportunities I explored was how YPO and the Gates Foundation could work together to do service projects around the world, kind of like the Rotary club does."

One would think that coming back to a city where she was born and grew up would make things easier, but the truth is that Heidi is not the same girl who left to pursue her studies a couple of decades ago. "You feel quite different in many ways because a lot of the people you come back to never left the city. They love their world. And I left that world a long time ago."

She found it easier to rebuild relationships with the people from home who had also stepped out of the Seattle world. "Some went to New York, others lived abroad. They had acquired a larger life experience and they knew what it's like to be the new one in town," Sinclair explains.

Spain, and the Madrid society specifically, were a tint more challenging. "Spain is more difficult because of the importance of family connections. I got very lucky because I was invited into IWF, which fuelled great personal and professional connections," she says:

> I remember someone I met in YPO who was fourth generation of a preeminent Spanish family and a very active socialite. His family seemed to be at the core of almost everything. It's true this exists everywhere, but I don't' feel it's as strong as what I witnessed in Madrid.

The characteristic cohesiveness of Latin family-driven networks creates a very protective and comfortable environment for family and friends. But it also makes arrival complicated for newcomers. Intense calendars of family occasions overlap with social pressure towards must-go events, leaving little time for new friends, let alone a spare seat at the table!

Another big difference was "the big long lunches" that are part of daily business and social rituals in Southern Europe. In Seattle it's often "just a bite to eat." Like in most Anglo-Saxon countries, lots of coffee cups are shared, or drinks at nice hotel lounges. Long meals are reserved for evening entertaining at home.

Heidi bought a new house upon her return to Seattle. She likes to "host a dinner around a specific topic, or even invite a speaker. It is very helpful to build relationships." Coming back to the United States has showed her how good Americans really are at building new relationships.

"People love to connect with each other. I used to think it seemed a bit superficial, but now I'm realizing that Americans are quite serious and committed to following up the relationship over the years," she reflects.

Sinclair finds Americans are fast and proactive when building new relationships, exchanging business cards, meeting again and actively developing trust. But she claims, "I can now see the power of these relationships is not dissimilar to those in Europe. Americans are very generous with their relations, and family is also important."

When asked what she considers to be key lessons in networking, she replies, "you have to drop your agenda." Sinclair believes that even while having an overall goal it is crucial to forget about private objectives in order to listen to others and understand what they need. She considers it imperative to take a larger view of the relationship, and to focus on the long run. "If not it becomes too deliberate, like you are trying to force something."

Heidi insists on avoiding pushy attitudes when networking: "If you are not able to connect with someone, don't try to force it. If it's not working, there's no chemistry, or the person is not interested, just drop it," she advises.

In her position at the Gates Foundation she was exposed to great expectations from many interest groups. Sometimes people were tempted to try too hard and insist beyond what felt natural or comfortable. Heidi reminds us that "if it's going to happen, it will happen naturally. Yes, putting inertia into things is important, but things can't be over pushed."

Something that Heidi has learned recently is how fundamental it is "to take the time" to build and strengthen relationships. She admits that she tended to take friendships for granted in the past. She is now convinced that time must be invested in every bond to make it stronger and richer.

Whether personal or professional, Sinclair believes that allocating time to each relationship is "as important as the task at hand." While smiling at the fact that she is learning this now, she realizes that she had been in a very comfortable environment during her years at Burson-Marsteller.

In her own words, "when you drop yourself into an unfamiliar environment, it forces you to rethink everything: what you do with your time, where your comfort zone is and when to leave it to explore new experiences."

Although Heidi has spent a lot of her work life in sales roles, she didn't really give much thought to networking. "I wasn't like: I have to meet these twelve people," she clarifies. But one thing she did do pretty often was attend a lot of conferences and events. Heidi recommends selecting a small group of regular events to get back to again and again. "It's a good way to really get to know the people attending."

People look forward to seeing each other at each yearly event, so that part of the fun in the conference is the chance to meet again and catch up. Heidi tries to go to about four conferences a year. She then organizes her travel calendar and work opportunities around these same gatherings.

In fact, that's the way she got to know Bill Gates. About two years before working for him they met up at one of the technology conferences they both attended yearly. Gates said that if she was ever interested in non-profit work she should come and join him.

At the time Heidi said she was very happy where she was and didn't think much else about it. But then his note arrived a year later and it triggered her curiosity. Bill put her in contact with the person in charge of recruiting the foundation's new communications team. That's how she became Chief Communications Officer for the Bill & Melinda Gates Foundation:

> After I talked to everybody I realized how much I missed my family in Seattle, and the amazing impact of the role I was being offered. Making the decision was easy. Implementing it was another story.

The Bill & Melinda Gates Foundation is guided by the belief that every life has equal value, and works to help all people lead healthy, productive lives. Based in Seattle, the foundation is led by CEO Jeff Raikes, co-chaired by William Gates Sr. Both Bill and Melinda Gates, as well as Warren Buffett, are co-chairs and trustees.

With close to 900 employees, and a financial asset endowment of $36.4 billion, the foundation supports projects in 100 countries. Rapid change and developments when Heidi was there made it especially important to build relationships both internally and externally.

During her time at the foundation Heidi stressed her networking skills to "find out what to do so that our work has more impact and it's easier to get it done." It was crucial to "figure out the personal approach with others in the foundation" in order to create more value, faster and for everyone.

Since this interview was published in the Spanish version of the book in 2008, Heidi moved on to start her own marketing, communications and philanthropic consulting firm, Heidi Sinclair & Co. She helped clients such as Richemont and Microsoft to "develop strategies, platforms and creative concepts that enable leaders, brands and organizations to achieve their highest potential."

Her new position as President of Weber Shandwick's global technology practice will surely bring even greater challenges and comparable successes to her amazing trajectory.

Heidi basically loves to make great things happen. She believes that global networks, glued together by intricate personal relationships, are crucial to build castles far greater than her individual effort could ever achieve.

CHAPTER 9

NETWORKING ACROSS DIFFERENT CULTURES

Jeff left the meeting feeling great. He had proved to his Japanese counterpart that he knew his stuff. Confident and eloquent, he even pointed out a number of improvement opportunities in the foreign operation that would render important benefits to the multinational business they both worked for.

Aiko was mortified. She had never been so shamelessly disrespected in her entire career. And in front of her team too! What had she ever done to deserve such a humiliating report of her area's shortcomings from a total stranger? She sincerely hoped never to see the arrogant foreigner ever again!

Networking across cultures is probably the riskiest activity on earth. And yet, it has become a life necessity for most executives everywhere. Perhaps the biggest risk of all is the feeling that all is going perfectly well, when, in fact, it couldn't be going any worse indeed.

Among the most important messages in this book, attention to the details of the other person's needs and reactions is the king. Almost everything I've written so far amply insists on the need to check and recheck whether the other person is comfortable with you or not.

If you apply this simple overarching principle, you should find your way around any culture in the world, because, even if you make initial mistakes, humans recognize good faith, respect, and honesty universally. The fact that you try to speak a few words of another person's language, or offer a pearl of their own culture's wisdom, is more important than actually speaking it fluently.

But nevertheless we can point out a few key elements to take into account when networking with people who have grown up to see the world in entirely different ways to yours.

9.1 GLOBAL CITIZENS

You and I are probably already part of an emerging new culture of global citizens. We read books coming from many countries, watch films in their original language made by Japanese, Americans and Danish directors. We travel a lot, we work with people from different countries.

This new emerging figure of the global citizen is the result of mixing all the colors of human approaches to life: the ones that existed before us, blended into history and literature, and the ones we grew up with ourselves. It is a lot easier to network with global citizens because they, or we, are naturally flexible and receptive to other ways of seeing the world.

But not everybody is as global as one would think. Remember that not everybody has had the rare opportunity you may have had to travel, to grow up speaking two or three languages. The large majority of the world stills grows up and dies in the same city that saw them come into the world. They may be on Facebook and watch US movies. That doesn't mean they like what they see on the internet. Their interpretation of the words and symbols that you take for granted may be entirely different.

Stay away from cultural stereotypes. They are disappearing as we speak, slowly but surely. Don't assume anything about the person you have in front of you. Just listen, observe, and ask questions. Looking at people with a clean slate is the best way to avoid clumsy mistakes that may be perceived as disrespect.

9.2 ESSENTIAL DRIVERS OF CULTURAL MINDSETS

I believe there are a number of basic parameters that distinguish people's approach to life. The following graph depicts a very simple framework to help you ask the right questions when you are trying to get to know somebody from a different world.

Three core parameters define a huge part of the way people respond to situations:

Time

■ Some people use time as their number one life indicator. They think that "time is money," and that wasting time or not using it efficiently is the worst mistake anyone could make.

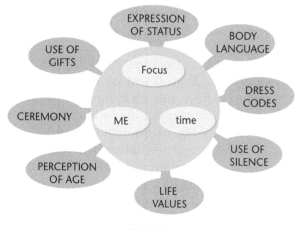

GRAPH 9.1

- Others pay little attention to the passage of time. They see time as something that can't be controlled or managed. Counting it and fussing over it doesn't make sense to them, and meetings can take as long as needed to close the deal at hand.

Focus

- Some people focus on work, business and practical matters over everything else. Setting concrete goals and action plans is the best way for these people to establish trust and build relationships.
- Other people focus on affection and emotional connection above all else. They don't ever consider doing business with someone they haven't met before, who doesn't share their life values or their choices around family, social status and sports.

ME (or not ME)

- Some cultures naturally put the individual's interest and needs above those of the group. Making ME the center of a presentation, talking about ME all the time, explaining how MY vision is crucial, building MY merits and MY career.
- Other cultures assume that the individual is always part of a group, and they organize almost everything in their societies to benefit

group dynamics, to the extent of leaving little space for individual expression.

I am describing only extreme interpretations of these parameters here to give you an idea of the range. If you ask yourself how the person in front of you seems to behave and act around these three parameters, you will understand why they react they way they do, and why their interpretation of events can be so different to yours.

A longer list of other factors feed into these three key parameters. When you approach someone from a different culture, ask yourself questions about these parameters. Every time you make the effort of offering the reaction they would expect, you show respect and the will to integrate into their world.

- *Dress code.* How can you adapt your personal style, without giving up your own values, to conform to the other person's comfort zone?
- *Body language.* How do people salute each other? How are hands used? When do people stand up or sit down? How do they react to you looking them in the eye or averting your glance? Is physical closeness and touching good or bad?
- *Use of silence.* How does the other person interpret silence? Does he or she prefer it? Does he or she avoid it? Does it have a hidden meaning like respect or assent?
- *Expression of status.* How does the other person behave with his or her superiors? And inferiors? How can you tell who is the most powerful individual in a group?
- *Gifts.* How much should you spend on a welcome gift or a thank you gift? What should you choose to offer? Is there any risk a gift may be interpreted as a bribe or pressure? When is a gift called for?
- *Ceremony.* How much does the other person insist on details and rituals around food, meetings, or other outings? What does each gesture mean to that person or to their culture?
- *Perception of age.* How do people regard the elderly in society and in business? What is more admired, youth or experience? How is personal status affected by age?
- *Life values.* How important is religion and spirituality to the other person? Do they believe in personal liberty or choose deterministic explanations of life? How much do they value risk?

When you go networking to other countries, think about all these questions and try to answer them when you get back to your hotel room or when you have breakfast in the morning.

Observe and learn from others. If you have a trusted friend who belongs to that culture, ask for advice. Many countries have very different customs from one region to the other.

Be very careful to reflect on the different answers to these questions in private one-to-one meetings versus group events. What may be acceptable in a private setting may be intolerable in the group setting and vice versa.

Pay attention to typical sayings, popular symbols, artistic expressions, stories and legends, and history. A people's culture is often expressed across all these symbolic vehicles. They are the very same vehicles they use to teach their young what life is all about.

Remember: sincere curiosity is a good networker's best friend. Invest as much time as you need in preparing to interact with people from another country. Show them you care enough to find out why they choose to see things in their own way.

9.3 JOSE A. MENENDEZ HERRERO, HEAD OF THE SHANGHAI FACTORY AT NOKIA SIEMENS NETWORKS

China's influence in global business is growing by the minute. We are all called to get a better understanding of how Chinese men and women do business, what they consider important to build trust and what they think of networking.

Jose is a Spanish executive who moved to Shanghai with his family more than two years ago, just after completing an executive MBA at IE Business School. Taking over the responsibility of the Shanghai factory, he is the only expatriate among the approximately 500 employees based on site.

In this interview he shares his impressions of Shanghainese networking practices, the role that networking plays in his job position, and what China is giving to his family.

Simply put, Jose hopes that his two pre-teen daughters "understand the value of effort, and why it's worthwhile to dedicate oneself to learning. Life isn't easy, and Chinese kids seem to be better prepared to invest in their own luck."

Little did Jose imagine, fifteen years ago, that he would one day be working in Shanghai for a real global company with a CEO from India and a diverse executive board that also merges cultural influences from all around the world.

"This is what I am trying to teach my daughters. Good luck can happen by chance, but most often it arrives when you have invested to make it happen", begins the Spanish executive. "Once I finished at university I had to do my military service, and I decided to study German while I was waiting."

A while later his notions of German were useful when he interviewed for a job at Siemens. "The interviewer was surprised to see that I was learning at my own initiative the language of headquarters, and I suppose it created the sense that I was open to German ways of working," he remembers.

Jose took a deep role to set up a manufacturing line for mobile networks products in Madrid area and due to that he immediately joined international expertise taskforces to transfer technology mainly from Italy and Germany at that time and later to share best practices also from Brazil and China. "At the very beginning there were few people with foreign language skills in my office, and somehow the opportunities for global interaction found their way to my desk."

These projects gradually nurtured flexible work approaches in Jose, encouraging him to collaborate easily with colleagues from different countries. He found it rather intuitive because "it was sufficient to be polite and respectful to network successfully at these meetings. But you also had to deliver on your promises in order to build your credibility."

Leadership today is strongly driven by results, based on facts and numbers. Being open to work with foreign colleagues was a qualifier, but in order to build influence you had to provide substantive results.

As Jose progressed in the company, he felt the need to expand his vision of business outside the Supply Chain. This is why he signed up for an executive MBA at IE Business School in 2007, taking classes on Friday afternoons and Saturday mornings while he carried on with a global responsibility and several international projects. He describes it as "a very challenging year. I prepared so many cases on air planes!"

It was just one of those airport afternoons, stuck in Helsinki preparing a case for class, when his boss called him up to propose the job in Shanghai. "I had visited the plant quite often since 2002, I knew the team and I was familiar with the city. My wife and I had discussed potential moves and Shanghai was a strong candidate for both of us."

Jose admits that it was, nonetheless, a bigger step for his family, considering "all my previous travels and global projects were helping me grow as a person. Thanks to close interaction with different cultures, I realized we want the same things and fear the same adversities." And he continues, "I felt my family was missing out on this part, and Shanghai was the opportunity to show them."

"Some people say that it's not easy to befriend the Chinese, but I have to ask: Have you tried?" Shanghai is a very international, striving city filled with expatriate executives in global positions from almost all business segments and facing similar challenges. People tend to group together around common interests: children at the same school, neighboring homes or mother tongue are typical.

Jose insists on the barrier that expectations can represent in this setting, "when you know you will be gone in three to five years, and the Chinese know it as well, you lose motivation to invest a lot of effort on networking with locals. They might shrug their shoulders to exclaim, 'Why should I get to know you if you're not staying?'"

This is a common barrier to networking across cultures. Unless you have been brought up to manage life-long relationships with people who live in different cities, countries or even continents, you aren't easily drawn to network with people you will lose touch with soon. It seems counter-intuitive. Yet you miss the opportunity to live unforgettable experiences. "I am pretty confident that if I stay much longer in the city I can make such strong friendships with Chinese, as I already start to have for example from the IE alumni network."

"Chinese are conscientious networkers," says Jose. Like everything else they do, effort and carefully trained skills are applied to develop strong networks. They understand the wisdom of building alliances to shape a better future.

"The biggest difference I have noticed is the enormous value Chinese place on every single interaction," explains the Spaniard. "You need to pay special attention to understand what they have achieved in life. Their achievements and current roles are the consequence of constant effort and discipline from an early age."

Disregard for a business card, for a correct hand shake or a respectful goodbye, can be construed as a lack of respect for the person's professional trajectory, to the point of making him or her feel sincerely humiliated, especially if it happens before other witnesses:

> In Western societies, for example, we may give a subordinate negative feedback in the middle of a team meeting. Nobody in the meeting associates this reprimand to the individual's value or questions

his past. But in China this action translates directly into the public questioning of an individual's entire professional track.

"It's a question of balance to them," and he goes on:

> your position in society is preceded by a long history of promotions and achievements. Not showing respect for it is like downplaying its importance. Making it worthless.

The Chinese strong devotion to effort and merit-driven success is also visible in Shanghai organizational structures. As Jose explains, "I am the only expatriate among my colleagues in the factory, and they look quite ok with that because they feel I can bring them added value in terms of knowledge and well trained global expertise that they eventually wouldn't access otherwise. Successful companies in Shanghai must have a minimum percentage of expats, just where the specific knowhow that they bring to make it grow locally is worthwhile for the company."

"In Europe we often complain about being stuck in a job where we aren't evolving any more. Chinese will simply resign if they feel they have no further development potential," he tells us. Chinese professionals are passionate about learning as much as they can to improve their chances for further success.

Today television, the internet and global travel are exposing us to different ways of approaching strangers, expressing welcome, shaking hands and sharing a meal. The clear-cut cultural stereotypes that we used to recognize so easily a decade ago are slowly fading into a common rule. As Jose expresses it, "there are things that aren't acceptable any place in the world. If you maintain strong respect and honesty, you shouldn't get into trouble."

When in doubt, as always, ask for advice from local colleagues or friends who can guide you towards specific gift guidelines or dress style, for example. "And if you can learn a few expressions in the other person's language, it can go a long way!"

Jose admits that his current level of Mandarin is just enough to keep simple conversations. People in Shanghai tend to speak Wu Chinese, rather than Mandarin, so it doesn't really help him get around the city. "But when I'm speaking to the workforce and I start or finish my speech with a few words in Mandarin, they realize I am making an effort to be close to them. I think this is universally appreciated by most people."

Work at the factory is very enjoyable, "partly thanks to the unique culture we have managed to create at Nokia Siemens Networks (NSN)," claims the executive. "Our values really walk the talk in terms of customer focus, ethics and teamwork." Siemens and Nokia decided to merge their telecommunication branches in order to create a new company in 2007 to provide solutions that improve communications to Telco companies:

> In top of complete solutions and managed services for Communication Service Providers, I always say that we make invisible products because we don't produce cell phones or end user devices well known by the final subscribers. Our products are hidden below antennas over roofs, connecting cities by optical fibre or stacked behind walls at customer premises to make wireless, fix and internet connectivity happen. As much as our customers are fully satisfied, we succeed.

Fast growth of worldwide connectivity requires extremely efficient implementation, where "a special openness and will to collaborate makes it easy to synchronize efforts." Networking is strongly encouraged in the company to activate idea exchange and grease up company joints, or as Jose puts it, "process goes a lot better when the human touch is driving it."

Last, but not least, the network provided by IE Business School alumni is another useful resource to navigate this unique international experience. It is the way we made this interview happen, in fact! Alumni based in Shanghai get together to attend expert conferences quite often happening in the city, have dinners from time to time "or even arrang[e] visits from local business schools and universities to the factory to show to the students a high efficient and added value supply chain."

Jose says it takes a lot of discipline to remain connected to home networks because of the time difference. "When Europe gets up we're ready to go home for the evening. But making time for a few Skype calls is important to keep your networks alive. Then you get home to family and you have lots of stories to tell."

Jose A. Menendez Herrero is a living example of the new generation of global executives who live in more than one country, speak several languages and appreciate the exotic flavours of remote typical dishes.

His groups of friends and colleagues at NSN, IE Business School and Shanghai are a little like his own private communications network. Human antennas and routers connecting him to the world with the most appreciated of invisible products: pure and simple human trust.

CHAPTER 10

A BETTER YOU REQUIRES A LONG-TERM APPROACH

Hwang Joo read a book at age 25 that convinced him he needed to get a lot better at public speaking. If anyone had asked him how long it would take him, his response would have been very optimistic. Like anyone picturing dreams of the future, Hwang Joo's image of himself was timeless.

Fifteen years later Hwang Joo still felt like he was 25 years old with another 15 years in front of him to improve his public speaking. As he nervously stuttered his way into a mediocre presentation of his department's results, he wished he had made the necessary time each week of the previous decade and a half. His timeless dream might have become a reality.

Writing up a strategic plan is tough. But it's not enough. You need to review it and compare to reality on a regular basis. The real value of the analysis and the effort invested in putting a strategy on paper is wasted, unless you stop from time to time in your frantic daily rhythm to check whether theory and practice are consistent or not.

A surprising number of companies regularly make a superhuman effort to define the strategy to adopt, yet then never check the plan until they are absolutely forced to. In the years following the establishment of "the plan" all the managers drift slowly away from the snapshot they have in their minds. They end up driving blind, because they know that "the plan" ceased to reflect reality long ago, and they and their colleagues have replaced it with different and often non-matching versions.

For entrepreneurs starting a new business, getting a strategic plan down on paper is almost unthinkable because they have no time for anything. They moan, they protest and they complain when the bank they want a loan from demands a snapshot of the situation in two years. Eventually they do come up with some kind of a document which they give to the bank.

There is no doubt that what appears on their paper seldom coincides with reality. Still, it is important because it supplies a frame of reference against which they can measure what they are doing. If in addition this plan is revisited on a yearly, or even half-yearly basis, it will become apparent that (1) the resources needed to operate the plan dwindle as theory is converted into practice, and (2) the decisions taken between plans, even if unrelated to the previous plan, are a better fit to the evolving long-term view.

The development of new ways to manage your contacts can also be improved noticeably if you are in the habit of checking what is happening and correcting the course with some degree of regularity. Once the CEO or the businessman becomes bogged down with steering the everyday course, it is very difficult not to lose what the Americans call "the big picture." By this they mean a panoramic view of the business, uncluttered with the day-to-day problems, a clear, objective and visionary perception.

This chapter will help you to set up a checking and adaptation system regarding your personal development which will allow you to continue to be both the master and designer of your own learning curve, one which you will regularly drag out into the daylight to inspect the overall view of yourself and your context.

My first recommendation is that you work on a weekly or fortnightly basis to record information. If you fail to record information, it will be difficult to revise it, or at the least your revisions will end up as very rough-and-ready conclusions, the upshot of which will be that you waste even more time perfecting your management system.

The second thing we notice is that there are two forms of revision. One form is more operational, and can be carried out every month or every six weeks, even perhaps once a quarter, as you see fit.

The other form is more strategic or overarching, and this needs attention every six months or perhaps once a year, depending on your preferences and needs.

In other words, the course revision and adjustment system consists of three important parts:

1. recording the data (weekly or fortnightly);
2. operational revisions (every 4–6 weeks);
3. a general or strategic review (every 6–12 months).

The more operational review is important to assess whether you are achieving your objectives, and if not, to learn from your failures and successes on the ground, or even to change your objectives.

If you have been managing to record the weekly readings for each progress indicator, you will now be able to assess how well you are using your time, what you have learned about new connections, and the development of existing ones. A disciplined manager who sets aside five minutes a week to jot down the week's data will usually spend two or three hours on the operational review.

The strategic review requires more time, from half a day up to a couple of days, depending on the situation and where you are in your career. It will give you a chance to re-establish your efforts and beliefs, so that you can ensure that you are on a pathway you like and you find motivational in the long term. This revision will include a SWOT analysis, the development of soft skills, and may even result in a radical career change.

The end purpose of this overarching review is to establish the two or three priority directions where learning is to be concentrated in the upcoming period.

10.1 OPERATIONAL REVIEW

The operational review helps you revise the evolution of your selected progress indicators in the preceding weeks. Here is a guide to the main areas and possible indicators you can use to check your progress.

The progress of your network

In Chapter 2 you performed a POTENCIA analysis of your network, and you were advised to select two or three priority parameters to work on.

For each parameter you should:

(a) come up with a tangible goal to achieve for each parameter;
(b) set up a measurable indicator to track this goal.

In the example shown in Chapter 2 we established Objectives, Transaction and Intermediation as top parameters to develop. The goals you could establish for each parameter could be like these:

- Network objectives: try to ensure that at least 50% of contacts speak Russian or are interested in learning Russian (in order to materialize the goal of learning the language where you are);

- Network Transaction: increase average transaction level by one point;
- Intermediation in the network: identify the main structural weaknesses of the network and plan the new developments you need.

The next thing to do is to set up some progress indicators to check what is happening each week. This way you can judge your own performance by looking back after only two or three weeks. The choice of the indicator is completely up to you, and the quality of your progress will depend on how well you choose it.

If you can't think of an obvious indicator to fix, you can always set up a subjective point system. By ranking a quality from 1 to 3 or 1 to 5 you can measure your weekly impression of it.

Here are a few examples of indicators you could choose for each of the goals we selected above.

1. Try to ensure that at least 50% of the contacts speak Russian or are interested in learning Russian:
   - Number of contacts who speak Russian
   - Number of contacts who have visited Russia more than once
   - Number of interactions with Russian speakers
   - Number of Russian cultural events you have attended
   - Number of Russian speakers who have contacted you.
2. Increase the average transaction level by one point:
   - Number of emails sent which contained useful information
   - Number of emails received which contained useful information
   - Number of useful interactions sustained (with exchange of value)
   - Number of relatively ineffective work conversations held
   - Score from 1 to 5 of the intensity of the transactions you have been involved in
   - Proportion of transaction calls with your boss.
3. Identify main structural weaknesses and remedy them:
   - Score from 1 to 5 for the clarity with which the structural weaknesses in your network are apparent
   - Density of your core network (equal to the number of connections which exist between each two contacts, divided by the total number of connections)
   - Number of new contacts who know nobody in your current network

- Number of events involving people you don't know which you attend
- Number of times at events you open conversations with strangers rather than talking with your colleagues.

Activity and output

In section 7 of Chapter 6 the importance of setting an objective in respect of use of time was discussed. A diary analysis exercise to work out how you divide your time between the various activities included in your contact management system was then included.

Placing a number behind each percentage is all well and good, but even as you do so, you must realize that you will fail to meet it sometimes. Previously established business priorities may get in the way, you may get sick, or something else could happen.

In other words, following up the real amount of time devoted to a job each week helps you to decide whether the goals you set are realistic. When you fail to meet them repeatedly, you may be forced to consider other hidden barriers to your networking: motivational reasons which lurk behind the typical excuse of "having no time."

Once again, you should set objectives and progress indicators for your time dedication. Typical indicators, measured per week unless otherwise indicated, include:

- Percentage of time devoted to managing networking
- Number of hours devoted to managing networking
- Number of hours devoted to visiting events and conferences during the month
- Percentages devoted to each type of contact
- Difference between the actual percentages and the objective division percentages for each type of contact
- Number of hours devoted to operational follow up and review
- Time since you made the last general review
- Number of hours devoted to learning activities: coaching, reading, courses
- Percentage of networking hours devoted to examination and analysis each month
- Number of exercises in the book completed
- Score from 1 to 5 for dedication to networking during the week

- Score from 1 to 5 for the output from networking activities this week.

New contacts

In the chapter devoted to this subject we broke down the steps in the first encounter procedure so that you could select those where you should do more, and we set out some guidelines about how to circulate.

Following up and checking this activity can therefore be organized in accordance with the recommendations and exercises provided here. You can use these same exercises to define appropriate follow-up indicators.

Meeting new contacts

Depending on what you are looking for, the main challenge may be establishing a new association, attending a certain number of events in the year, or selecting useful events in order not to waste time on pointless fairs. Remember the 6H method from Chapter 7 will help you select the best occasions.

On your map of circles you may have set objectives about a new circle to be developed, or you may decide that you must be involved in a project within your company.

Go back and read once more the section on meeting new contacts, and choose two or three objectives to achieve. Write them down and then think about the indicators to help you monitor your own progress.

A manager intending to set up a company in a sector other than the one he was familiar with, let's say, large-scale distribution, might set the following objectives and indicators:

- Attend three key events in the large-scale distribution sector in Europe this year.
- Indicators: number of events analyzed using the 6H method, number of events in which you have participated
- Register with foreign commerce chambers and publish articles in their monthly publications
- Indicators: number of articles published, number of chamber of commerce events attended, number of contacts made in the chamber of commerce.

First conversations

In the section on first conversations you were advised to analyze your recent encounters. You had to write a maximum of three pieces of positive advice and one negative about what you should do or avoid doing in first encounters.

Review your responses to define two or three "SMART" goals. You may then assign progress indicators in a similar way to what we just did in the previous section. Then go back over the table in section 7.2.1 on the important items to look out for in first meetings. Decide whether you should define goals around hygiene, style, attitude or your promotional instruments.

Do the same with the table in section 7.2.2, which concerned the "during" part. Set up a series of performance indicators covering approach, conversation, your presentation of yourself and rounding off.

Finally, take another look at the section about what happens after first conversations. Decide whether to set improvement goals on the following questions:

- Do you have an effective contacts classification system? (Here you can measure the number of cards you can't classify, the time it takes to classify cards or the general fit of the classification to your business decisions.)
- Do you have the necessary discipline after the events to register the information about the contact? Have you set up smooth and quick information storage procedures?
- And what about your backup reinforcements: how do they stand?

Better contacts

Chapter 8 dealt with the daily advance of individual relationships. Another look at this section will allow you to select improvement goals on the following aspects:

Is the accounting on current relationships clean and easy to gauge? When was the last time you did an in-depth revision of the balance sheet of each "relationship account"? What percentage of your contacts have no return? Which ones need more attention from you because they've been in the red for some time?

- Which of the laws of sustainable development are you good at implementing? Can you see one that you should especially improve?

- What objectives could you set regarding the multimedia management of your contacts?
- What about "rare gems" in your network? Should you think about recruiting anyone in particular? Could you become one yourself?
- How would you score your ability to manage conflicts between contacts? What difficulties do you experience? What improvement goals can you set?
- How would you score your recommendations?
- And how about your risk management? Can you foresee and calculate the risks involved in a network movement before you make it? Dare you make it even though it is risky? How accurate is your risk assessment?

Operational progress form

Graph 10.1 can help you write down all your goals and indicators, and track down weekly readings in the columns on the right.

10.2 PANORAMIC REVISION

Reading this book and doing all the set analysis exercises is the first panoramic revision you will have made of your networking procedures. You've probably spent a large number of hours on the job.

It will be up to you to decide when to do your panoramic revisions and how much time to devote to them. Here you have a summary table, with a recommendation for the frequency with which you should do each one, and a space to put down the results of each analysis.

You can begin each panoramic revision by checking Graph 10.2 to decide which parts to focus on this time. Ideally, the operational reviews will tell you what goals need a deeper, structural approach.

The first goal of this panoramic revision is to show the direction in which you should be moving. With this in mind, it might be advisable to re-do the mission exercise and the SWOT analysis for each revision. You will be amazed to discover how much they both change as you evolve and mature.

You also want to prioritize which goals to work on during the upcoming quarter or half-year. A specific column has been included in the table to help you prioritize your objectives. Remember not to try to improve everything at once. We'll discuss this right after the pause!

	Area in need of work			Objective (s)	Indicator	W1	W2	W3	W4	Learning curves
Network progress	P1									
	P2									
	P3									
Activity and Output										
First meetings	Collection									
	First conversations	Objectives based on advice and anti-advice								
		Before items (Graph 7.3)								
		During items (Graph 7.4)								
		After								
Ongoing Development	Relationship accounts									
	Sustainable development laws									
	Multimedia management									
	"Rare Gems"									
	Conflict management									
	Recommendations									
	Risk management									

GRAPH 10.1

Exercise index	Chapter or section	Recommended frequency	Comments and conclusions	Objectives derived	Objectives ranking (10)
My last 5	1	Every 2 months			
Current network generators	2.1	Every 12 months			
POTENCIA analysis of the network	2	Every 12 months			
Reputation	3.9	Every 12 months			
Trust levels	4.2	Every 2 months			
Emotional intelligence diagnosis	4.6	Every 3–6 months			
Invisible obstacles analysis	5.4	Every 12 months			
Discover your mission	6.2	Every 3–6 months			
Your personal SWOT	6.3–6.6	Every 3–6 months			
Diary analysis	6.7	Every 1–2 months			
Inventory of available resources	6.7	Every 12 months			
Analysis of 6H events	7.1	Every event			
Circles map	7.1	Every 12 months			
Sundry analyses, first conversations	7.2	Every 1–2 months			
Sundry analyses, developing connections	8	Every 1–2 months			

GRAPH 10.2

10.3 LEARNING SOFT SKILLS IS DIFFERENT

Intuitively everybody realizes that change is costly because we have all been involved in failed attempts to change, and we have seen others unsuccessfully try it as well. Going on a diet after Christmas, wanting to stop smoking or cutting the number of hours in the working day are all examples of how easy it is to want to change, and how difficult it is to actually do it.

An executive who wants to improve his managerial skills will have to deploy more time and effort in doing things which in the past he did without thinking. The reason behind this is what some call the law of mental equivalence.

This law states that there is a dynamic balance between what people do and what they think and feel. It is dynamic because none of the dimensions is immobile. If we make waves in one of them, the other two will tend to realign with it, or push it back to the way it was before.

GRAPH 10.3

So if you decide to change your time management practices, for example, you decide to use the first half hour of each day to organize priorities. So far, so good.

But the first day, during your 30 minutes of thought, you have to restrain your own hand as it heads for the phone to make an urgent call. You need to convince your mind that this is not a waste of time and that the consequences of delaying that call are not as serious as you think. You want to have a couple more cups of coffee, or to take a relaxing stroll to shake the stress out of your system.

You've broken the balance between behaviour, thinking and feeling. You still think that spending the first half hour of the day organising your life is a luxury you can't afford. You feel uncomfortable and nervous for every one of the 30 minutes you spend not doing what you used to do before.

The fastest way to feel better again is to stop the new 30-minute routine. The old balance is achieved, and the stress or extra effort you had to apply to get through the day is no longer necessary.

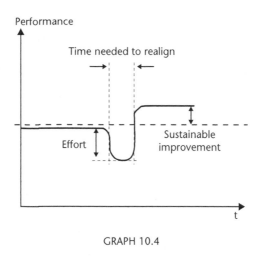

GRAPH 10.4

As the graph shows, introducing a change in your routines and behaviors lowers your performance because you require more time to do the same things. You need to stop and think before you do stuff that you used to do with your eyes closed.

If you do resist the temptation to forget your new resolution, however, and if you maintain the new habit, you will eventually develop new thought patterns and emotional sensations to reach a new balance of your three dimensions. Once a new balance is achieved, your newly increased performance will sustain itself naturally.

You may begin to sense a new feeling of total relaxation when you switch off your mobile phone. Or you may find yourself telling everyone you know how useful and efficient it is to invest the first half-hour of the day in organizing your agenda.

Another important fact of executive development is that you need to choose the number and impact of changes you try at once. Graph 10.5 shows what happens when you implement many changes at once. The effort needed to perform is significantly higher, and the time needed to reach a new balance is longer.

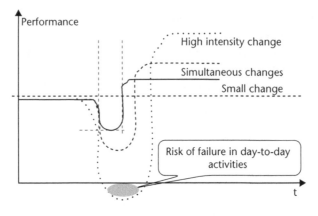

GRAPH 10.5

Your best strategy is to introduce one change at a time, as shown in Graph 10.6.

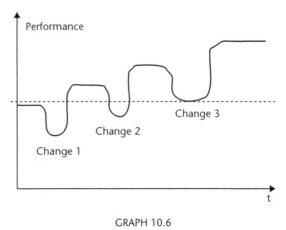

GRAPH 10.6

Don't assume that the ranking column suggested in Graph 10.2 above is silly or a waste of time. Pacing the expenditure of the energy you devote to developing your networking skills is almost as important as the development itself.

10.4 ADDITIONAL RESOURCES TO HELP YOU

Be sure to seek out and incorporate into your development process the whole range of learning resources out there. You can stimulate your progress via different combinations of sensory perceptions. You never

240

know which of your five senses will provide you with the next important step forward.

Build yourself a toolkit of stuff that helps you learn from yourself. Here are a few primers to help you put it together:

Reading: books, editorials, specialist magazines, dedicated websites, other media

_____

_____

_____

_____

_____

_____

Conferences on the subject matter, seminars on actual skills, courses and distance-learning courses (MBAs and other masters courses)

_____

_____

_____

_____

_____

_____

Catalysts: a coach, online communities, experts on the subject, specialist consultants in specific subject areas, etc.

_____

_____

_____

_____

_____

_____

Models and references: people from your everyday life whom you consider examples of success in the behavior patterns you intend to develop. You can choose different models for each actual skill, and observe what they do that you could incorporate. You can also chat with them and seek their advice.

_____

_____

_____

_____

_____

Sports, games and other experiences that test the skills you want to develop. Taking part in an NGO or joining an amateur dramatic group, for example. These other situations provide low-risk environments where you can practice new tricks without risking how they will go down in your workplace.

_____

_____

_____

_____

_____

The training sections of many large businesses are now designing individual training trajectories for high potential managers. You should do the same for yourself, based on the development objectives you define during each panoramic revision.

The table which follows may help you to plan the time and cost deriving from the training trajectory you design to cover a year.

10.5 HERE WE GO...TAKE A BITE!

The doughnut awaits your bite. Just in case you need a detailed guide to follow this first time, you can follow these instructions:

(1) Make a two-hour space in your diary for next week.
(2) Buy a notebook just for this, or open a folder on your computer for all relevant information.

	January	February	March	April	May	June	July	August	September	October	November	December	YEAR TOTAL
READING BOOKS													
MAGAZINES													
JOURNALS													
WEBS													
BLOGS													
COST/MONTH													
HOURS/MONTH													
TRAINING CONFERENCES													
COURSES													
MASTERS													
SEMINARS													
COST/MONTH													
HOURS/MONTH													
CATALYSTS COACH													
ONLINE FORUMS													
CONSULTANTS													
COST/MONTH													
HOURS/MONTH													

GRAPH 10.7

(continued)

		January	February	March	April	May	June	July	August	September	October	November	December	YEAR TOTAL
MODELS	COST/MONTH													
	HOURS/MONTH													
EXPERIENCES	SPORTS													
	NGOS													
	CLUBS													
	COST/MONTH													
	HOURS/MONTH													
	TOTAL MONTHLY COST													
	TOTAL MONTHLY HOURS													

GRAPH 10.7 Continued

(3) When the date and time arrive, switch off your mobile phone, make sure that nobody is going to interrupt, and begin by revising Graph 10.2. Choose three exercises from the table to do, including the SWOT analysis if possible.

(4) Devote the first hour and a half of your meeting with yourself to complete the three exercises you chose. When the hour and a half is over, leave them as they are. Save them with the date in your exercise book and/or folder.

(5) Devote the last half hour of your time space to writing all the next steps that occur to you, the people you want to call, the books and websites you want to check, the remaining steps to finish your exercises and complete your SWOT.

(6) Set aside a date and time to complete each of these steps in the next fortnight and book a further two-hour space in your diary.

(7) Once again, when the date and time arrive for your second meeting, switch off your mobile phone. Make sure that you will not be interrupted, and complete the exercises proposed in section 10.4 to complete your training trajectory and identify the learning resources you will need.

(8) Before finishing this second meeting, set up your contact classification system and do the exercise of time allocation suggested in section 6.7.

(9) Put imaginary appointments with yourself in your diary to meet these time allocation objectives. The more clearly defined your next step is, the more likely it is that you will take it.

(10) Undertake your first contact management action, and then write down your impressions in your notebook.

Congratulations! You are officially on your way to a much better you, with a much better network.

10.6 GHASSAN E. NUQUL, VICE CHAIRMAN OF NUQUL GROUP BOARD, AND A MAKER OF POSITIVE WAVES

Ghassan Nuqul is an articulate man. The clarity of his words generates waves of value for his family, for his company, and for his country. He creates positive ripples for the Arab world, and for all those of us who still don't get it.

Because he strongly believes "you should never spare an effort", he made this last interview possible at the very last minute. The thoughts he shares with us here about networking, business, and life in general, are living proof of how he practices what he preaches: "If you don't have passion for it, please don't do it!"

Networks of people are like ripples on the surface of a pond after a stone hits it. Ideas and emotions spread through personal ties at the speed that trust enables, moving us along choices and events that shape us as individuals, while they create the future we share with others.

The logo of the Jordan-based Nuqul Group happens to resemble a stone, creating ripples of positive value around it. In 1952 a Palestinian refugee laid the first stone of the international conglomerate that today employs 5,800 workers around the world. His name was Elia Nuqul, and if you visit the group's webpage at www.nuqulgroup.com, his smiling image will greet you with pride and good wishes.

Ghassan feels that his role in life was the direct product of his father's expectations: "I am eldest son to my father, who arrived in Jordan in 1948 with a big family and without a penny. As a refugee he had been deprived of his scholarship at university to study litigation, so he came to Jordan with a lot of ambition."

Political instability and a complex economy didn't make his life any easier, but "his sacrifice, his hard life gave me the incentive and the drive to come back to the Nuqul Group as an educated young man in 1985 to continue his mission," explains our friend, and he goes on: "He gave me a platform, he gave me a name, and a value system. The honest and true drive of my work to this day comes from the journey this man began."

These are men who understand the crucial importance of their family name. Gurus today insist on cultivating a personal brand as if they were inventing something new in networking and business. The Nuqul family, however, has known this for a long time. When Ghassan's mother considered marrying Elia, "her well-to-do friends advised her not to marry a man of a lower condition. My father didn't persuade her with talk about money or riches. He promised her that he would build a name she could be proud of. And so he did!" Yes, this is certainly a line of wave makers.

Possibly influenced by his American University studies, Ghassan decided to write down a mission statement for himself upon his first arrival to the family business. "I wanted to make a difference in my family, my company and my country. Today it still holds true. I need to make a positive difference around me. Sure it takes a toll on me and on my time. But I believe this is why I am in this life."

With 40% of his time spent on committees, boards, conferences and Trusts, Ghassan feels he is "ambassador to my family and to my name. I affect positive change for my country and I get to influence how things are done to benefit my people. It is my duty and my obligation!"

The vice chairman has come to believe that "all this time does not only serve my family and business, it also helps me to learn through all the networking and interaction with people from different sectors and other places."

Nuqul is convinced that "networking is an essential element of the equation of business. It is critical to show the people you deal with what you stand for, and then everything else becomes easy." His daily experiences confirm how face-to-face interaction shows a person's good ethics, demonstrates an open mind, and illustrates personal values to every stakeholder of any business: clients, suppliers, associates, media representatives, government figures, etc.

"Networking is not a one time thing," he claims. "It's a continuous interaction that transmits the solid achievements of numbers, market share or reputation to others. People see the person, they can connect and relate to the person and emotions behind the information. Networking means being active in the social scene, participating in NGOs and corporate social responsibility, influencing economic policy...any situation in which you as an individual can contribute."

Ghassan insists on the fact that "you must enjoy doing it. It's not something you do because you have to. If I go to my boards or charity organizations without enthusiasm for what we are trying to achieve it will show. People would look at me as if I was not up to the expectations they have of a Nuqul. Believe me when I tell you that I represent my company, my family and our values of enthusiasm and entrepreneurship in every interaction."

But the Nuqul group is not only present in Jordan. An industrial and investment group with presence in the Middle East and North America, the 31 companies and 5,800 employees export their products all over the world. International networking is also a big part of the group leader's job.

"Politics can be complicated some times, but business today is very open because we have more similarities. We speak the same language, international law agreements and transparency lay open rules that help to open borders and bring mindsets closer," argues Ghassan. "When I network internationally I am very conscious of the fact that

I represent my country and the Arab world in general. I always try to make the best impression possible."

But making a good impression is only the beginning. "You learn new ideas and concepts when you interact with new cultures and different visions. Then you need to come back to your country and try to make a positive difference based on what you have learned." And he goes on, "today it is as crucial to network internally among your people as it is to go abroad and network externally because everything is open."

Among Mr. Nuqul's favourite platforms is the prestigious Young Presidents Organization (YPO), of which he is an active member: "First it helps you develop relationships on the professional and on the personal level. They organize many events ranging from business seminars to touristic activities and even family programs about raising children, for example. Not only myself, but also my wife and children can interact with their counterparts while discussing and sharing a wide range of life interests."

"This kind of platform is ideal to find people like you who come from very different realities. You build bridges, remove stereotypes, reduce inhibitions, and of course you do good business as well. If I need to look for an international supplier I start by looking in YPO. This group offers great guarantees of credibility and good standing of its members," describes this insightful networker.

For someone with the roles and responsibilities of Mr. Nuqul, the World Economic Forum at Davos is also an ideal platform for international networking. "You meet leaders in politics, the arts, environmental organizations…you go to lunches and seminars, you speak as panelist of debates…the amount of knowledge and sharing around issues you don't normally think about in your day to day is inspiring and enriching. We are all there to become better human beings."

"Without a doubt, networking is a piece and parcel of becoming a leader," he concludes. Ghassan strongly recommends readers to "never underestimate any conference or the smallest meeting. Invest your best effort and time. Any given reunion can change your life."

An example of this was the trip he made to Kuwait as part of His Majesty's official delegation. Ghassan was a member of the Economic Consultative Council to His Majesty King Abdullah II at the time. "I attended a small breakfast with counterparts from Kuwait, and the idea of a Jordanian–Kuwait holding company came up. I became the vice chairman of the company, which has since made a lot of investments in Jordan and elsewhere."

"If I had not made the time for that small meeting, justifiably so with all my other obligations, I would never have met these people from top notch families in Kuwait. Thanks to this occasion I met many others I still interact with today to do good business and make a positive difference for all involved," he claims.

Nuqul advises us to "never spare an effort. Due your due diligence before you accept, of course. Always look for those opportunities where you as an individual can make a difference. Make mistakes, they are good to learn from, and be persistent. Be brave. Be bold. Don't shy away from giving your opinion. And most importantly, you must want to serve. It's not about popularity."

I personally couldn't agree more. This is a man who walks his talk, making waves of positive change with everything he does and says. An irreplaceable tribute to the Nuqul legacy, Ghassan Nuqul is an example not only to every family business leader, but also to executives from around the world. We all represent our family's name.

CONCLUSION

Networking is essentially a very meaningful act of human creation. Not a day goes by without teaching us a new lesson about the nature of our species. Each knowledge bead you acquire about the enormous diversity of ethnicities and religions we embody will also reveal deeper truths about who you want to be and who you wouldn't want to become.

Two people who meet for the first time are like two high-speed trains racing towards a collision of conflicting expectations, different mental maps, cultural visions of life and emotional needs to fulfill or demand.

Often we bring all our best and most presentable charms to the table, with all the affection and good will we have within us, and it still doesn't work. The reliable future we're seeking turns out to be an unrealistic illusion. We're left with personal regret or professional disappointment.

Sometimes we truly believe we are doing just that, with affection and generosity and plenty of sweet icing on our cake. But deep down we're trying to manipulate the situation. It takes real courage to look in the mirror and admit it to ourselves.

Other times we're the ones pursued by people with too much interest, or passion, admiration and praise. We experience the uncomfortable satisfaction of being the one who chooses or rejects. We may do it haughtily, with disdainful superiority. Or we may feel deep and genuine empathy towards the emptiness that drove that person to seek us out. Still, how could we be the response to a gaping hole that only he or she can truly complete?

Once in a while, however, on a few special occasions, the two trains merge into a single graceful motion, combining loads of unpredictable

250

factors with a precision impossible to dissect or explain. A rich exchange of ideas and emotions begins and continues to flow at a changing rate that wraps around time and circumstance like the sound of a melody does to the mood of its composer. Sometimes explosive, sometimes slow or even tedious, some melodies suddenly end with a discord, while others play on forever.

Our human brains evolved to their present size and complexity in response to an environment whose greatest survival threats came from other humans. Consequently, each of us is no more than the sum of the contacts and the "non-contacts" experienced in our lives, who in turn left their singular imprints on our personality.

Networking is about assuming risk. It's about creating new opportunities where there was nothing before. It's the beginning and the end of everything that is human. Connecting to other people will teach you more about life than any book you will ever read. It will make you more human.

Make sure you take advantage of every new human interaction to learn a little more about who you are, who you want to be and who you don't want to be. Accept the results of each action, whether rejection or praise, as the answer the world gives you to that eternal, magnetic, existential question: why am I the way I am?

It's been a pleasure meeting you throughout these pages. I sincerely hope you succeed in all your future endeavors, one cup of coffee after another.

It will probably take you more than six cups, but then again, you never know! The next stranger you meet might just be the one you were looking for.

Over everything else, enjoy the thrill!

NOTES

1 ONLY SIX?

1. P.S. Dodds, M. Roby, and D.J. Watts, "An Experimental Study of Search in Global Social Networks", *Science* (8 August 2003).

2 YOUR PRESENT

1. Granovetter, M., "The Strength of Weak Ties", *American Journal of Sociology* (May 1973),78, 6: 1360–80.
2. R.S. Burt, *Structural Holes: The Social Structure of Competition* (Cambridge, MA: Harvard University Press, 1992).

3 A BETTER YOU STARTS WITH A NEW UNDERSTANDING

1. R.L. Graham and J. Nesetril, *The Mathematics of Paul Erdós* (Berlin: Springer, 1997). See also A.K. Peters, *The Man Who Loved Only Numbers* (New York: Hyperion, 1998).
2. Norman L. Biggs, E. Keith Lloyd, and Robin J., *Graph Theory: 1736–1936* (Oxford: Clarendon Press, 1976).
3. See series of articles on Rényi's life in the Hungarian language in *Matematikai Lapok* (1970): 3–4.
4. Stanley Milgram, "The Small World Problem", *Physiology Today* (1967), 2: 60–7.
5. Albert-László Barabási, *Linked: How Everything is Connected to Everything Else and What it Means for Business, Science and Everyday Life* (New York, NY: Penguin, 2002).
6. Malcolm Gladwell, *The Tipping Point: How Little Things Can Make a Big Difference* (New York: Little, Brown & Company/Back Bay Books, 2000).
7. Peter D. Killworth and H. Russell Bernard, "The Reversal Small World Experiment", *Social Networks* (1978–79): 159–92.
8. See www.oracleofBacon.org. Brett Tjaden was the original conceiver of the idea, receiving help from Russ Haddleton and Glenn Wasson, and then Patrick Reynolds. See site credits for more details.

9. See reference to Hawoong Jeong's list of most connected Hollywood actors, depicted in Chapter 5, section 3. Barabási, *Linked*, see note 8 above.

10. Vilfredo Pareto and Alfred N. Page (1971), translation of *Manuale di economia politica* ("Manual of political economy"), (New York, NY: A.M. Kelley).

11. See <http://ngm.nationalgeographic.com>. Virginia Morrell, *Animal Minds* published March 2008.

12. Jerome Barkow, Leda Cosmides, and John Tooby, *The Adapted Mind: Evolutionary Psychology and the Generation of Culture* (New York, NY: Oxford University Press, 1992).

13. Michael D. Lemonick and Andrea Dorfman, "One Giant Step for Mankind", *Time* magazine, Europe edn (23 July 2001), 158.

14. Richard Dawkins, *The Ancestor's Tale: A Pilgrimage to the Dawn of Life* (Boston, MA: Houghton Mifflin, 2004).

15. Ryan Raauma, and K. Sternera, "Catarrhine Primate Divergence Dates Estimated from Complete Mitochondrial Genomes", *Journal of Human Evolution* (2005), 48: 237–57.

16. Frank Brown and Ian McDougall, "Strategic Placement and Age of Modern Humans from Kibish, Ethiopia," *Nature* (February 2005), 433: 733–6.

17. Nigel Nicholson, *Managing the Human Animal* (New York, NY: Crown Publishers, 2000).

18. Robin Dunbar, "Neocortex Size as a Constraint on Group Size in Primates", *Journal of Human Evolution* (1992), 20: 469–93.

19. J. Kleinberg, "Navigation in a Small World," *Nature* (2000) 406: 845.

20. I. de Sola Pool, and M. Kochen, "Contacts and Influence," *Social Networks* (1978), 1(1): 5–51.

21. D.J. Watts, and S.H. Strogatz, "Collective Dynamics of 'Small-World' Networks," *Nature* (1998), 393: 440–2.

22. D.J. Watts, P.S. Dodds, and M.E.J. Newman, "Identity and Search in Social Networks," *Science* (2002), 296: 1302–05.

23. Frans de Waal, *Chimpanzee Politics: Power and Sex among Apes* (Baltimore: Johns Hopkins University Press, 2000).

24. Ronald S. Burt, *Structural Holes: The Social Structure of Competition* (Boston, MA: Harvard University Press, 1995).

25. Ronald S. Burt, "Bandwith and Echo: Trust, Information and Gossip in Social Networks", in J.E. Rauch and A. Casella (eds), *Networks and Markets* (New York: Sage Foundation, 2001), pp. 30–74.

26. Gladwell, *The Tipping Point*; see note 6 above.

4   THE PART OF THE ICEBERG THAT SITS UNDER THE WATER

1. Jose Luis Alvarez and Silviya Svejenova, *La gestión del poder* (Barcelona: Granica, 2003).

2. Sandro Costaldo, "Trust Variety: Conceptual Nature, Dimensions and Typologies", IMP 2003 conference, Bocconi University, Lugano, Switzerland.

3. Daniel Goleman, *Emotional Intelligence: Why It Can Matter More than IQ* (New York: Bantam Books,1998).

5 BARRIERS TO BEING A BETTER YOU

1. Francis H. Cook, *Hua-Yen Buddhism: The Jewel Net of Indra* (University Park, PA: Pennsylvania State University Press, 1977).

6 YOUR FUTURE

1. Herminia Ibarra, *Working Identity: Unconventional Strategies for Reinventing Your Career* (Cambridge, MA: Harvard Business Press, 2003).

7 NEW CONTACTS

1. Robert A. Caro, *The Years of Lyndon Johnson: The Path to Power* (New York: Alfred A. Knopf Inc., 1982); *The Years of Lyndon Johnson: Means of Ascent* (New York: Alfred A. Knopf Inc., 1990); *The Years of Lyndon Johnson: Master of the Senate*. New York: Alfred A. Knopf Inc., 2002).

INDEX

255